AMERICAN RACIST

AMERICAN RACIST

THE LIFE AND FILMS
OF THOMAS DIXON

ANTHONY SLIDE

THE UNIVERSITY PRESS OF KENTUCKY

Publication of this volume was made possible in part by a grant
from the National Endowment for the Humanities.

Scholarly publisher for the Commonwealth,
serving Bellarmine University, Berea College, Centre
College of Kentucky, Eastern Kentucky University,
The Filson Historical Society, Georgetown College,
Kentucky Historical Society, Kentucky State University,
Morehead State University, Murray State University,
Northern Kentucky University, Transylvania University,
University of Kentucky, University of Louisville,
and Western Kentucky University.

Editorial and Sales Offices: The University Press of Kentucky
663 South Limestone Street, Lexington, Kentucky 40508-4008
www.kentuckypress.com

08 07 06 05 04   5 4 3 2 1

Library of Congress Cataloging-in-Publication Data
Slide, Anthony.
American racist : the life and films of Thomas Dixon / Anthony Slide.
p. cm.
Filmography: p.
Includes bibliographical references (p.   ) and index.
ISBN 0-8131-2328-3 (acid-free paper)
1. Dixon, Thomas, 1864-1946. 2. Motion pictures—United States—History—20th
century. 3. Dixon, Thomas, 1864-1946—Film and video adaptations.
4. Dixon, Thomas, 1864-1946—Political and social views. 5. Authors, American—20th
century—Biography. 6. African Americans in motion pictures. 7. African Americans in
literature. 8. Racism in motion pictures.
9. Racism—United States. 10. Racism in literature. I. Title.
PS3507.I93Z86 2004
818'.5209—dc22
2004006074

This book is printed on acid-free recycled paper meeting
the requirements of the American National Standard
for Permanence in Paper for Printed Library Materials.

Manufactured in the United States of America.

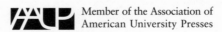
Member of the Association of
American University Presses

It's what we call fiction, but I think fiction's
the very best history we can read.
It may not have happened just that way
but it's true all the same.

> **Marse Rooney, the Negro schoolteacher
> in Thomas Dixon's *The Man in Gray* (1921)**

quod semper, quod ubique, quod ab omnibus
What always, what everywhere, what by all has been
held to be true

> **motto of the Ku Klux Klan**

Get your facts first, and then you can
distort them as much as you please.

> **Mark Twain to Rudyard Kipling (1899)**

CONTENTS

Acknowledgments

I am grateful for individual help provided by Raymond Allen Cook, Robert Gitt, Evelyn Baldwin Griffith, Larry Karr, Emily Leider, Arthur Lennig, Howard Prouty, and, most of all, James Zebulon Wright, who offered open and frank comments on his distant cousin Thomas Dixon Jr. Both Arthur Lennig and James Zebulon Wright took time out of their busy schedules to read the manuscript, and I am grateful for their comments and corrections. When I mentioned to film critic Joel Siegel that I was working on a book concerning Thomas Dixon, he astonished me with the revelation that his mother-in-law, Charleen Swansea, was Dixon's great-great-granddaughter and put me in touch with this remarkable woman. My thanks to you both.

Thomas Dixon left no major archival collection of papers (or films, for that matter) at any library or similar facility. However, I would like to acknowledge the institutional assistance provided by the staff of the Margaret Herrick Library of the Academy of Motion Picture Arts and Sciences; Gregory Farmer at Chapman University; the Asheville-Buncombe Library System (Zoe Rhine); Alice L. Birney, American Literature Manuscript Historian at the Library of Congress; Robert Anderson and Helene Mochedlover in the Literature Department of the Los Angeles Central Library; the Film Study Center of New York University (Ann Harris and Antonia Lant); the staff of the Doheny Memorial Library of the University of Southern California; Fred G. Turner at the Olivia Raney Local History Library of the Wake County Public Libraries system; and Megan Mulder of the Z. Smith Reynolds Library of Wake Forest University.

ACKNOWLEDGMENTS

Dixon's library of books is housed at Gardner-Webb University, and I much appreciate the help and friendship of its library director, Valerie M. Parry. The largest collection of Dixon papers—some 239 items—is to be found in the Rare Book, Manuscript, and Special Collections Library of Duke University, where I was helped by Research Services Librarian Janie C. Morris and researcher Rod Clare.

I am deeply indebted to Gary Dartnall and Tim Lanza of the Douris Corporation, successor company to the Raymond Rohauer Collection and owner of whatever copyrights still exist in the writings of Thomas Dixon.

Finally, thanks to Angelique Cain Galskis and Leila Salisbury at the University Press of Kentucky for believing in the project.

AMERICAN RACIST

Introduction

Although some of his novels still remain in print, Thomas Dixon is relatively unknown today. His fame, or more precisely infamy, rests on his being the man behind *The Birth of a Nation*, responsible for the original story and concept. As such, Dixon is regarded as a major representative of Southern racism. Like the director of *The Birth of a Nation*, D.W. Griffith, Thomas Dixon was a proud son of the South, who learned of its history from his father. Griffith heard of the great Civil War battles from his parent, while Dixon was told by his father and his uncle, Colonel Leroy McAfee, how they had helped organize the local Ku Klux Klan in 1868–69. Both men told their fathers' stories in *The Birth of a Nation*. Both were children of Reconstruction, both felt the South had been maligned, and both wanted to tell the true story as they knew it to be. "The true story" became almost a mantra for the two men. Griffith tried to recount what he believed to be the truth of the Civil War and Reconstruction in *The Birth of a Nation*, utilizing a medium with which he was familiar and which he had largely helped popularize. Dixon used the popular novel to the same end. In his mind, a Northerner, Harriet Beecher Stowe, had libeled the South in *Uncle Tom's Cabin*. Thomas Dixon set out to put the record straight with *The Leopard's Spots* (1902), *The Clansman* (1905), and other novels.

As one of the greatest of nonfictional Southern writers, W.J. Cash, has pointed out, the Civil War may have temporarily destroyed the South, but it left intact the Southern mind and will. The tragedy and sorrow of the Reconstruction period fortified and confirmed that mind-set, and from it, in natural succession, developed the fertile and creative works of Thomas Dixon and D.W. Griffith.

Raymond Allen Cook wrote the only published biography of Thomas Dixon, *Fire from the Flint*. Its subtitle, *The Amazing Careers of Thomas Dixon,* properly acknowledges that the subject was not only a prolific and controversial novelist but also a popular lecturer on the Chautauqua circuit, a lawyer, a minister, a playwright, and above all, a spokesman for his generation of Southerners. Back in 1959, Cook wrote effusively on Dixon, arguing that his personality "is one of the most compelling in American history. Rarely does a man achieve great success in more than one field. More rarely still does a man achieve fame in three or more fields."[1] Unfortunately, what Cook fails to note is that the compelling nature of Dixon's personality is his blatant racism, to which others have been drawn for more than a century in either outrage or support. Many would agree with F. Garvin Davenport Jr.'s assertion that Dixon was "a spokesman for southern Jim Crow segregation and for American racism in general."[2] Yet he did nothing more than reiterate the comments of others, including poet Richard Watson Gilder: "I do not see, in short, how the Negro is ever to be worked into a system of government for which you and I would have much respect."[3]

Aside from his vast contributions by way of the written and spoken word, Thomas Dixon was also a filmmaker, responsible in some way or another—often in a major capacity—for eighteen American feature films produced between 1914 and 1937. The most famous is, of course, the first, *The Birth of a Nation,* and just as Dixon and his collaborator, D.W. Griffith, used that initial production to tell the history of the Civil War and Southern Reconstruction as they believed it to be, so did Dixon embrace the motion picture—although he preferred to call it the cinema[4]—as a means of propagandizing many of his ideals and philosophies. Socialism, communism, and feminism were just three of the isms that he discussed on screen.

To some the link may be insidious, to others appropriate, but both Griffith and Dixon used the screen as much to propagandize as did Leni Riefenstahl in the 1930s with *Triumph of the Will* and its glorification of the Nazi Party.[5] Thomas Dixon was as intense in his vindication of the South and its history as was Riefenstahl in her early vindication of Nazi Germany. For Riefenstahl, Nazism was her subject. For Dixon, the South was not merely his subject but his cause. Whether the issues are right or wrong, few filmmakers can claim to have influenced audiences as much as Griffith, Dixon, and Riefenstahl have. And certainly no other filmmakers from the silent era, let alone the early years of the twentieth century, have produced a film that remains controversial almost ninety years after its original release. Like the director of *The Birth of a Nation*, Dixon has suffered rejection and ridicule. His name is no longer deserving of respectful prominence in the history of American popular culture.

The eighteen novels that Dixon published between 1903 and 1939 have been described by one critic as "flaming stories of love, adventure and intrigue."[6] The same description might equally be applied to the twelve or more plays that he wrote and to Dixon's film productions. They are almost all stirring social melodramas, morality plays in which the morality is that of their auteur and, more often than not, that of the general American populace. With *The Birth of a Nation*, D.W. Griffith recognized the power of the motion picture to influence and arouse its audience. Dixon learned a lesson from his friend and mentor. If the motion picture was to Griffith the "universal language," to Thomas Dixon it was the "university of man." He wrote, "The class rooms, with row on row of seats in our Theatres, are already heated and lighted and provided with ushers."[7]

It is worthy of note that whereas *The Birth of a Nation* remains one of the most influential films of all time, and one that routinely appears on one-hundred-best lists or similar tabulations, none of Dixon's novels have achieved such status. In 1925, when *Publishers Weekly* documented the best-selling fiction of the past quarter century, no novel by Dixon was included. The list was headed by Sinclair Lewis's *Main Street* and included Edith M. Hull's outrageous *The Sheik*, which was to become a major star vehicle for Rudolph Valentino, but, despite selling hundreds of thousands of copies, neither *The Leopard's Spots* nor *The Clansman* boasted comparable sales.[8]

The more one reads the works of Thomas Dixon, the more one realizes—as Dixon scholars have yet to do—that although he is no expert at plot development, he is a master at self-plagiarism. He is unwilling to let go of several of his best scenarios. The storyline of *The Traitor* is recycled seventeen years later as *The Black Hood*. *The One Woman* becomes *Companions*, while *The Foolish Virgin* serves as the basis for Dixon's film *The Mark of the Beast*. Plagiarizing from oneself is no crime; somewhat more questionable is Dixon's plagiarism of Walt Whitman's *Specimen Days and Collect* (1882–83) for his scenes of Washington life at the close of the Civil War in *The Clansman*.

For Dixon, the motion picture was no mere toy nor just another popular form of entertainment. As he wrote in 1923, "The moving picture man, author and producer and exhibitor should take himself more seriously. He is not merely the purveyor of a form of amusement. He is leading a revolution in the development of humanity—as profound a revolution as that which followed the first invention of printing. The new film press uses the rays of the sun to etch thoughts on yellow parchment—instead of dull printer's ink."[9]

Just as Thomas Dixon's name is seldom associated with the motion picture, outside of *The Birth of a Nation*, so he has generally disappeared from view in most critical and broad-based studies of American literature in the twentieth century. His first three novels are dismissed as "unashamedly racist," and his later works, with "Dixon's extremist views focused on other issues," are "of no literary merit."[10] Dixon himself might have responded to such criticism by saying, "I had a message and I wrote it as vividly and simply as I knew how."[11] While of limited, if any, literary worth, his novels demonstrate a skill in storytelling; polemical in content, they affected the thinking of millions of Americans from both the South and the North.

Dixon's first biographer, James Zebulon Wright, whose work was never published but in my opinion is the best account, had to admit, "I admire Thomas Dixon more than anything in the world. . . . I can admire him because, once logically arriving at a conclusion even though today it is known to be fallacious, he was brave enough and strong enough to suggest a remedy to the problem."[12] Dixon's courage as both a writer and a preacher is beyond dispute. One may vehemently reject his arguments, but one should never deride his honesty or his integrity or his forthrightness.

No pun is intended, but Dixon's life and career cannot be discussed in terms of black-and-white—not even the black-and-white of the silent motion picture. Dixon is a complex character, and while his on-screen commentary on race, on miscegenation, on women's suffrage, on socialism, and on communism may appear outmoded, one should never doubt Dixon's integrity or his supreme faith in his Southern philosophy. A populist author, he provided Americans with as much satisfying reading matter as John Grisham does a century later. Neither Dixon nor D.W. Griffith is a racist in the modern sense of the word, and they should not be branded as such. They are idealists in a world that today they would regard as out-of-step.

Both would have strongly protested any effort toward suppression, as now generally takes place, of screenings of *The Birth of a Nation*. Or any other film for that matter. Both men were ardent fighters against motion picture censorship, often addressing audiences on the subject. "The itch for censorship is a contagious mental disease," argued Dixon. "Once it starts it goes on. It spreads from one nosey mind to another. . . . God almighty never made a man or a woman good enough, broad enough, wise enough to hold the autocratic power to press hands on the throat of an author and say, 'You shall think only as I think and write only what I say shall be written.'"[13] Thomas Dixon and D.W. Griffith have another link besides that of the South and *The Birth of a Nation*. Both can be considered auteurs in an industry where few are worthy of such a title. Both men produced, wrote, and directed their own films, and both could boast of immediate name recognition with their contemporary audiences. From the American silent film era, only pioneering female director Lois Weber is comparable, but her films are infinitely more liberal than those of Dixon and Griffith and far more female-oriented. Where Dixon and Griffith differ is that the latter tended to concentrate on Victorian morality on screen, whereas Dixon promoted a considerable number of issues, many of which were distinctly twentieth-century. Griffith's arguments for tolerance and peace, as in *Intolerance, Broken Blossoms,* and *Isn't Life Wonderful,* were of little interest to Dixon. Here again, to some extent, the author is closer in outlook to Leni Riefenstahl than to D.W. Griffith.

Dixon belonged to the "magnolia and moonlight school of Southern literature," and that myth of the Old South has been perpetuated on screen from the early years of the twentieth century. Dixon's South was the South of *The Birth of a Nation* and *Gone with the Wind,* a romantic vision, tinged with violence, but a "nation" from which the Southern white aristocracy would ultimately rise triumphant. Dixon expressed his love for his "country" through the heroine of his last novel, *The Flaming Sword:* "I've been North. The spring up there is cold. Flowers bloom and birds sing a little, but with a kind of restraint. Down here nature laughs and tells us to laugh. The sunshine fills the world with joy and our hearts sing. It's glorious" (p. 30).

But his love of his country is also tinged with blatant racism; as he wrote in *The Clansman,* "But for the Black curse, the South would be to-day the garden of the world!" (p. 282). Brian R. McGee has argued that Dixon's writings are evidence of a search for an American utopia, neither Southern nor Yankee, but one "where Aryans North and South unite to protect their racial heritage."[14]

Dixon's filmic concept of the South is one exemplified in John Ford's *Judge Priest* (1934) and its sequel, *The Sun Shines Bright* (1954), where Henry B. Walthall and Charles Winninger, respectively, declaim the glory of the Old South and proudly wave the Confederate Flag as the strains of "Dixie" are heard on the soundtracks. It is the South in which Shirley Temple dances with Bill "Bojangles" Robinson, the quintessential and subservient Southern Negro, in *The Littlest Rebel* and *The Little Colonel* (both 1935), where another child star, Bobby Breen, sings to happy Negro plantation slaves in *Way Down South* (1939), where Bing Crosby croons in *Mississippi* (1935), where Mary Brian and Charles "Buddy" Rogers are sweethearts in *River of Romance* (1929), and where Tom Sawyer and Huckleberry Finn live. Even the South of the present is as dated as that of old in Hollywood's *Carolina* (1934), with the romantic coupling of Janet Gaynor and Robert Young. The South of the motion picture was a world inhabited by faithful Negro servants, exemplified by Clarence Muse, Eddie "Rochester" Anderson, and Stepin Fetchit, and, on the distaff side, by Louise Beavers and Hattie McDaniel.

With important Negro roles played by Caucasian actors in blackface, *The Birth of a Nation* is no aberration, as some historians might suggest. Blackface was a part of American entertainment as far back as the minstrel shows of the 1840s; and white twentieth-century vaudeville entertainers such as Tess Gardella, billed as Aunt Jemima, always appeared on stage in blackface. The sound motion picture might arguably have begun with *The Jazz Singer* in 1927, which featured the most famous of all blackface entertainers, Al Jolson. As late as 1930, Jolson starred in *Big Boy* entirely in blackface as the faithful Negro jockey Gus, who wins the Kentucky Derby for his Southern "owners."

Southern mythology had no better champion on the printed page prior to Thomas Dixon than Joel Chandler Harris, whose Uncle Remus character is the happy and contented Southern African American of legend. Walt Disney's popular 1946 screen adaptation of the Harris stories under the title *Song of the South* was proof that the myth was very much alive in postwar America, a country that celebrated the return of its soldiers from battle with *The Best Years of Our Lives*, in which not one black American is visible. It is not the South depicted as intolerant on screen as early as *I Am a Fugitive from a Chain Gang* (1932). It is the South that seems only in recent decades to have lost its virginity, and thus its appeal to filmgoers. It was not until 1947 that African American novelist Frank Yerby brought his Southern (and unfortunately somewhat dull) vision of the South to the screen in *The Foxes of Harrow*, and it was a Frenchman, Jean Renoir, who directed Hollywood's first major and feature-length look at what Dixon would have described as "poor white trash" in *The Southerner* (1945). It might be galling to Thomas Dixon, but nothing more aptly demonstrates the one-time appeal of the Old South than the eight versions of *Uncle Tom's Cabin* filmed between 1903 and 1965.

At the start of his career at American Biograph, D.W. Griffith directed a number of films with Southern themes, including *The Planter's Wife* (1908), *In Old Kentucky* (1909), and *The House with Closed Shutters* (1910); the charm of the Southern landscape was evident in the director's *A Romance of Happy Valley* (1919), and an unreconstructed Confederate living in France is prominent in *The Girl Who Stayed at Home* (1919). Dixon also featured Southern characters with high, if not always palatable, ideals in his films, and the South is important to the two screen adaptations of *The Foolish Virgin* and in his original production of *The Mark of the Beast*. Griffith and Dixon are the only true Southern filmmakers from the so-called golden age of the motion picture, although an argument might certainly be made for the inclusion of John Ford as at the least an honorary Southern filmmaker—a Southerner through his marriage to Mary McBride Smith, whose family plantation had been burned by General Sherman on his infamous march to the sea. Since the passing of Griffith and Dixon, the only true Southern filmmaker is documentarian Ross McElwee, whose original and self-absorbed 1985 production, *Sherman's March*, was likened by *People* magazine to *Gone with the Wind* as if made by Woody Allen. With its examination of the filmmaker's highly personal relationships and its nonglamorous, handheld camera style, *Sherman's March* would have horrified both Griffith and Dixon.

From a modern perspective, Thomas Dixon should be grateful to the motion picture in that Martin Scorsese's 2002 production *Gangs of New York* probably alerted the majority of Americans for the first time to the reality that many Northerners were not sympathetic to the Civil War as a vehicle for the freeing of slaves. If Dixon had produced the film, it would have depicted the reality of Negroes lynched in New York and the burning of a city orphanage for African American children, but these incidents were only hinted at in Scorsese's production and its interpretation of the 1863 Conscription Act, which forced the Civil War draft on poor white Americans while permitting the rich to buy themselves out for three hundred dollars.

American Racist: The Life and Films of Thomas Dixon certainly does not overlook its subject's life and nonscreen career, but the emphasis here is on Dixon as a member of the film community. A study of Dixon as a filmmaker is very much valid in that, to a large extent, after the success of *The Birth of a Nation*, he ceased to concentrate on the written page and immersed himself in the projected image. As a 1916 reporter commented, "He will tell you, with a ring of sincerity in his voice and a flash of idealism in his eyes, that the cinema can be made to give the strongest interpretation of great world movements."[15]

Through documentation and analysis of his films, the reader is introduced to the novels that influenced them or from which they are adapted. The medium of the motion picture is, of necessity, lighter in substance than that of the novel, but through his films, Dixon could introduce a wider audience to his ideas and beliefs. Through this book, it is hoped that a new generation will rediscover the many talents of Thomas Dixon and, perhaps, will be less willing to dismiss him as totally without merit or decency. After all, by denouncing Dixon without due consideration, we debase ourselves and lessen our argument against him. "My books are simply merciless records of conditions as they exist, conditions that can have but one ending if they are not honestly and fearlessly faced," argued Dixon.[16] Because Dixon dealt with recent historical reality in such a frank and, to him, honest fashion, his novels were often condemned by contemporary critics; one wrote, "His realism is the realism of the open sore; his art the art of the billboard."[17] Such a comment is both an assault on and an affirmation of Dixon's pragmatic integrity. There are some who argue that Dixon is both a racist and a bad writer and as such should be consigned to obscurity.[18] But that is an overstatement on both counts.

There is much that is wrong, perhaps even evil, in the works of Thomas Dixon. Yet who can boast of so much influence on not only a generation of readers but also a generation of moviegoers? On February 9, 1861, Lawrence M. Keith, a South Carolina delegate to the Convention of Seceded States, said, "Our separatism is final, absolute and eternal." Thomas Dixon might similarly have described his accomplishments as final, absolute, and eternal.

1

THE LIFE WORTH LIVING

In 1905, Thomas Dixon Jr.[1] published the autobiographical *The Life Worth Living*. "It is not often that we are given such an insight into a public man's private life," wrote a reviewer in *Public Opinion* (June 24, 1905), and yet the publication was hardly a surprise in that Dixon from early manhood was very much a public figure, one who had never shied away from controversy. Whatever his beliefs, no matter how inflammatory they might be, Thomas Dixon stood behind them, uncompromising and proud. Most liberals and all African Americans regarded him as an unreconstructed Southerner. He was most certainly a Southerner. Unreconstructed? That is a matter of serious, and ultimately unresolved, debate. Was Dixon's life the life worth living? Based on his literary and motion picture output, it was.

Thomas Dixon was a populist novelist and a racist. As the latter, he was little different from the majority of his era. At the same time, he was ahead of his age, for example, in his endorsement of animal rights. His love of dogs is evident from *The Life Worth Living*. As a ten-year-old boy, Dixon was baptized into his father's church and reborn. In the process, he was required to repent of his sins—and the only guilt that he felt was the revengeful killing of a dog. An impulse of hate had led to the killing, and by admitting to the sin, Dixon experienced religion for the first time.

It is very obvious that Dixon believed in the Bible's interpretation of man's dominion over animals rather than ownership of them. His denunciation of hunting is evident from the comments of the heroine in his last novel, *The Flaming Sword*, as she refuses to participate in the cruelty of a coon hunt. Similarly, after watching a mother coon defend her three babies against attack by a dog, Dixon decided as a child never to hunt coons again. Abraham Lincoln as a boy in *The Southerner* refuses again to participate in a coon hunt after witnessing its horror, depicted by Dixon in graphic detail. In *The Sins of the Father*, the central character, Major Norton, releases a tortured fox from a trap, urging the animal to "Go—go— I'm sorry I hurt you like that!" (p. 258).

There is another area in which Dixon's political correctness is unusual for his age. In his unpublished journals of the 1930s, Dixon wrote that "Capital Punishment is a mistake," arguing that state-sponsored killing does nothing more than "kick" the criminal "out of his body" and that through his death the criminal "may obsess some one (weak) to commit another crime."

Dixon's attitude toward a dog is perhaps unfortunately symbolic of his attitude toward the Negro population of the United States, over which he believed the white man also had dominion. The subtitle of Dixon's first novel, *The Leopard's Spots*, provides a clear indication of his bias: *A Romance of the White Man's Burden, 1865–1900*. (He always used lower case in reference to the Negro, and while this may seem derogatory from a modern viewpoint, it should be noted that the *New York Times* also referred to the "negro" as late as the 1920s.) Yes, as his supporters have argued, Thomas Dixon loved the Negro, but his affection was that of a master toward a well-behaved household pet. The similarity between a dog and Dixon's Negro is accentuated by a comment from Northerner Helen Lowell in *The Leopard's Spots*: "I've seen those beautiful Southern children kiss their old black 'Mammy.' It made me shudder, until I discovered they did it just as I kiss Fido" (p. 317).

Certainly, there is no evidence of any personal animosity toward African Americans. "Tom Dixon didn't hate Negroes," wrote his friend Lee B. Weathers. "He loved them because he understood and sympathized with them."[2] Dixon might write graphically and with fervor of the lynching of a Negro, but in his own household, African Americans were always considered a part—admittedly a lowly part—of the family, and there was never any animosity toward them. "I was placed in my cradle by the hand of a slave, a black saint from whom I first learned of God and eternity," he wrote in his autobiography.[3] In many of his non-Southern novels there are African Americans in minor and subservient roles in whom Dixon, for all his patronizing, can find no fault. Typically, in *The Love Complex*, the leading character has a "colored woman," Mandy, who cleans his rooms: "By Southern training and inheritance she was a motherly soul" (p. 33).

Dixon claimed that his closest friend as a child until he went to college was an African American boy named Dick, whom he regarded as his brother: "His skin was very black, his nose very flat, but there was no evil in his young heart and I loved him from the first."[4] Dick also appears as a character in *The Leopard's Spots*, introduced in, and the subject of, chapter 13. The early life of the Dick of the novel is identical to that of Dick in Dixon's autobiography, with the only difference being that the Dick of *The Leopard's Spots* is later lynched for the rape and murder of a white teenager. Dixon was notorious for recycling his own writings, and it may well be that in old age he decided to recreate his fictional Dick as a real-life childhood companion. Dick may have been a figment of Dixon's imagination, but there is no question that in his last years it was Negro servants who took care of him, and at his funeral a Negro maid named Blanche sat in the front row beside his wife.

James Zebulon Wright has questioned whether the African Americans who came into contact with the private Thomas Dixon were aware of his published proposals for them. Probably not. At an April 25, 1994, symposium at the Library of Congress on *The Birth of a Nation*, one of the participants, John Hope Franklin, professor emeritus of history at Duke University, recalled that fifty-five years earlier he had routinely passed "a courtly gentleman outside the courthouse." That gentleman, who greeted the African American student with a warm smile, was Thomas Dixon. Franklin, displaying a racial antagonism of which Dixon is generally accused, chose to misinterpret that smile as one of secret delight at keeping "the likes of me" out of any government office.

The Ku Klux Klan figures prominently in Dixon's first novels, and his name is permanently linked to the original organization and the principles on which it was founded. But Dixon was no fan of the modern, twentieth-century Klan; from his pulpit and in his novels, it was attacked as vehemently as Dixon himself was attacked by the new Klan and its leaders. On January 22, 1923, Dixon appeared at the Century Theatre, Detroit, praising the Reconstruction Klan as "the bravest and noblest men of the South" but denouncing the modern Klan as "unprincipled marauders."[5]

In February 1923, Dixon was challenged to a debate by the Reverend Dr. Oscar Haywood, national Klokard or lecturer of the KKK, who claimed that the former's attacks on his organization were unjust.[6] Dixon did not respond, but a year later, he told the *New York Times* that the modern Klan was "a growing menace to the cause of law and order . . . a provocation to violence and disorder." Dixon had refused to join the Klan because he would not wear a hood:

> The disguise is a dangerous weapon in the hands of many irresponsible and reckless people and a lawless phase of an organization which politically might do a whole lot of good. . . .
>
> I am opposed to the present-day Ku Klux Klan because I believe it a menace to American democracy.[7]

Stirring as Dixon's words are (as always), his comments contain evidence that he did not in any way renounce the entire history of the Klan. The Ku Klux Klan was founded in Pulaski, Tennessee, in late 1865 or early 1866 and formally disbanded in January 1869 on orders of its Grand Wizard, Nathan B. Forrest. Dixon viewed the Klan, as originally constituted, as an organization that might hold some political sway against the forces of radical Reconstuctionism. The Klan was on a par with his romantic vision of the Old South, honorable knights riding not in shining armor but in white bedsheets against the forces of legalized disorder. His attitude was identical to that of D.W. Griffith, who, in the prologue to the sound reissue of *The Birth of a Nation*, noted that the Klan served a purpose "then" (i.e., during Reconstruction).

Since his death, right-wing elements in American society have used Dixon's writings to their own end and often in disregard of his opinions. In 1965, a paperback edition of *The Clansman* appeared from Professional Services, Inc., of Phoenix, Arizona, with a front cover depicting Robert M. Shelton, the Imperial Wizard of the United Klans of America, against a backdrop of a flaming cross. In 1994, the Noontide Press of Newport Beach, California, reprinted *The Reconstruction Trilogy* as a single paperback, with an introduction by Sam Dickson, who wrote:

> The more intelligent and proud blacks are now recognizing their own destiny lies not in integrating with whites and becoming chocolate covered white men, but in pursuing their own separate African-American identity.
>
> Nevertheless, undeterred by facts, experience or evidence, the liberals, the integrationists, and multiculturalists fanatically press on, always convinced that they are just one more civil rights bill, one more Supreme Court edict, one more welfare program away from the utopia that seems ever to hover on their horizon. Indeed, the more their programs are demonstrated to have failed, the more angrily and furiously they persevere.
>
> Not contented to try to integrate the races already

within the country, they now promote an even more radical program of "multiculturalism," seeking to flood the country with scores of different immigrant groups. . . .

The liberal who constantly accuses racial separatists of "hate" has done nothing but cause hatred. Hatred will best be avoided by separation. Tibetans and Scots, for example, do not hate each other for the precise reason that each folk has its own country apart from the other.

Despite the unwillingness of liberals to face facts, reality cannot be avoided. This country is on a collision course with reality. Ultimately, reality will be heard, even by those, or most especially by those, who want to ignore it. (xix–xx)

Sam Dickson lists his home as Marietta, Georgia. Newport Beach is located in Orange County, the home of the John Birch Society.

Unquestionably, comments by modern members of the Ku Klux Klan reiterate those of Thomas Dixon in *The Leopard's Spots* and elsewhere. When Atlanta attorney James R. Venable was named chairman of the National Association of Ku Klux Klans in the 1960s and later named himself Imperial Wizard of the National Knights of the Ku Klux Klan, he said, "I can't see how any white man can think the nigger is equal. . . . In Africa, the richest land in the world, he's never been able to build a skyscraper. Without the Klan we all would have been spotted, or some other color."[8] From a lawyer, the speech is far from eloquent, but the message is that of Thomas Dixon from more than a half century ago.

To a modern constituency, Thomas Dixon is an archconservative. At the height of his fame, Dixon might well have been considered by many as a liberal. "A liberal says that we don't have to live with what we have. We can change—even undergo drastic changes," noted James Zebulon Wright. "None of Thomas Dixon's ideas fitted the prevailing ideas of the age and state in which he lived. He was never a Southern demagogue. . . . He was a reformer and liberal in the best 19th century tradition."[9]

The son of a Baptist minister of English, German, and French ethnicity who was married to the daughter of a wealthy plantation owner, Thomas Dixon Jr. was born in King's Mountain, North Carolina, on January 11, 1864, just as the Civil War was winding down to its tragic conclusion; the bitterness of Reconstruction was but a year away. His mother's parents had been prominent slaveholders in South Carolina, while his father had "freed" his slaves at the close of the Civil War, except for an elderly "mammy" who remained as one of the family. By all accounts, Dixon's early life was at times a lonely but never an unhappy one. He saw firsthand the carpetbaggers, the new breed of Negro politicians that he so despised, and the rise and the fall of the Ku Klux Klan. A major influence in Dixon's childhood was his mother's brother, Leroy McAfee, who at the age of twenty-five had been a colonel in the Confederate Army and who was later a leader of the Ku Klux Klan in Cleveland County, North Carolina.

In 1879, Dixon enrolled at Wake Forest College, which served as a seminary for potential Baptist ministers and which was also attended by Dixon's two brothers, Clarence and Frank. (There were also two sisters, Delia and Addie May.) The Dixon children were exceptionally intelligent, charismatic individuals and would often correspond with each other in Latin or Greek; they were all the subjects of entries in *Who's Who in America* prior to their thirtieth birthdays. Dixon was one of the organizers of the college's first student newspaper, the *Wake Forest Student,* whose first issue, published in January 1882, featured an essay by Professor William Royall titled "African Slavery in America—Its Good Results—Why These Should Be Noted," described by James Zebulon Wright as "the sort of writing one saw later in Dixon's own work."[10] The *Wake Forest Student* was also the outlet for Dixon's first play, *From College to Prison*, published in January 1883; it was a drama of a student arrested as a member of the Klan.

Upon graduation from Wake Forest in 1883 with a master of arts degree and with more honors than any other student before him, Dixon enrolled at Johns Hopkins University, where he met and became close to a fellow student, Woodrow Wilson, some years his senior. It was the latter who introduced Dixon to the editor of the *Baltimore Mirror*, where he was briefly employed as a drama critic. Dixon became enamored of the theatre and on his twentieth birthday made his first visit to New York and experienced for the first time what the city had to offer in terms of both dramatic and operatic entertainment. He left Johns Hopkins, enrolled at Frobisher's School of Drama in New York, and enjoyed his first professional stage experience as a player in Richard Foote's Shakespearian Repertoire Company. Dixon paid Foote, a theatrical shyster, three hundred dollars for the opportunity to appear as the Duke of Richmond in *Richard III*.

Ultimately, Dixon's efforts to join the New York theatrical community proved abortive, and in April 1884, he returned to family life in Shelby, North Carolina. Never lacking enthusiasm, Dixon entered politics and on his twenty-first birthday was elected to the state legislature. But Dixon lost interest in politics as quickly as he had found it, and in 1885, he became a student at the Greensboro Law School of Dick and Dillard. In 1886, he was admitted to the bar, ordained as a Baptist minister, and married to Harriet Bussey, herself the daughter of a Baptist minister. The couple met in March 1885 while participating in the Mardi Gras celebrations in New Orleans. It is difficult to imagine either having an overly festive time. In photographs, Harriet appears as a somewhat buxom lady, mannish in facial appearance, and one may well surmise that she had a domineering spirit that was more than helpful in prodding Thomas Dixon when necessary—not that there was much need.

Harriet Bussey was not Dixon's first love, nor was she his last. As a fourteen-and-one-half-year-old, he had fallen in love with Mollie Durham, who died while he was at Wake Forest. "In all the novels, plays and pictures which I have written since," wrote Dixon, "I have never sketched a heroine but that something of the tenderness and beauty of this little sixteen year old girl was suggested."[11]

Dixon quickly became noted as a flamboyant and sensationalist preacher who moved away from what he perceived as the strictures of the Baptist ministry to become head of a new congregation, the Raleigh Tabernacle. The showmanship that he evinced early in his career as a preacher was to dominate all aspects of his later life. Dixon is the nineteenth- and early-twentieth-century equivalent of today's televangelist, but with an honesty and integrity unknown to the latter. His fame spread beyond the South, and in November 1887, he became a minister at Dudley Street Church in Boston. Here, Dixon experienced Northern racism for the first time when the Negro nurse of his young baby was refused admission to the hotel where he was staying with his wife. The family moved to another, more liberal establishment. (The child, Thomas Dixon III, lived for many years in Los Angeles, where he died in October 1953 at the age of sixty-three.) Also in Boston, Dixon first became aware of Northern antagonism toward the South through a lecture, "The Southern Problem," by Baptist minister Justin D. Fulton.

From Boston, Dixon moved on to New York and to the Twenty-third Street Baptist Church. He used his pulpit to attack local government corruption as represented by Tammany Hall and boasted the largest congregation of any Protestant minister in the United States. On August 22, 1891, *Harper's Weekly* identified Dixon, along with Theodore Roosevelt, music director Walter Damrosch, and others, as among the city's top thirteen young men of distinction. Facing opposition from some members of the board of the church and because he desired "to lay aside" his "denominational baggage"—"I wish to have a perfectly free pulpit, in which to preach to their last logical conclusion those things which have become to me of supreme importance"[12]—Dixon decided to move on and form a new church, the People's Church (sometimes described as the People's Temple), in the auditorium of the Academy of Music, where on his first visit to New York in 1884, he had heard Adelina Patti sing in *Les Huguenots*. She also sang "Home Sweet Home," which Dixon considered to be the sweetest of all songs. (A leading member of the Klan, Captain Plato Durham, who is buried in the same cemetery as Dixon, once rode on horseback from Shelby to Charleston in order to hear Adelina Patti sing.) For the next four years Dixon was to enjoy unprecedented attention and publicity.

At this time, Thomas Dixon was very much the social crusader, taking on issues with an intensity that anyone of a liberal persuasion would admire. His condemnation of Tammany Hall was so virulent that in September 1896, he was briefly arrested for, of all things, killing seventeen robins on Staten Island. Dixon might argue for the annexation of Hawaii and attack William Jennings Bryan, but basically, he must be acknowledged as a preacher for social justice. The living and working conditions of the poor of New York angered Dixon deeply, and he was to continue his attacks on such circumstances in his second novel, *The One Woman*. In line with the anti-imperialist stance of his novels, Dixon argued for Cuban independence from Spain, with his church becoming headquarters for the Cuban liberation movement.

Thomas Dixon was somewhat aloof as a public speaker, having little interest in the individuals to whom he was preaching, but to his audience he was a mesmerizing figure. A contemporary critic wrote of him:

> His dark eyes seem really luminous; his high, thin nostrils are sensitive to emotion; his every motion on the platform is a definition of grace and vigor; his articulation is marvelous for its distinctness and rapidity, and his voice preserves its southern sweetness and carries like a bell. In speaking, he goes against the theories of elocution so far as to fold his long arms over his chest and to clasp his hands behind him; ofttimes he thrusts his hands into his pockets. A favorite gesture is to strike his fingers through his fine shock of black hair, or to toss it back when the vigorous motions of his shake it about his forehead. Before the footlights he is as goodly a figure as heart could desire. It matters little to his auditors what the philosophy of his discourse may be; their only dread is that which Ben Jonson [sic] ascribed to those who heard

Lord Bacon, "lest he make an end." He has had many imitators, but none successful, for his oratory is unique, and as an orator he can claim most justly, what he has no right to claim as a novelist, style.[13]

Dixon had also commenced his publishing career, and by the end of the nineteenth century, he was responsible for several volumes of nonfiction: *Living Problems in Religion and Social Science* (C.T. Dillingham, 1889), *What Is Religion? An Outline of Vital Ritualism* (Scott Publishing Company, 1891), *Dixon on Ingersoll: Ten Discourses Delivered in Association Hall* (J.B. Alden, 1892), *The Failure of Protestantism in New York and Its Causes* (Victor O.A. Strauss, 1896), as well as a popular collection of his sermons: *Dixon's Sermons: Delivered in the Grand Opera House, New York, 1898–1899* (F.L. Bussey, 1899). Dixon's views were also propagated in a weekly newsletter from the People's Church, titled *The Free Lance*, of which he wrote, "It will be the champion of the weak, the foe of every wrong, and on every page an independent patriot fighting for the larger life of the new Church and the new Nation."

Despite his obvious success, Dixon was forever dissatisfied with his work, and on January 15, 1899, he announced his resignation as pastor of the People's Church. As he later explained to the *New York Herald* (April 30, 1906), it was "for reasons of conscience" not only that he chose to resign but also that he rejected the title of reverend. Dixon continued to lecture, but on the Chautauqua circuit, where tents provided popular summer venues for leading personalities and respectable entertainers of the day. According to Raymond A. Cook, during a four-year period, Dixon was heard by more than five million attendees, with audiences sometimes exceeding six thousand per program.[14] Dixon was a wealthy man with a stately colonial home, Elmington Manor, in Old Tidewater, Virginia, acquired in 1897, and an eighty-foot-long schooner named *Dixie*. A typical dinner for Dixon, his wife, and their two sons aboard the boat consisted of oysters on the half shell, terrapin stew, and duck, all either caught or shot by Dixon himself.

But still, Thomas Dixon considered himself unfulfilled. There was yet another new audience waiting—a literary one. In a comment "To the Reader" prefacing his last novel, *The Flaming Sword*, Dixon wrote, "A novel is the most vivid and accurate form in which history can be written." As he entered on a new chapter in his life, Thomas Dixon was with his first novels to both prove and dispute such a statement.

2

SOUTHERN HISTORY ON THE PRINTED PAGE

While on one of his lecture tours, Thomas Dixon witnessed George L. Aiken's stage adaptation of Harriet Beecher Stowe's *Uncle Tom's Cabin*, which had first been published in serial form in the antislavery newspaper the *National Era*, and in book form in 1852 as *Uncle Tom's Cabin, or Life Among the Lowly*. An ardent abolitionist, Harriet Beecher Stowe argued that tacit support of slavery by the Northern states was immoral, and it is generally accepted that her novel was a primary factor in bringing about the Civil War. "So this is the little lady who made this big war," said Abraham Lincoln upon being introduced to her. Of Simon Legree in *Uncle Tom's Cabin*, one of the characters in Dixon's first novel, *The Leopard's Spots*, comments: "The picture of that brute with a whip in his hand beating a negro caused the most terrible war in the history of the world. Three millions of men flew at each other's throats and for four years fought like demons. A million men and six billions of dollars worth of property were destroyed" (pp. 404–5). "If ever a book proved that politics and literature are inextricably bound, *Uncle Tom's Cabin* is it," wrote Vivian Gornick in the

Los Angeles Times (December 15, 2002), upon publication of a new edition by Oxford University Press. Her comment might equally apply to Dixon's *Reconstruction Trilogy*.

Both Yankee and Southerner chose to view *Uncle Tom's Cabin* as political propaganda. But, as W.J. Cash wrote in 1941, "Mrs. Stowe did not invent the figure of Uncle Tom, nor did Christy [with his minstrels] invent that of Jim Crowe—the banjo-picking, heel-flinging, hi-yi-ing happy jack of the levees and the cotton fields. All they did was to modify them a little for their purposes. In essentials, both were creations of the South—defense mechanisms, answers to the Yankee and its own doubts, projections from its own mawkish tears and its own mawkish laughter over the black man, incarnations of its sentimentalized version of slavery."[1]

Dixon was obviously aware both of the novel and of its impact, but it was the play that upset him so much that he wept at its misrepresentation of Southerners.[2] He determined that he would write a sequel to *Uncle Tom's Cabin*, featuring one of Mrs. Stowe's most prominent characters, Simon Legree. The impetus for Dixon's career as a writer may have been *Uncle Tom's Cabin*, but the literary formula was provided by Polish author Henryk Sienkiewewicz (1846–1916), winner of the 1905 Nobel Prize for Literature and best remembered today for *Quo Vadis?* (1896). Dixon greatly admired Sienkiewewicz's trilogy on Polish history, *With Fire and Sword*, *The Deluge*, and *Pan Michael*.

Although he did not admit it in relation to the writing of *The Reconstruction Trilogy*, Dixon equally admired British novelist Hall Caine (1853–1931). There are a number of similarities between the two men, both being propagandizers with a strong sense of morality and a sentimental attachment to the area about which they wrote. For Dixon, it was the South, and for Caine it was the Isle of Man, off the northwest coast of England. Hall Caine knew as much as Thomas Dixon about self-promotion, at one point describing himself as "the Shakespeare of the novel." Caine's 1894 novel *The Manxman* broke the formula of the three-volume novel popular up until that time. It was filmed in 1929 by Alfred Hitchcock as his last silent film, and, again as with Dixon, many of Caine's novels later became motion pictures, most notably *The Christian* (1897) and *The Eternal City* (1901).

On publication of *The Manxman*, Dixon wrote: "The marvelous power of this book is something immortal. I have never read a book of more resistless power. No man can write the truth and not preach. Talk about preaching! I try to preach, but when I read such a book I think I would crawl on my hands and knees around the world if I could write one like it. When a thousand preachers shall have died and been forgotten that book shall preach to generations yet unborn, preach to millions unchanging truths of the human heart and human life."[3] "I made no effort to write literature," wrote Dixon of his own efforts, a comment with which many critics were in agreement. "It has always seemed to me a waste of time to do such work. Every generation writes its own literature. My sole purpose in writing was to reach and influence with my argument the minds of millions. I had a message and wrote it as vividly and simply as I knew how."[4]

Thomas Dixon was to be the voice of the silent South, as he put it, slandered and misrepresented by Northern writers. He was no apologist for the Old South, as was writer Thomas Nelson Page, but rather its defender, a white slave to a system and society that endorsed black slavery. He did not support the Confederate cause—Dixon's beliefs were of reconciliation and union—but he did view any Southern state in general, and North Carolina in particular, as being representative of any American state, North or South. White Northerners and Southerners were united in common causes and beliefs, as he saw it, with only the Negro an alien. *The Leopard's Spots* opens on the field of Appomattox as General Lee watches the ragged troops of Cox's North Carolina regiment march by. The last act of the Civil War tragedy has been played out, and General Joseph Eggleston Johnson has surrendered to Northern Army commander William Tecumseh Sherman.

Surrender!
A new word in the vocabulary of the South—a word

so terrible in its meaning that the date of its birth was to be the landmark of time. Henceforth all events would be reckoned from this; "before the surrender," or "after the surrender." (p. 2)

The first book of the novel is subtitled "Legree's Regime" and deals with the rise to power in postwar North Carolina of Harriet Beecher Stowe's villainous Simon Legree. Now forty-two years old, Legree, "whose cruelty to his slaves had made him unique in infamy in the annals of the South" (p. 86), has sold his slaves and become the ultimate carpetbagger, inciting the newly free Southern Negroes to vote at his command. In Raleigh, North Carolina, he is elected Speaker of the House. At his last appearance in the novel, Legree is claimed to have amassed a fortune of fifty million dollars. Dixon quotes Abraham Lincoln's 1858 statement:

I am not, nor ever have been in favor of bringing about in any way the social and political equality of the white and black races. . . . I will say in addition to this that there is a physical difference between the white and black races which I believe will forever forbid the two races living together on terms of social and political equality; and inasmuch as they can not so live, while they do remain together, there must be the position of the inferior and the superior; and I am, as much as any other man, in favor of having the superior position assigned to the white race. (pp. 67–68)

But two years have passed since the end of the Civil War, Lincoln has been assassinated, and Congress has passed Thaddeus Stevens's infamous bill, dividing the Southern states into military districts, enfranchising the entire African American population, and disenfranchising one-fourth of white Southerners. Various acts of terror, murder, and rape against the white population are documented in gory detail by Dixon; these lead to the legitimate establishment of the Ku Klux Klan and equally, although certainly Dixon does not see it as such, the establishment of white law by lynching. He evokes an air of mysticism to the Klan:

> The origin of this Law and Order League which sprang up like magic in a night and nullified the program of Congress, though backed by an army of a million veteran soldiers, is yet a mystery. The simple truth is, it was a spontaneous and resistless racial uprising of clansmen of highland origin living along the Appalachian mountains and foothills of the South, and it appeared almost simultaneously in every Southern state produced by the same terrible conditions. (p. 151)

> This Invisible Empire of White Robed Anglo-Saxon Knights was simply the old answer of organized manhood to organized crime. Its purpose was to bring order out of chaos, protect the weak and defenseless, the widows and orphans of brave men who had died for their country, to drive from power the thieves who were robbing the people, redeem the commonwealth from infamy, and re-establish the civilization. (p. 152)

The second half of the novel deals with the love affair between Sallie Worth, a daughter of the old-fashioned South as well as a daughter of Southern aristocracy as represented by General Daniel Worth, and Charles Gaston, a son of "what is known in the South as poor white trash" (p. 185) but who becomes governor of the state.

Even by the elementary standards of criticism that one might use to judge the entire creative output of Thomas Dixon, *The Leopard's Spots* is not a great piece of literature. It is poorly, almost crudely, conceived, with the emphasis on propaganda rather than literary construction. The *Independent* (June 26, 1902) concluded, "In this novel Mr. Dixon shows himself an orator rather than a literary artist." Another contemporary reviewer commented,

"The love story and the political thesis were so poorly blended that the book may fairly be called a failure from the strictly literary point of view, in spite of its evident adaptation to its author's primary purpose."[5] To the *Dial* (May 1, 1903), *The Leopard's Spots* seemed to be "thrown into the form of a novel, so far as it can be said to possess form at all."

Dixon's primary purpose was twofold: to denigrate the Reconstructionist Southern Negro and to argue against any integration, particularly through marriage, between the black and white races. A one-legged Confederate soldier, Tom Camp, representative of the poor Southerner, admits, "I always hated a nigger since I was knee high" (p. 28). The racism here is blatant and deeply disturbing for the power Dixon displays in its manifestation. Six Negro troopers invade a marriage party and carry off the bride. The white guests pursuing the troopers are urged to shoot and kill the bride, which they do: "there are things worse than death!" (p. 126). After teenager Flora is raped and murdered by a former slave, her father stops the funeral—"Don't put her in that grave! A nigger dug it" (p. 380)—until his Confederate colleagues have excavated a new burial site.

With emancipation, the danger that the Negro represents to Southern civilization cannot be overestimated. The Reverend John Durham is forced off the sidewalk by a drunken Negro in federal uniform: "Gradually in his mind for days this towering figure of the freed negro had been growing more and more ominous, until its menace overshadowed the poverty, the hunger, the sorrows and the devastation of the South, throwing the blight of its shadow over future generations, a veritable Black Death for the land and its people" (p. 33).

It is at a political convention that Charles Gaston delivers an eight-page speech that is the raison d'être for *The Leopard's Spots*. He argues that there is not room enough for both the Negro and the white races on this continent (p. 443); he speaks against "the negro supremacy under which our civilization is being degraded" (p. 444) and says, "This is a white man's government, conceived by white men, and maintained by white men through every year of its history—and by the God of our Fathers it shall be ruled by white men until the Arch-Angel shall call the end of time!" (p. 446).

Miscegenation is an important issue in *The Leopard's Spots*, and this is never more clearly discussed by Dixon, and with such obvious delight in ridicule, as when dealing with the liberal Northern politician Everett Lowell. Lowell is the mentor of George Harris, the baby carried across the ice by escaped slave Eliza Harris in *Uncle Tom's Cabin*. Educated at Harvard, Harris is a "gentleman and scholar" (p. 390). An honored guest in Lowell's home, Harris makes the unfortunate announcement, "I am madly, desperately in love with your daughter" (p. 394), resulting in an interesting exchange of dialogue:

> "Why is such a hope unreasonable, sir, to a man of your scientific mind?"
>
> "It is a question of taste," snapped Lowell.
>
> "Am I not a graduate of the same university with you? Did I not stand as high, and age for age, am I not your equal in culture?"
>
> "Granted. Nevertheless you are a negro, and I do not desire the influence of your blood in my family."
>
> "But I have more of white than negro blood, sir."
>
> "So much the worse. It is the mark of shame."
>
> "But it is the one drop of negro blood at which your taste revolts, is it not?"
>
> "To be frank, it is." (p. 395)

Lowell throws Harris from his home, arguing that social rights and political rights are not interwoven:

> I happen to know the important fact that a man or woman of negro ancestry, though a century removed, will suddenly breed back to a pure negro child, thick lipped, kinky headed, flat nosed, black skinned! One drop of

your blood in my family could push it backward three thousand years in history. If you were able to win her consent, a thing unthinkable, I would do what old Virginius did in the Roman Forum, kill her with my own hand, rather than see her sink in your arms into the black waters of a Negroid life! Now go!" (p. 398)

George Harris is now forced to turn to Simon Legree for help but begs "in vain for the privilege of serving in the meanest capacity as his slave" (p. 407). Harris deliberately begins a life of crime, and as he visits Colorado, Kansas, Indiana, and Ohio, he comes across ash heaps where African Americans have been burned alive. Never in the South, under the harshest conditions of slavery, has any Negro been so brutalized. Through the educated George Harris, the underlying and obvious message of *The Leopard's Spots* is proven to be correct: "The Ethiopian can not change his skin, or the leopard his spots" (p. 463). Through George Harris's later life, Dixon emphasizes that the condition of the Negro is, in reality, no different in the North than in the South, and perhaps, in the days of slavery, somewhat better in the latter.

Dixon claimed to have spent more than a dozen years researching *The Leopard's Spots,* but only sixty days in the actual writing of the novel, which was initially titled *The Rise of Simon Legree,* in the log cabin studio at Elmington Manor. When the manuscript was complete, he sent it to an old friend, Walter Hines Page, who had been a student at Johns Hopkins University and was now editor of the *Raleigh State Chronicle* and a partner in the publishing house of Doubleday, Page, and Company. Page and Dixon shared the same view on emancipation, with Page writing in reference to the period immediately after the Civil War, "Negro men, who had wandered a while looking for an invisible 'freedom' came back and went to work on the farm from force of habit. They now received wages and bought their own food. That was the only difference that freedom had brought them."[6]

Page, who was anxious to publish works by Southern authors,

read Dixon's manuscript within forty-eight hours and was, according to Dixon, so impressed by the novel that he told the author to create his own scale of royalties. Eventually, the novel sold more than one million copies and made Dixon the modern equivalent of a millionaire.[7]

"For Thomas Dixon, writing *The Leopard's Spots* was a sort of attenuated ink blot test," wrote Joel Williamson. "The image held up was the South in the nation after the Civil War. Into his interpretation of that image, Dixon poured a lifetime of emotion, and at least a dozen years of travel, observation, and brooding about himself and his society. Through it all, the characters are rearranged and moved to suit Dixon's own psychic needs. It was his fantasy life, his dream life, the life he felt he should have been living all along. The actual writing was a way of reliving his life as in retrospect he would have it."[8]

There is a strong link between hero Charles Gaston and Thomas Dixon, not only through young Dick but also in the manner in which General Worth dismisses Gaston as a suitable husband for his daughter, just as Dixon had initially been rejected by his future father-in-law. There is also an element of Dixon in Rev. John Durham, who adopts Charles Gaston and rejects the offer to head a rich church in Boston. Dixon accepted such an offer, and he must always have contemplated what his life might have been had he stayed in the South.

Joel Williamson maintains that Dixon wrote *The Leopard's Spots* because of a deep emotional problem, the belief that his mother had been sexually violated as a child.[9] There is, of course, an obsession here with the violated woman, with the aborted kidnap-rape of the young bride and the rape-murder of Flora. James Zebulon Wright has suggested to me that, based on portions of the author's autobiography not in the published version, Dixon's first sexual experience was with his faithful Negro friend, Dick.[10] If that is true, then obviously Dixon's writing provides a treasure trove for amateur psychologists. Another critic, Sandra Gunning, has suggested a homosexual or, at the least, a homosocial relationship between the young Charles Gaston and his faithful Negro friend, Dick.[11] Is it possible that Dick rapes the teenage girl because he pines for his childhood love, Gaston? And why does this rapist possess a phallic name?

But there is also a deliberate attempt by Dixon to titillate his female readership. *The Leopard's Spots* was published at a time when many women were experiencing a form of sexual awakening, thanks to the opportunity for the first time to enjoy the male body outside of marriage. At the turn of the century, women were able to attend boxing matches, to view the seminaked protagonists whose brief and clinging costumes emphasized their sexuality. The early motion picture recognized the importance of the female gaze, offering lengthy filmed records of prominent boxing bouts, which might be viewed with comparative ease by all manner and classes of females.

In *The Leopard's Spots* and elsewhere, Dixon emphasizes the physical aspects of the African American male. Strippings to the waist (and beyond) together with whippings, emphasizing the cut of the lash on the body, play a prominent role in Dixon's novels. The "saturnalia of debauchery," about which Upton Sinclair writes in *The Jungle* (1906), with white women admiring "big Buck Negroes" engaged in fistfights, is prevalent in the writings of Thomas Dixon. His descriptions of the physical size of his Negroes' bodies might make unnecessary any written hint as to the size of their genitalia. Yet, in recognition of the long-held superstition that a large foot indicates a large penis, in *The Clansman* Dixon actually has a group of white men fascinated by the large footprint left by a black rapist. The pervasive and sexual smell of sweat hangs heavy in the Southern air as "a great herd of negroes" invades Mrs. Gaston's home and garden and she becomes aware of "the unmistakable odour of perspiring negroes" (p. 139). There is no effeminate Uncle Tom in Dixon's world. When he writes of Negro blood, it is semen to which he is referring, one drop of which will make the child of a white woman black.

Recently, Philip Dray has noted the sexual retribution central to the lynching act, the castration of the victim. Dray claims that the lynchings were sexual events, with "the lynching of the alleged rapist . . . itself an act of rape, more specifically gang rape."[12] Certainly, Dixon does not flinch from lurid descriptions of lynchings, with victims generally stripped and with the obvious hint of castration.[13]

Thomas Dixon was arguably one of the first popular authors to pander to female fantasies, regardless of how offensive the notion of rape as pleasure may be to modern feminists.[14] A couple of decades later, Edith M. Hull was drawn to this same feminine fantasy, and in *The Sheik*, which was filmed in 1922 with Rudolph Valentino in the title role, she has a white woman carried off into the desert (and unthinkable debauchery) by an Arab sheik. In the 1926 sequel, *The Son of the Sheik*, Valentino is stripped to the waist and whipped in a scene that might be right out of a Thomas Dixon novel. While he was codifying the racist image of African Americans, Dixon was also clearly establishing their sexual identity for a white female readership.

But the sexual imagery is not only for female readers. Gay men may have enjoyed some descriptive passages that border on homoeroticism, while white males could fantasize and yet distance themselves from the sexual assault and rape at which Dixon hints so vividly. In his mind, white men do not rape women—white or black—and when an interracial relationship occurs, as in *The Sins of the Father*, it is the black woman who seduces the white male.

One of the few positive reviews of *The Leopard's Spots* was in the *Saturday Evening Post* (April 12, 1902). The reviewer, Lilian Bell, had, it is believed, a personal interest in Dixon beyond that of a concerned critic. Bell maintained that the "facts" in Dixon's novel were generally unknown even to the enlightened and thinking classes of the North:

> In *The Leopard's Spots* the hitherto silent, misunderstood and maligned South has found a fiery pen and an eloquent voice lifted in dignity in its defense. The general mass of readers will condemn the book as too radical,

35

prejudiced and highly colored. I, for one, from absolute knowledge of my facts, do not hesitate to say that the book is moderate in tone considering what might have been written. . . .

But whether you believe it all, accept it all, or like it all, have the justice to read it. It cannot fail to hold for each reader some one new thought, some one new fact, some one new reason. Those of purely Northern blood have put the question. For thirty-five years those of purely Southern blood have held their peace and struggled. Now for the first time there speaks through the medium of the novel the history of thirty-five awful, never-to-be-forgotten years.

Describing the novel as "ill-natured," the literary journal the *Dial* (June 1, 1902) provided a backhanded complement: "He is full of hatred against the negro, who was rather the tool in the hands of designing whites than an actor on his own responsibility in the scenes complained of. Yet his book will not have been written in vain if it points out the dangers of ruling a people against its will, the awful perils of governing without the consent of the governed." The *Dial* returned to the novel on May 1, 1903, with a discussion of the work of Booker T. Washington and W.E.B. Du Bois, noting, "He [Dixon] has much to learn from either one of them."

Dixon responded to his critics with a letter in the *New York Times* that concluded with an almost threatening tone: "I have given voice to the deepest soul convictions of these eighteen millions of our people on the gravest problem of the twentieth century. They are so situated geographically that they control enough votes to elect the President with the aid of but two Northern States. Is it not time to make an honest effort to understand them? I have tried to introduce you to them."[15]

The Leopard's Spots was the first in Dixon's *Reconstruction Trilogy*, but the author took a break after its publication to work on the first in a second trilogy—on socialism—titled *The One Woman* (discussed in chapter 7). If nothing else, the title reminds the reader that while white heroines figure prominently in *The Reconstruction Trilogy*, African American women are curiously absent except in the form of the sympathetic "mammy." Why is the rape of slave women by their white masters nothing more than an undiscussed irrelevancy? What happened to female slaves after emancipation? Why did they not provide a restraining hold on Dixon's slavering, oversexed Negroes? Do Thomas Dixon's black women represent nothing more than the sometimes unwilling architects of miscegenation?

As Sandra Gunning has written, "The Klansmen make a brief appearance in *The Leopard's Spots* . . . , but they ride in full force into the pages of *The Clansman*,"[16] the second book in the *Reconstruction Trilogy*. Their prominence is emphasized not only by the title but also by the dedication: "To the memory of a Scotch-Irish leader of the South, My Uncle, Colonel Leroy McAfee, Grand Titan of the Invisible Empire Ku Klux Klan." It might well be argued that the novel is nothing more than a cheap justification for the Klan; Congress makes errors and the Klan corrects them. It is all very convenient, if somewhat implausible.[17]

The Clansman is in no way a sequel to *The Leopard's Spots*, but rather almost a rewriting of the same theme. It is as if Dixon is trying to improve himself as a writer at the expense of his reader, but he fails dismally as the pages of *The Clansman* desperately cry out for a competent editor. The book begins in a leisurely style, with too much emphasis on the Washington political scene, and ends in a mad, intertwined rush of plot and Klansmen. The change of primary location from Dixon's home state of North Carolina to South Carolina was necessary because South Carolina was one of only two Southern states of the Reconstruction period that had Negro majorities in their legislatures (the other state was Mississippi).

Like *The Leopard's Spots*, *The Clansman* begins at the close of the Civil War as the newspapers report that Lee has surrendered. In Washington, D.C., Elsie Stoneman is tending to the wounded,

37

providing them with the opportunity to listen to her banjo playing and singing, the delights of which the reader can scarcely imagine. "The banjo had come to Washington with the negroes following the wake of the army. She had laid aside her guitar and learned to play all the stirring camp-songs of the South" (p. 9)—all of which would appear to contain the word *nigger* in their titles. At the hospital, Elsie meets Mrs. Cameron of South Carolina and helps her locate her wounded son, Colonel Ben Cameron, who is under sentence of death for violating the rules of war as a guerilla raider in the invasion of Pennsylvania.

Because she is the daughter of Austin Stoneman, Elsie is able to take Mrs. Cameron to meet with President Lincoln and gain a pardon for her son (which is initially rejected by Secretary of War Edwin Stanton). Dixon's white villain Austin Stoneman is based very literally on Thaddeus Stevens (1792–1868), an abolitionist and instigator of the Reconstruction program for the defeated South. Should there be any doubt as to Stoneman's identity, Dixon labels him the "Great Commoner," just as Stevens was known as the "Old Commoner." For twenty years, Stevens lived with his housekeeper, Lydia Smith, the daughter of a Negro mother and a white father, who could easily pass as white and was, presumably, Stevens's mistress. Similarly, Stoneman lives with Lydia Brown, "a mulatto, a woman of extraordinary animal beauty and the fiery temper of a leopardess" (p. 56), identified in one chapter heading as "The First Lady of the Land." Also in the Stoneman household is the Negro Silas Lynch, whom Stoneman has sent to college and helped enter the Methodist ministry, playing a similar role here to that of George Harris in *The Leopard's Spots*.

Dixon was proud of his characterization of Austin Stoneman as Thaddeus Stevens:

> I drew of old Thaddeus Stevens the first full length portrait in history. I showed him to be, what he was, the greatest and vilest man who ever trod the halls of the American Congress. I dare my critic to come out from

under his cover and put his finger on a single word, line, sentence, paragraph, page, or chapter in *The Clansman* in which I have done Thad Stevens an injustice. If he succeeds, I will give a thousand dollars to endow a chair of Greek for any negro college he may name, for I take him to be a "missionary" to the South.[18]

It is not the law of libel—one cannot libel the dead—that prevents Dixon from calling Stoneman by his historical name, but rather a change in the circumstances of his family life—Stevens was a bachelor without children—and the eventual change in attitude toward the South at which the novelist hints. In reality, Thaddeus Stevens remained committed to Negro suffrage and believed, rightly as it transpired, that the gains he had won for the African American would ultimately be lost. His biographer, Fawn M. Brodie, points out that "Stevens should not be blamed for the fictions of Reconstruction, which cling tenaciously in the Southern folk memory. One of these holds that Reconstruction consisted of 'Negro rule' and the 'Africanization' of the South. In only two states, Mississippi and South Carolina, did the Negroes control the state legislature, and in both these states the Negroes greatly outnumbered the whites in the total population. Everywhere else 'Negro rule' meant simply that a minority of Negroes were elected to the state legislatures, where they were largely dominated by Radical white men."[19]

That one of those black-controlled states was South Carolina is enough for Dixon to label Stevens/Stoneman as a traitor to his race. In counterpoint, Dixon's admiration for Lincoln shines through on page after page. That almost childlike adoration is expressed in the words of Phil Stoneman to Margaret Cameron: "On the surface, easy friendly ways and the tenderness of a woman—beneath, an iron will and lion heart. I like him. And what always amazes me is his universality. A Southerner finds him in the South, the Western man in the West, even Charles Sumner, from Boston, almost loves him. You know I think he is the first great all-round American who ever lived in the White House" (p. 72).

In a chapter titled "A Clash of Giants," Lincoln and Stoneman argue over the future of the South, with Lincoln's views very much echoing those of Dixon:

> I believe that there is a physical difference between the white and black races which will forever forbid their living together on terms of political and social equality. (p. 45)

> The negro has cost us $5,000,000,000, the desolation of ten great states, and rivers of blood. (pp. 45–46)

> Within twenty years, we can peacefully colonize the negro in the tropics, and give him our language, literature, religion, and system of government under conditions in which he can rise to the full measure of manhood. This he can never do here. It was the fear of the black tragedy behind emancipation that led the South into the insanity of secession. We can never attain the ideal Union our fathers dreamed, with millions of an alien, inferior race among us, whose assimilation is neither possible nor desirable. The Nation cannot now exist half white and half black, any more than it could exist half slave and half free. (pp. 46–47)

> We fought the South because we loved her and would not let her go. Now that she is crushed and lies bleeding at our feet—you shall not make war on the wounded, the dying and the dead! (pp. 54–55)

Stoneman's response is quick and to the point: "The South is conquered soil. I mean to blot it from the map" (p. 49).

Historical events take control as Lincoln is assassinated, with Elsie, Mrs. Cameron's daughter Margaret, and Austin Stoneman's son Phil in the audience at Ford's Theatre. (In *The Birth of a Nation*, only Elsie and Phil are present in the auditorium.) Lydia Brown and Silas Lynch urge Stoneman on with his plans for the South, including the confiscation of white land and its division among the Negroes. Ben's father, Dr. Cameron, is arrested and charged with complicity in Lincoln's murder. (Dr. Cameron is supposedly based on Dr. J. Rufus Bratton of York, South Carolina, who was chief surgeon at two Confederate hospitals and active in the local Klan organization.)[20] Outraged at the hanging of Annie Surratt, the new president, Andrew Johnson, demands Secretary of War Stanton's resignation, but it is refused. In direct conflict with Johnson, Stoneman fights for his impeachment. Stanton resigns and dies in despair, allowing for the release of Dr. Cameron. "A new mob of onion-laden breath, mixed with perspiring African odor, became the symbol of American democracy" (p. 155).

Thomas Dixon seizes the opportunity to attack special interest groups in Congress:

> The first great Railroad Lobby, with continental empires at stake, thronged the Capitol with its lawyers, agents, barkers, and hired courtesans.
>
> The Cotton Thieves, who operated through a ring of Treasury agents, had confiscated unlawfully three million bales of cotton hidden in the South during the war and at its close, the last resource of a ruined people. The Treasury had received a paltry twenty thousand bales, for the use of its name with which to seize alleged "property of the Confederate Government." The value of this cotton, stolen from the widows and orphans, the maimed and the crippled, of the South was over $700,000,000 in gold—a capital sufficient to have started an impoverished people again on the road to prosperity. The agents of this ring surrounded the halls of legislation, guarding their booty from envious eyes, and demanding the enactment of vaster schemes of legal confiscation. (pp. 152–53)

Book 2 of *The Clansman* concludes with a sick Austin Stoneman agreeing to visit Piedmont, South Carolina, at the instigation of daughter Elsie, who has fallen in love with Ben Cameron, and son Phil, who is in love with Margaret Cameron. The family takes up residence at the home of Marion Lenoir and her mother. After an encounter with a Negro trooper and former family slave named Gus, Ben Cameron is arrested on a trumped-up murder charge, and his father is also later detained. Phil arranges the release of Ben, and Dr. Cameron is released because of his position in the community.

After the first election of the Reconstruction, the South Carolina legislature consists of 101 Negroes and 23 white men, and Silas Lynch is elected lieutenant governor. Ben becomes involved in the local organization of the Klan, against the wishes of his father: "a secret society such as you have planned means a conspiracy that may bring exile or death. I hate lawlessness and disorder. We have had enough of it. Your clan means ultimately martial law" (p. 262). While Austin Stoneman remains in the background, in what Dixon describes as "mental twilight," his son Phil becomes "as radical in his sympathies with the Southern people as his father had ever been against them" (p. 276).

The plot reaches its climax not with the central players but with Mrs. Lenoir and her daughter Marion, who have been saved from bankruptcy by the unexpected generosity of Stoneman, paying twenty dollars an acre for their land. Gus, in company with "four black brutes," bursts into their home. "We ain't atter money" (p. 304), he laughs, as the mother is tied up and Marion is raped. (There is no evidence that Mrs. Lenoir suffers the same fate as her daughter.) In the morning, the two women agree upon a suicide pact, and Marion puts on a dress of spotless white that she wore the night Ben Cameron kissed her (after she had rescued her horse from a burning stable). The mother obviously has some misgivings, but, urged on by her daughter, she walks to the cliff above the river, earlier described as Lover's Leap. "Then, hand in hand, they stepped from the cliff into the mists and on through the opal gates of Death" (p. 308).

Marion Lenoir is, of course, *The Clansman*'s substitute for

Flora of *The Leopard's Spots*. Her death not only serves to provide a justification for the appearance of the Ku Klux Klan but also conveniently disposes of the one woman standing between Ben Cameron and Elsie Stoneman.

Gus is the prime suspect in the rape, and to prove his guilt, Dr. Cameron invites his son to witness an experiment. He believes that impressions remain in the brain and images in the eye. By using a microscope to examine Mrs. Lenoir's eye, Dr. Cameron obtains what he claims to be an image of Gus but which his son sadly tells him is nothing more than an image in his eye, not the mother's.[21] More convincing evidence is a footprint found at the Lenoir home and believed to be that of Gus.

In Dr. Cameron's foolish belief that through Mrs. Lenoir's eye he establishes the Negro as the perpetrator of the crime, the father is himself identified as a victim of the Old South. He sees what he wants to see, and what he wants is for Gus as the former slave, representing all former slaves, to be the primary villain in the downfall of the South as he knew it.

The Klan gathers in a cave by the river, and the hapless Gus is led in. Dr. Cameron hypnotizes him, and Gus describes his crime while breaking into fiendish laughter. His body is found in Lynch's yard, and across the breast is pinned a scrap of paper with the letters *K.K.K.* An outraged Austin Stoneman warns his son that the Camerons "are on the road to the gallows" (p. 328), but in anger, Phil tells him "that if it comes to an issue of race against race, I am a white man" (p. 329).

In answer to the speedy rise to power of the Klan, Stoneman has Ben Cameron arrested and sentenced to death. Phil visits Ben in the Charlotte prison and changes places with him. (This plot device is obviously borrowed from the Sydney Carton–Charles Darnay switch in Charles Dickens's *A Tale of Two Cities*.) An appeal against the execution can only be made through Austin Stoneman, and he has secretly left town. Margaret Cameron rushes to find Stoneman before Phil is killed. In a matter of three pages, all the principals arrive at the Cameron residence, with Ben in full

Klan regalia. He and his Klansmen have rescued Phil. Ben points to the fiery crosses burning on the mountains around Piedmont, indicating that the white Southerners are victorious: "Civilization has been saved, and the South redeemed from shame" (p. 372).

The incredibly rushed ending is standard, occurring in many of Dixon's novels. He spends too many pages on political and moral exposition, and too few on the climax of the novel. Stoneman races to save his son, but as far as one can ascertain, he is saved by Ben, making Margaret's rush to find Stoneman irrelevant. Dr. Cameron has tried earlier to reason with Stoneman, but ultimately it is the Klan that delivers salvation.

In acknowledgment of the supposed Scottish ancestry of the Ku Klux Klan, despite the fact that the link is nebulous and the fiery cross unknown in Scottish history, Dixon spends time emphasizing the ancestral connection. In his preface, Dixon claims the young South was "led by the reincarnated souls of the Clansmen of Old Scotland." Margaret Cameron tells Phil Stoneman that her family is old-fashioned Scotch Presbyterian—Dixon misusing the term *Scotch* in place of *Scottish*.

According to Dixon, *The Clansman* was based on several thousand books and pamphlets[22] but written in a mere thirty days, with its author working sixteen hours of each of those days. At its publication by Doubleday, Page, and Company in January 1905, *The Clansman* garnered a mixed reception from the critics. "*The Clansman* may be summed up as a very poor novel, a very ridiculous novel, not a novel at all, yet a novel that very properly is going to interest many thousands of readers of all degrees of taste and education, a book which will be discussed from all points of view, voted superlatively good and superlatively bad, but which will be read," wrote a breathless F. Dredd, who obviously believed in sentences without end, in the *Bookman* (February 1905). "There is less vulgarity in the story than might be expected," wrote the *Outlook* (February 4, 1905), "but restraint has not yet done its full work. The best men, both North and South, will turn from this repellant portrayal of our country and our countrymen." While the *Saturday Review* (May 13, 1905) complained, "Mr. Dixon . . . has lost his sense of perspective," the *New York Times* (January 21, 1905) hailed the novel as "a thrilling romance."

A lengthy discussion of the novel appeared in *Current Literature* (February 1905), with Charles C. Winery commenting on "the orgy of Reconstruction" and making unfortunate reference to Dixon's calling a spade a spade. "It is sufficiently certain at all events," wrote Winery, "that the author has few of the qualifications for purely historical writing; his tone, his lack of poise and detachment, his disregard of perspective, inevitably vitiates everything that he says. . . . [*The Clansman*] does not promote a correct, unprejudiced understanding of the Reconstruction period."

To Dixon, all criticism was irrelevant. "Whether *The Clansman* is literature or trash is a question about which I am losing no sleep," he wrote to the *New York Times* on February 22, 1905. "This generation will not decide it and in the next I'll be dead and it will not matter."

The Ku Klux Klan may be central to both *The Leopard's Spots* and *The Clansman*, as well as to the final volume in the trilogy, *The Traitor*, but it is the issue of the Negro, his subjugation and his post–Civil War welfare, that is central to Dixon's writings here and in much of his output. As he explains in his preface to *The Clansman*, it is the second in a series of historical novels "on the Race Conflict." Racial destiny is the issue. As it is explained by Dr. Cameron to Austin Stoneman, "For a Russian to rule a Pole . . . , a Turk to rule a Greek, or an Austrian to dominate an Italian, is hard enough, but for a thick-lipped, flat-nosed, spindle-shanked negro, exuding his nauseating animal odor, to shout in derision over the hearths and homes of white men and women is an atrocity too monstrous for belief" (p. 290).

The Civil War abolished slavery and permanently established the Union, but it did not solve or address the issue of the African American. A century later, what Dixon found amusing, a reader must find distasteful, as, for example, when Marion Lenoir shows Elsie Stoneman a wren's nest and tells her that the male's mating call is "Free-nigger! Free-nigger! Free-nigger!" (p. 198). Any discussion of the Negro question, as Dixon generally referred to it, is complex and, to a large extent, outside of the scope of this work. The vitriolic attacks on Dixon and his writings are race-based, and Dixon's response was never conciliatory; if anything, the animosity only strengthened his point of view.

Dixon did not believe in slavery. Like his father, he "believed that slavery would die of its own weakness in the South, as it had died in the North."[23] As Robert E. Lee is quoted as saying in *The Man in Gray: A Romance of North and South*, "Slavery must perish in the progress of human society" (p. 27). The slave ships landed their human cargo at Northern ports. In a speech almost identical to that delivered by Dr. Cameron to his son Ben in *The Clansman*, Dixon noted, "Slavery was not a Southern institution. It was a national inheritance."[24] In his love of the Negro, of which he frequently wrote, Dixon always claimed that "he should have the opportunity for the highest, noblest and freest development of his full, rounded manhood."[25] The problem was that Dixon's notion of this development excluded a life and career in the United States, South or North.

The charge of racism that, justly from a modern perspective, is leveled at Dixon is not based so much on his defense of the Ku Klux Klan of the immediate Reconstruction period, but rather on his ultimate solution to the Negro problem. Almost a century prior to the publication of *The Leopard's Spots*, the American Society for Colonizing the Free People of Colour of the United States had been founded with the notion of repopulating the American Negro in Africa. Within less than two decades, Jamaican-born Marcus Garvey, whose arrival in the United States was concurrent with the publication of *The Clansman*, was to promote the Back to Africa movement, while at the same time expressing admiration for Thomas Dixon's work. Garvey was black; Dixon was not. But both were ultimately disgraced by a liberal establishment.

Always, Dixon believed that what he wrote and what he spoke was based on a love and sympathy for the Negro race. The Negro could not be assimilated into white society, and therefore, the obvious answer was to create an all-black society—elsewhere. It took Spain eight hundred years to expel the Moors, but Dixon believed it would take only two hundred to expel the Negro, whom he estimated would number sixty million by the end of the twentieth century. Dixon could be restrained in his argument. For example, in his 1905 essay on Booker T. Washington, he expresses his warmest admiration for the Negro educator but, ultimately, questions the educating of the African American in the United States: "We owe him a square deal, and we will never give it to him on this Continent."[26] He could also be vitriolic: "the conflict between the two races is absolutely irreconcilable. . . . Physical contact, mere proximity of the two races, is a constant menace, no matter whether they meet as equals or as master and servant."[27] Prejudice against the Negro was based on the instinct for self-preservation, Dixon told the *New York Times*. "The negro is the menace . . . to one element of the American's strength—his race integrity."[28]

To further his argument, Dixon turned to Abraham Lincoln, and in his 1913 novel, *The Southerner*, he has the president deal squarely and frankly with the issue: speaking to a number of representative Negroes, Lincoln says, "The Colony of Liberia is an old one, is in a sense a success and it is open to you. I am arranging to open another in Central America. It is nearer than Liberia—within seven days by steamer. . . . I ask you to consider it seriously, not for yourselves merely, nor for your race and ours for the present time, but for the good of mankind" (p. 272).

To Senator Winter, Lincoln explains, "I am not, nor ever have been, in favor of bringing about in any way, the social and political equality of the white and black races. . . . I will say in addition to this that there is a physical difference between the white and black races which, I believe, will forever forbid the two living together on terms of social and political equality. I have always hated Slavery from principle for the white man's sake as well as the negro's. I am equally determined on principle that the negro race after it is free shall never be absorbed into our social or political life!" (pp. 345–46).

And finally, in summation, Dixon writes of Lincoln on the penultimate page of the novel: "His prophetic soul had pierced the future and seen with remorseless logic that two such races as the negro and the Caucasian could not live side by side in a free democracy. The Radical theorists of Congress were demanding that these black men emerging from four thousand years of slavery and savagery should receive the ballot and the right to claim the white man's daughter in their marriage. They could only pass these measures over the dead body of Abraham Lincoln" (p. 543).

The Reconstruction Trilogy ended in 1907 with the publication of *The Traitor*, discussed in chapter 11, but it did not mark a close of Dixon's writings on Southern history. He presented an apologist fiction of the life of Abraham Lincoln in *The Southerner,* set against the story of two brothers, Ned and John Vaughan, both in love with the same woman, senator's daughter Betty Winter. Ned fights on the Confederate side in the Civil War and his brother fights for the North. After Ned is shot and dies in his brother's arms, John plans to assassinate Lincoln but is won over by his oratory. The novel concludes with Sherman's taking of Atlanta, but Lincoln's assassination is briefly alluded to on its last page. "The picture drawn by Mr. Dixon is so clear, vivid and truthful that, for the sake of it, the book is well worth reading," reported the *New York Times* (July 13, 1913).

Another Civil War hero, at least to the South, Jefferson Davis, was the subject of *Victim* (D. Appleton and Company, 1914). "The book is much like its predecessors, having less venom, however, owing to the absence of the carpetbagger and the free and enfranchised negro," commented the *Nation* (July 30, 1914). "Barring its partisanship, it presents a vivid and truthful picture of war days in the South, particularly at Richmond."

The best—from a modern perspective—of the later Southern historical novels is *The Man in Gray: A Romance of North and South*, which deals with the murderous and fanatical career of John Brown, focusing on the 1856 massacre of the Southern settlers at Pottawatomie and the 1859 seizure of Harpers Ferry. Framing the

John Brown segment is the story of Robert E. Lee, here presented as a noble and sincere Southerner who frees one of his slaves early in the novel and plans the eventual release of all the family slaves. It is not the slavery of the South but the wage slavery of the North that Lee denounces. The novel begins on the Lee plantation just before he leaves to take up the appointment of superintendent of West Point. The visit of Phil Sheridan from Ohio provides for a tour of the estate and a positive view of the slave population, who are well cared for, educated, paid small sums of money, and allowed to sell their own produce. Much is made of the difference between the Southern black slave and the poor Southern white.

John Brown is depicted as one who "early learned to love the pleasure of hating. . . . He made witch-hunting one of the sports of New England. When not busy with some form of the witch hunt, the Puritan found an outlet for his repressed instincts in the ferocity with which he fought the Indians or worked to achieve the conquest of Nature and lay up worldly goods for himself and his children" (p. 102). "Our early Slave traders were nearly all Puritans. When one of their ships came into port, the minister met her at the wharf, knelt in prayer and thanked Almighty God for one more cargo of heathen saved from hell" (p. 104).

Again, Dixon returns to an attack on Harriet Beecher Stowe, coupling her name with that of John Brown, the two most powerful elements in the cause of the Civil War. As chapter 35 begins, "John Brown's body lay moldering in his grave but his soul was marching on. And his soul was a thousand times mightier than his body had ever been" (p. 309).

"It actually happened," wrote Dixon in his preface. "Every character in it is historic. I have not changed even a name. Every event took place. Therefore it is incredible. Yet I have in my possession the proofs establishing each character and each event as set forth. They are true beyond question."

While at work on *The Man in Gray*, Dixon wrote to D.W. Griffith that he wanted the director to "do" both Lincoln and Lee. In a reference to *A Man of the People*, he wrote, "I lost money this season in the plays—but the picture is there—big, universal in appeal, stirring in effects."[29] In 1930, Griffith did direct, as his first sound feature, *Abraham Lincoln*, but Dixon played no part in its creation. Stephen Vincent Benét provided the script, although both he and the director would have preferred to make a film based on Benét's *John Brown's Body*.

However, the motion picture was still in its infancy when Dixon completed *The Reconstruction Trilogy*. The obvious means by which the author might further expound his "message" was not through a motion picture that was never longer than one reel or ten minutes in length up to this time, but rather the theatrical experience, an experience of which Dixon was very much enamored.

3

SOUTHERN HISTORY ON STAGE

"The book cries out for the stage—the Third avenue stage," wrote Ward Clark about *The Traitor* in the *Bookman* (September 1907). "It is as full of situations, thrills, climaxes, 'curtains,' as a home of melodrama is of gallery gods." By 1907 it was an irrelevant comment. Thomas Dixon was already fully aware of the theatrical potential of his novels. However, prior to his arrival in the theatre, it would seem that the American theatrical experience of the South was largely limited to adaptations of *Uncle Tom's Cabin*. There had, of course, been minstrel shows on the vaudeville stage and elsewhere since the mid-1800s, and in December 1893, "a coloured company" appeared at New York's Olympic Theatre in *Slavery Days*, a romantic picture of the Old South.

The Civil War produced plays as instruments of both Northern and Southern propaganda. The first Southern effort was *The Vigilance Committee,* by "Mr. Ottolengui, a Citizen of Charleston," first performed in that city in June 1861. It was followed by *The Roll of the Drum; or, The Battle of Manassas* (1861); *The Scouts; or, The Plains of Manassas* (1861), *The Vivandiere* (1863); *The Virginia Cavalier* (1863); and *Miscegenation; or, A Virginia Negro in Washington* (1864), among many others from a substantial number of authors, all of which, for obvious reasons, did not make it across the Mason-Dixon Line.

The first drama to denounce slavery after *Uncle Tom's Cabin* was J.T. Trowbridge's *Neighbor Jackwood*, which opened in Boston in 1857. The play was based on the case of Anthony Burns, a runaway slave captured in Boston and forcibly returned to the South. Slavery was strongly denounced by Dion Boucicault, a playwright primarily associated with Irish melodramas, in *The Octoroon*, first performed in New York in 1859. Described as "old-fashioned" when it was revived in New York in November 1879, *The Octoroon* was influenced by *The Old Plantation, or, The Real Uncle Tom* (also produced in 1859), in which George Jamieson portrayed an Uncle Tom far removed from Harriet Beecher Stowe's creation.

A more curious work is Bartley Campbell's *The White Slave*, which opened at New York's Fourteenth Street Theatre on April 3, 1882, and concerned a supposed octoroon slave who is in reality a white woman. "It is based—as Mr. Campbell's plays are invariably based[1]—upon a preposterous and altogether unacceptable motive. Its elements are, in brief, a hero who is singularly virtuous and astonishingly idiotic; a heroine who is not unattractive or unsympathetic; an abundance of the stale and monotonously pious negro fraternity; a steam-boat which takes fire and explodes; two death scenes, and a dozen expedients which have been used so often in dramas of the class to which Mr. Boucicault's *Octoroon* belongs," wrote the *New York Times* (April 4, 1882).

The White Slave is of primary interest in that it was most appealing to D.W. Griffith. The director acquired the screen rights in 1920 and tried to persuade Paramount in the late 1920s and both Fox and Universal in the 1930s to produce a screen adaptation.

However, to all intents and purposes, the theatre was Yankee dominated, a description that Dixon and others would claim was equally appropriate when describing *Uncle Tom's Cabin* on stage. Harriet Beecher Stowe's work had first been adapted by C.W. Taylor for presentation at New York's National Theatre on August 23, 1852, with him as Uncle Tom and St. Clair, Topsy, and Eva strangely missing from the production. On July 18, 1853, the National Theatre welcomed the definitive adaptation by George L. Aiken, with G.C. Germon as Uncle Tom and with St. Clair, Topsy, and Eva restored to the storyline. The production ran at the National for more than three hundred performances. There were at least two versions of *Uncle Tom's Cabin* expressing Southern sympathies. *The Southern Uncle Tom* opened in Baltimore in January 1852, even before the serialization of the Harriet Beecher Stowe novel was completed, and in October 1852, Clifton Tayleure presented his *Uncle Tom* with a positive Southern image.

Dixon's first love was the theatre, and his choice of both his political and his religious careers was obviously influenced by their potential for oratory and dramatic presentation. Once he was assured that his novel *The Clansman* was a commercial success, Dixon determined to adapt it for the stage. What might appear from a modern perspective as nothing more than racist cartoon characters on the printed page became living, breathing reality on the legitimate stage. Dixon studied dramatic technique under Kentucky-born William Thompson Price, who had been drama critic of the *Louisville Courier-Journal* and the *New York Star* and founded the American School of Playwriting in 1901. A young theatrical agent, Crosby Gaige, read Dixon's play script and submitted it to a former newspaperman and would-be producer, George H. Brennan. The latter established the Southern Amusement Company to produce *The Clansman* on stage, with Dixon owning a half interest in the organization. In all, Dixon claimed that it took three months to write the four-act play, one month to select the cast, and five weeks to rehearse. The large cast of twenty-nine was, of course, exclusively white; all African Americans were portrayed by white actors in blackface.[2]

The first scene of act 1, titled "The Fall of the Master," takes place outside the Cameron home in Piedmont, South Carolina. Placards indicate the location of the polling places. A Negro preacher harangues the crowd of African Americans who discuss how and the number of times they are going to vote. A Negro peddler has promised forty acres and a mule for every black man who votes the right ticket. There is much of what passes in Dixon's work as Negro humor, with one of the group, Dick, announcing, "I ain't er nigger. . . . I'se er dark skinned white man."

Austin Stoneman enters from the Cameron house and is hailed as the secret commander of the Black League. Dr. Cameron appears almost immediately, and the two men hold a brief conversation before Stoneman exits toward the polls, and Cameron's daughter, Flora, appears. At great length, Cameron warns her to stay close to the house because "the negroes are crazy today." He also explains that the family is now very poor and is forced to turn its home into a boardinghouse. Nellie Graham, described as "A Daughter of the South" but with no further identification, arrives and is soon followed by her schoolmate Helen and Elsie Stoneman.

After some exposition as to the heroics of Ben Cameron, the latter arrives and is left alone with Elsie Stoneman. There is some talk of the racial situation in the South, and Ben criticizes Elsie for allowing Silas Lynch to talk to her as a social equal. Lynch and Stoneman appear and Ben leaves. Stoneman suggests to Lynch that Ben Cameron would make a fine Southern leader if he will take the oath of the Black League. Stoneman invites Lynch to join him in the Cameron home, but he is threatened by Nelse, "an old fashioned negro" and faithful family retainer. Nelse's wife, Eve, appears and there is further humor as the two discuss the election in the presence of Flora. (In act 2, it is revealed that Nelse and Eve are not married, and there is considerable "humor" as to the situation and Nelse's wooing of Eve.)

Lynch reappears with Gus, and the audience learns that the polling place has been closed to prevent the white population from voting. Ben and his father discuss the situation, and the former suggests they organize in secret as in Tennessee—the Ku Klux Klan—but Dr. Cameron expresses opposition: "Promise me never to lift your hand in violence—without my advice. We are the last of our tribe—the rest sleep in unmarked graves. We must stand close, my boy, you and I."

Stoneman advises Ben that he is unofficially the head of the Black League and asks him to join them: "You must lead the negroes or be crushed by them." Ben appears to consider the offer, but Elsie, Lynch, Gus, and others arrive with a telegram, announcing that the state legislature will consist of 22 white men and 101 Negroes. At the same time, a proclamation appears in front of the Cameron home promising bayonets to enforce the marriage of blacks to whites. Ben tears down the poster, and when ordered by Stoneman to put it up again, he responds, "I'll see you in hell first!"

Act 2, titled "The Slave in the Master's Hall," opens six months later in the parlor of the Cameron home, the day of its sale for taxes. Dr. Cameron and Helen discuss the situation, and Flora brings news of Elsie Stoneman's expected arrival from Washington, D.C. Ben Cameron enters with news that Silas Lynch, the new lieutenant governor, is about to arrive, along with William Pitt Shrimp, a white man who is governor of the state but also involved in the Black League. Lynch orders Shrimp to issue a proclamation disarming the six white military companies in the state, who represent a threat to his interests, which include the purchase of the Cameron home. The auction begins, but just as it appears that Lynch will acquire the home, Elsie Stoneman arrives and enters a higher bid. She then leaves for the station to meet her father, in the company of Nellie and Helen.

However, Nellie returns upon word that General Forrest, "the unconquered hero of the South," is about to arrive. She listens as Forrest addresses Ben and Dr. Cameron:

Dr. Cameron, I stood in the gallery of your legislative hall in Columbia yesterday, and looked down on your Black Parliament at work—watched them through fetid smoke, vapors of stale whiskey and the deafening roar of half drunken brutes, while they voted millions in taxes their leaders had already stolen, and I had a vision. I stood beside the open grave of the South! Beneath that minstrel farce I saw a tragedy as deep and dark as was

ever woven of the blood and tears of a conquered people.
I heard the death rattle in the throat of my race, barbar-
ism strangling civilization by brute force.

As Dr. Cameron claims the danger is exaggerated, Gus and Shrimp
appear, announcing the disbandment of the white military companies in the state and requesting Ben Cameron's sword. Both Ben and
Dr. Cameron are arrested. Faithful Nelse asks Shrimp, "Is I yo' equal?"
When Shrimp replies in the affirmative, Nelse knocks him down with
the words, "Den take dat fum yo' equal!" (In *The Clansman*, it is
faithful Negro Jake who delivers the same line and the same blow to
the white Captain Gilbert, who has arrested Dr. Cameron.)

Act 3, "In the Claws of the Beast," opens a week later in the
Cameron home, decorated for Flora's thirteenth birthday. Gus can
be seen above the fence watching as Flora, Helen, Eve, and Nelse
talk. When Ben appears, he reacts angrily as Flora shows him a
box of candy, given to her by Gus. (No explanation is provided as
to why he and his father have been released from jail.) Elsie arrives
and Flora asks her to wait while she goes down to the spring to
feed a pet squirrel. As twilight falls and the moon rises, Stoneman
enters and challenges his daughter to say whether she is pledged to
Ben Cameron. He tells Elsie that Ben is the leader of the Klan in
South Carolina. Elsie does not believe him, but when she confronts
Ben, he explains, "The secret Klan is our only way. We are the
guardians of civilization in the South—until the day dawns. My
men are a band of young knights, circled with bayonets who yet
dare to ride with their lives in their hands and songs on their lips—
ride to the defense of the weak and the innocent."

Elsie insists that Ben must choose between her and the Klan.
Ben bids her goodbye as Nellie appears. She understands because
she has suffered too (but in what manner is not revealed). When
Ben tells her of his need for a scout and a spy, Nellie gladly joins the
Klan. Eve appears, carrying Flora's bonnet, found by the "ribber,"
and the family learns that Flora has disappeared. Dr. Cameron waits
with a neighbor, listening for one shot indicating that Flora has

been found or two that she is dead. As the curtain falls, two shots are heard offstage.

Act 3 concludes with a new title, "The Hunt for the Animal." The Klansmen are gathered as Gus is dragged in. As in the novel, Dr. Cameron hypnotizes the terrified Negro, who reveals how he approached Flora not planning to hurt her but that in her fear of him, she threw herself off the cliff. As Gus is dragged off, Ben announces that tonight he will disarm every Negro in the country. Gus is to be executed with his body hanging from the Court House balcony until he is dead. "Cut down the body—drag it at a horse's heels through the camp of negro soldiers—blow your whistles, rouse them from their sleep and let them see and hear—and then boldly fling him on the doorstep of the negro Lieutenant Governor of South Carolina!" The curtain falls as Ben orders, "Go!"

Act 4, titled "The Ku Klux Klan," opens in the library of Lynch's home. Shrimp tells Lynch what has happened and, in fear, appoints Lynch acting governor. Lynch reveals to the audience that Stoneman has been armed by the president with a proclamation of martial law, as Stoneman himself appears. Stoneman orders Lynch to issue a warrant for young Cameron's arrest and demands that his daughter identify Ben as the leader of the Klan. When he is brought before her, she refuses, announcing her love for Ben: "Yes, before the world, I say it without shame! I am his and he is mine—and his people shall be mine."

Ben Cameron is taken away, and Stoneman announces his plan to leave for Washington. Nellie tells Elsie to plead with Lynch while she goes to rouse the Klan. Lynch agrees to commute the sentence of death if Elsie will become his wife (although the ultimatum is given in very veiled and vague terminology). A guard takes Elsie to her room and Stoneman reappears to learn from Lynch that he is "in love—madly in love with a beautiful white girl." Stoneman nods in approval, only to discover the identity of the beautiful white girl: "My family has a record of a thousand years of achievement in the old world and this. I have no ambition that it should end in a brood of mulatto brats."

Lynch asks that a minister be brought immediately and warns Stoneman that if he tries to shoot him, Elsie will instantly be killed.

> Stoneman: Have I not struck the chains of slavery from your race?
> Lynch: You've stripped the rags of slavery from a black skin, but what are you going to do with the man. This man with a heart that can ache and break—Oh! If I could take the stain from this skin, the kink from this hair, I'd bathe in hell fire.

There is the sound of horses' hooves, the door is flung open, and the Klansmen enter. Ben uncovers himself, and Elsie is led in by another Klansman.

> Ben to Stoneman: Will you appeal to the President against us again, sir?
> Stoneman: Yes—one more appeal—that the army be withdrawn and water be allowed to find its own level.
> Elsie (throwing herself into his arms): Ben!

The curtain falls.

At best, *The Clansman* is nothing more than great melodrama, outrageously overwritten and overwrought. It is not what the play contains but what it lacks that draws the attention of the reader. There is little explanation as to General Forrest's identity or the reasoning behind the Klan. There is even less explanation of the power held by Austin Stoneman. What purpose does the character of Helen Lowell serve? How has Nellie Graham suffered? Why are the final lines uttered by Ben Cameron, Austin Stoneman, and Elsie Stoneman so weak and ineffectual? One can only surmise that a hot-blooded Southern audience, sitting in an equally hot Southern theatre, felt a passion that a modern reader can never hope to attain.

The most serious moral issue raised by *The Clansman* has to do with the lynching of Gus. What exactly was his crime? At worst, he is a stalker, but in reality, he is nothing more than a former faithful slave to the Cameron family who is besotted with young Flora. At no point in the play does he express any sexual interest in her. "Come back. I ain't gwine hurt yo," he calls to her as Flora runs away. Flora's death is nothing more than misadventure; she threw herself off the cliff and into the river because both her brother and her father had filled her with a deep distrust and fear of all African Americans.

The Clansman opened in Norfolk, Virginia, on Friday, September 22, 1905, complete with white actors in blackface playing the Negro roles and live horses, themselves in full Klan regalia, galloping across the stage, carrying the hooded Klansmen.[3] At the end of the third act, Dixon appeared on stage, telling his audience: "My object is to teach the north, the young north, what it has never known—the awful suffering of the white man during the dreadful reconstruction period. I believe that Almighty God anointed the white men of the south by their suffering during that time immediately after the Civil War to demonstrate to the world that the white man must and shall be supreme. To every man of color here to-night I want to say that not for one moment would I do him an injury. . . . I have nothing but the best feeling for the Negro."[4]

These were heady words, and Dixon was obviously having the time of his life with the opportunity to appear on stage with his play. In fact, the promise of a speech by Dixon at some point during the evening was a definite selling point for the production: "There is no doubt that his plays would not have been so eagerly attended if it had not been known that the author often accompanied the troupe and would respond to a curtain call."[5]

The Clansman began a highly profitable tour of the South—generally playing only a few days at each location—with successful stops in Richmond, Virginia; Raleigh, North Carolina; Columbia, South Carolina; Charleston, South Carolina; Montgomery, Alabama; Chattanooga, Tennessee; Knoxville, Tennessee; Nashville;

and New Orleans, later moving on to Southern-friendly cities such as Columbus, Ohio; Indianapolis; and Topeka, Kansas. The enthusiasm of the Southern audiences was matched by the negativity of Southern newspaper critics. The *Richmond News-Leader* called the play "about as elevating as a lynching." To the *Charleston News and Courier* it was "one of the most remarkable exhibitions of hysterics to which we have been treated in many long days." "What a pity there is no way to suppress *The Clansman*," wrote the *Montgomery Advertiser*, while the *Chattanooga Times* called the play "a riot breeder . . . designed to excite rage and race hatred."

Southern clergymen were equally outraged. To the Reverend Dr. L.G. Broughton of the Atlanta Baptist Tabernacle, *The Clansman* was "a slander of the white people of the south . . . so vile . . . that I cannot find words sufficiently strong to denounce it. . . . For God's sake, the negro's sake, and our sake, give the negro a rest from abuse and incendiarism!"[6]

A lengthy and informative review of the play as performed in Charleston, South Carolina, on October 25, 1905, appeared in the *New York Evening Post*:

Picture, if you will, a Southern playhouse crowded to the doors on a sultry night with whites. There are no negroes in the gallery, which is unusual. The audience is of the best and the worst. There are present those to whom the ghastly picture of a land rent with race feud, aggravated by prejudice and by political buccaneering and chicanery, is little obscured by time. The younger generation, which had no part in the war and its disastrous sequel, is as bitter as the fathers. There is the spirit of the mob. There is something in the stolidness of the crowd, before the raise of the curtain, that is out of keeping with the temperament of the people. It is as if they were awaiting the return of the jury, knowing already what the verdict will be. They know, but they must hear it again, and again. The orchestra is playing a lively air—but an orchestra is

superfluous. The people have come not to be amused—
and that is a feature which is startlingly evident to every
close observer.

There is comedy, or what passes for comedy, in the
play. True, there are laughs, but it is not hearty, whole-
some laughter. There is an hysterical note in that laughter; and it hushes as if by common consent. Every
reference to the maintenance of the power of the white
race is greeted with a subdued roar.

. . . In *Uncle Tom's Cabin* the negro was shown at his
best. In *The Clansman* the negro is shown at his worst.
The glamour of his love of humor, his songs and plea-
sures, his faithfulness, is stripped from him. True, there
is a "good nigger" in the play, but he evokes little interest. The daring pen of Mr. Dixon has presumed to place
before the eyes of a Southern audience a picture approaching as nearly as possible to the "unspeakable crime."

When the cause of the carpet-baggers and the Black
League seemed in the ascendant there was hissing. But it
was not such hissing as one hears directed toward the
eyebrows of the villain in the ordinary melodrama. The
whole house, from pit to roof, seethed. At times the actors could not go on.[7]

Thomas Dixon responded angrily to editorials attacking *The
Clansman*:

Many of these editors have attacked the play with unre-
strained fury—not by reason of its immorality or untruth-
fulness, but upon the remarkable ground that it stirs the
audience to depths of emotion which obliterate reason
and will cause riot and bloodshed.

Such a contention is, of course, childish twaddle, and
yet the persistence with which this declaration is repeated
by editors in nearly all the cities of the Black Belt of the

South is another pointer to the fact that the drama is by far the most powerful of all forms of art. . . .

The accusation that I wrote *The Clansman* to appeal to prejudice or assault the negro race is, of course, the silliest nonsense. For the negro I have only the profoundest pity and the kindliest sympathy.[8]

George H. Brennan promoted the play with a lurid brochure, describing it as "The Greatest Success in the Theatrical History of the United States." According to Brennan, a million and a half people saw the play, and that same number were turned away (or perhaps turned off?). He boasted of a "Specially Selected Metropolitan Cast of Forty Principals; Small Army of Supernumeraries and Troop of Horses; Carloads of Scenery, Mechanical and Lighting Effects."[9]

The production moved north, with performances in Syracuse; Philadelphia; Washington, D.C.; and Baltimore. Ultimately, two companies of players were active performing *The Clansman* over a five-year period. When the secondary company appeared in Shelby, North Carolina, in 1906, with Thomas Dixon himself reportedly playing the leading role, Dixon's father saw the play and told his son, "My only criticism is, Son, I felt once or twice you bore down a little too hard on the Negro. He wasn't to blame for the Reconstruction. Low vicious white men corrupted and misled him."[10]

Less than three months after George Bernard Shaw's *Mrs. Warren's Profession* had been forced to close as an offense to public decency, *The Clansman* opened in New York at the Liberty Theatre on January 8, 1906, with a cast of little-known actors including De Witt Jennings (as Nelse) and Holbrook Blinn (as Austin Stoneman), both of whom would have long careers on screen as character players. "There will perhaps be many people who will feel that a play which avowedly depends for its interest upon sectional feelings and sympathies, which involves so much tearing open of old sores, may do more harm than good," commented a critic in the *New York Times* (January 9, 1906). However, "A large and noisy audience without discrimination vigorously applauded every highly flavored sentiment and clamored for the author until at the close of the second act he responded with a little speech in which he declared that the reception of his play proved 'there is no longer a North and a South.'"

A lengthy review in the *New York Dramatic Mirror* (January 20, 1906) began with the ominous words, "It is difficult to do justice to so bad a play as *The Clansman*." After admitting, "this peculiarly obnoxious melodrama contains some effective episodes," the anonymous critic continued:

> As a piece of constructive playwriting *The Clansman* is altogether amateurish.
>
> Whatever one may think of the nature of the drama—and the critic is with difficulty choking down the anathemas with which he would like to blight its abominable existence—one must admit that the night meeting of the Klan was an impressive stage episode. . . . The only light was a greenish one from the right side of the stage, which gave the white robed figures a ghastly appearance and seemed to color their voices—for voices have color in technical parlance—with a subterranean hue. It is no wonder that nervous women have become hysterical at that point of the performance.

In protest of the New York presentation of the play, the Constitutional League of New York, founded by John E. Mulholland and Henry H. Tremaine to urge the rigid enforcement in the South of the Fourteenth and Fifteenth Amendments to the Constitution, employed two young boys, outside the theatre, to distribute a pamphlet by Kelly Miller of Howard University. The twenty-one-page document, "An Open Letter to Thomas Dixon, Jr.," dated September 1905, is a remarkably reasoned and quietly persuasive literary work by an African American scholar. It begins with Miller's noting, "Your race has inflicted accumulated injury and wrong upon mine. Mine has borne yours only service and good will." At its heart, Miller's demand was: "Will you please tell a waiting world just what is the psychological difference between the races? No reputable authority, either of the old or the new school of psychology, has yet pointed out any sharp psychic discriminant. There is not a single intellectual, moral or spiritual excellence attained by the white race to which the Negro does not yield an appreciative response" (p. 5).

Miller provides page after page of documentation, refuting all of Dixon's arguments for the inferiority of the black race in America, and ends with a frank indictment of Dixon's racism: "Those who become inoculated with the virus of race hatred are more unfortunate than the victims of it. Voltaire tells us that it is more difficult and meritorious to wean men of their prejudices than it is to civilize the barbarian. Race hatred is the most malignant poison that can afflict the mind. It freezes up the fount of inspiration and chills the higher faculties of the soul. You are a greater enemy to your own race than you are to mine" (p. 20).

Concurrent with the New York presentation of *The Clansman*, Booker T. Washington visited the city to raise $1.8 million for his Tuskegee Institute. Dixon had expressed "the warmest admiration" for Washington, while denouncing the work of the Institute as "dangerous" in that it educated a Negro for whom there was no future.[11] As Booker T. Washington entered Carnegie Hall on January 22, 1906, to speak before an audience that included George Foster Peabody, Mrs. John D. Rockefeller, and Mark Twain, he was handed a note from Dixon in which the author promised ten thousand dollars if Washington would declare publicly that he wished no social equality for the Negro. Washington did not dignify Dixon's challenge with a response. The latter refused to modify his racist comments, and at New York's Baptist Church of the Epiphany a week later he told his congregation: "We must remove the negro or we will have to fight him. He will not continue to submit to the injustice with which we treat him in the North and the South. . . . When the negro smashes into your drawing room some day in the future with a repeating rifle in his hand, his flat nostrils dilated, his yellow eyes and teeth gleaming, you will make good on your protestations of absolute equality or he will know the reason why."[12]

A theatrical response to *The Clansman* came from playwright Edward Sheldon (1886–1946), whose major contribution to the American theatre is the 1913 drama *Romance* (which was filmed in 1920, starring the star of the original stage production, Doris Keane, and again in 1930 as a vehicle for Greta Garbo). Sheldon's first play, *Salvation Nell*, which opened in New York in 1908, was influenced by the work of Ibsen and starred the legendary Mrs. Minnie Maddern Fiske. His second play, *The Nigger*, which opened at New York's New Theatre on December 4, 1909, is, despite its politically incorrect title, a prominent defense of miscegenation. The central character, Philip Morrow, is a white supremacist who becomes governor of a Southern state, only to discover that his grandmother was a Negro. The villainous Clifton Noyes, a distiller opposing a prohibition bill, uses Morrow's ancestry to blackmail him. Rather than deny his black ancestry as his fiancée, Georgiana, suggests, Morrow decides to devote his life to the betterment of his people—the Negro race. As Morrow explains to his fiancée, who still loves him, "You see, what my gran'fathah did t' my gran'mothah isn't all—it's what ev'ry white man has done t' ev'ry niggah fo' the las' three hundred yeahs! An' it's time for someone to pay up, even if he wasn't extra keen on bein' the pa'ticulah chosen man."

George Jean Nathan described *The Nigger* as one of "the ten dramatic shocks of the century." Outside of *The Clansman*, *The Nigger* was the first play to confront racism, lynching, and interracial marriage. It was published in book form (by Macmillan) in 1910, at which time the *New York Dramatic Mirror* (September 28, 1910) commented, "It crystallizes the testimony of the best thinkers on one of the painful of national problems." Dixon was obviously not among those "best thinkers." The play was filmed in 1915, partly on location in Augusta, Georgia, as *The Nigger*, by producer William Fox and director Edgar Lewis, with William Farnum as Morrow and Claire Whitney as his fiancée. Because of the sensitivity of the title, in some areas of the country, the film was screened as *The New Governor*, which does detract from the shock effect that Sheldon obviously intended.

At the film's release, Edward Sheldon spoke at some length to *Motion Picture News* (March 20, 1915). Sheldon's comments suggest that his attitude toward the Negro was not far removed from that of Thomas Dixon:

> I did not intend it for "a play with a purpose" as some of my kind critics have supposed. I penned it as drama pure and simple. Of course in the action and characterization and in the telling of the story the negro problem crops up.
>
> As I have pointed out in the play the negro problem is in my belief due largely to bad whiskey. There is hardly one of the "usual crimes" of the Southern negro, for which the penalty is usually lynching, that has not alcohol as an underlying cause. Take liquor out of the South and the race problem would cease to be one. The negro is naturally primitive. Alcohol brings the worst in him to the surface. It makes him worse than the brutes.

Thomas Dixon expressed considerable respect for the play:

> *The Nigger* seemed to me a most skillful, philosophical argument for the mixture of races, the old doctrinaire abolitionist idea from New England put in dramatic form. I couldn't imagine a better presentation of the theme that the two young people ought to forget his drop of African blood and be happy. That was the impression Sheldon's drama left on me and that, I take it, was the purpose of the plot. The South would not for a moment listen to the final scene in which the girl offered to marry the hero. Had that scene been eliminated, the drama would have been successful in the South, for Sheldon constructed a series of thrilling and highly dramatic episodes.[13]

With the triumph on stage of *The Clansman*, Dixon adapted his second novel, *The One Woman*, as a play, and then turned to the third volume of *The Reconstruction Trilogy*, *The Traitor*, and adapted it for the theatre, working in collaboration with Channing Pollock, a former drama critic who was the author of many popular books and plays from 1900 onward and in 1914 became active as a screenwriter. Pollock, who always proudly proclaimed that he fought sex, crime, and sophistication in the drama, received top billing because, certainly as far as the New York stage was concerned, he was the far more prominent of the two. Dixon's acceptance of Pollock as a collaborator is curious in that the two would seem to have little in common, and at his death in 1946, Pollock was to leave his papers to the African American college, Howard University, in Washington, D.C., where he was born. Certainly, Pollock was considered a superior and more commercial playwright than Dixon, and it was his name that came first in the billing. *The Traitor* was one of the least successful of Pollock's plays, although thanks in large part to the popularity of the novel on which it was based, the four-act drama did find an appreciative Southern audience when it opened in the spring of 1908.

Much more successful was Dixon's drama of Southern miscegenation, *The Sins of the Father*, which he wrote as a three-act play in 1909, some three years prior to its publication as a novel. "In all my novels and plays dealing with the race problem, I try to bring my audience up against a dead wall. I want them to see that the conflict between the two races is absolutely irreconcilable," Dixon explained. "*The Clansman* presents the social aspects of the question, and *The Sins of the Father*, my new play, treats it from the domestic point of view. Physical contact, mere proximity of the two races, is a constant menace, no matter whether they meet as equals or as master and servant."[14]

The Sins of the Father opened at the Academy of Music in Norfolk, Virginia, on September 21, 1910, before a typically enthusiastic Southern audience. In what might read as an extraordinary example of life imitating theatrical melodrama, according to

Dixon and his biographer, the day after the premiere, the leading man was attacked and killed by a shark while bathing at Wrightsville Beach. Rather than cancel the next presentation—at Fayetteville, North Carolina—Dixon agreed to go on in his place. It is a great story, but its truth is somewhat in doubt. The theatrical trade papers of the day contain no reports of the leading man's death, and after Richmond, *The Sins of the Father* did not move on to Fayetteville but played at the Masonic Opera House in Covington ("best offering ever here"), the Masonic Opera House in Clifton Forge ("very good house"), and the Academy of Music in Roanoke, all in Virginia, before moving on to the Academy of Music in Durham, the Opera House in Greensboro, and the Masonic Opera House in Rocky Mount, all in North Carolina. The play was scheduled to open at the Academy of Music in Petersburg, Virginia, at the end of September 1910 but "failed to appear," and it is perhaps then that the change in leading men took place.[15]

As Major Daniel Norton, Dixon toured the South and the western United States for thirty weeks, although the response to the production in major cities, such as Chicago, was poor. According to Dixon, his innate sense of the dramatic transformed him into a naturalistic actor:

> I have always been immensely interested in plays as a writer, but this Winter as an actor, I learned many things about pleasing audiences that I never should have discovered in any other way. My experience has convinced me that my play which failed, failed because it was miscast. . . . An actor must convey the fundamental idea of the author or he overturns the equation of the reasoning and destroys the logic of the drama. He must not only comprehend the entire significance of his role, but also depict it so vividly that others cannot help seeing it. He must be the type for which the role calls, and furthermore, he must have individual personality enough to inspire the type with animation.[16]

According to Dixon's great-great-granddaughter, Charleen Swansea, the Dixon family was of the opinion that he was "absolutely lousy on stage."[17]

It was Dixon's hope that *The Sins of the Father* would open in New York in the fall of 1910, but there was very obviously no audience for such a production there. His one-act play about an elderly slave, *Old Black Joe*, opened in New York on February 17, 1912, but it was not until 1919 with the presentation of his anti-communist melodrama *The Red Dawn* that Dixon's name came again before New York theatergoers—and then only as an object of ridicule.

Thomas Dixon's last play to be produced on the New York stage was *A Man of the People*, which opened on September 7, 1920, at the Bijou Theatre. The three-act drama dealt with the Republican National Committee's request that Lincoln stand down as candidate for president at the end of his first term in office and Lincoln's conflict with George B. McClellan. The third-act climax had Jefferson Davis and Robert E. Lee receiving news of General Sherman's capture of Atlanta. Lincoln reappeared in the epilogue to deliver his second inaugural address. The president was portrayed by Howard Hall, an actor with a reputation from earlier decades as a melodramatic impersonator of Lincoln. The *New York Times* (September 8, 1920) was relatively enthusiastic, describing the play as "always interesting, generally well-written, and only slightly theatrical." But the production suffered from comparison with John Drinkwater's drama in six scenes, *Abraham Lincoln*, which had opened in New York on December 15, 1919, at the Cort Theatre, with Frank McGlynn in the title role. *A Man of the People* was published in November 1920 by D. Appleton and Company— the only one of Dixon's plays to appear in book form—and, as on the stage, it was discussed in relationship to the Drinkwater play (also published in book form) and found wanting; "melodramatic and inferior" was the opinion of *Booklist* (November 1920), whereas *Abraham Lincoln* was described by drama critic Burns Mantle as "truly a great play."[18]

Thomas Dixon never lost his enthusiasm for the theatre, and there were other plays, including *The Almighty Dollar* (1912); *Robert E. Lee*, a play in five acts (1920); and even a 1913 dramatization in three acts of *The Leopard's Spots*. However, after the printed page, after the dramatic stage, the next outlet was most obviously the motion picture.

4

SOUTHERN HISTORY ON FILM

While there is no question that Thomas Dixon enthusiastically embraced the motion picture from about 1910 to 1915, there is no documentation as to when he first became interested in the new medium. Whether he saw a film while the art form was still in its infancy in the 1890s, or whether he was a visitor to the nickelodeon theatres of New York in the first decade of the twentieth century, is unknown. The record is silent, but what is obvious is that Dixon realized the screen potential of his play *The Clansman*. The hooded figures of the Klansmen riding across the stage would be even more impressive, and would carry far more dignity and authority, if presented on the motion picture screen. The proscenium arch could disappear and the Klan could once more ride to glory across a motion picture simulation of the Southern landscape—or, better still, across that actual Southern horizon.

Dixon's initial idea was to utilize the actors under contract to appear in the play as performers in a screen adaptation. The film would be shot on location as the players moved from Southern town to Southern town. "In these Southern towns all the Southern atmosphere would be free for the asking," wrote actress Linda Arvidson, who was also Mrs. D.W. Griffith. "Houses, streets, even cotton plantations would not be too remote to use in the picture. And there was a marvelous scheme for interiors. That was to drag the 'drops' and the 'props' and the pretty parlor furniture out into the open, where with the assistance of some sort of floor and God's sunshine, there would be nothing to hinder work on the picture version of the play."[1] An obscure but pioneering filmmaker, William Haddock, was hired to direct, and he spent two or three weeks filming on location in Natchez, Mississippi. After realizing the impossibility of filming actors as they moved from city to city, he quit the company and returned to New York.[2] It was all rather primitive, but no more primitive than was the production of many one- and two-reel films of those early years.

"From the first I believed that the success of *The Clansman* on the screen would be as great as the play and I determined to submit the story to the motion picture magnates," wrote Dixon.[3] The author went on to claim that he spent two years in search of a visionary producer and eventually canvassed unknown forces entering the industry.

In reality, Dixon and his theatrical producer George H. Brennan contracted with the Kinemacolor Company of America in September 1911 to undertake the physical production of the film version of *The Clansman*. Unlike the majority of films of the period and earlier, which were shot in black and white with tints and tones added in the laboratory upon processing, *The Clansman* was to be shot in color—not full color, but an approximation of the real thing.

Kinemacolor was the earliest commercially successful natural-color film process, utilizing a two-color additive system. It was first demonstrated in London in May 1908 and was used with considerable success to film *Delhi Durbar*, a massive spectacle of British Imperialism in India, in 1911. After a major presentation at New York's Madison Square Garden in December 1909, two American businessmen, Gilbert H. Aymar and James K. Bowen, acquired the system and formed the Kinemacolor Company of America in April 1910.

After filming a series of travelogues and establishing a studio at Whitestone, Long Island, Kinemacolor decided to move its primary production facility to Los Angeles and set up a studio at 4500 Sunset Boulevard. Here, additional work on the screen adaptation of *The Clansman* got under way, with a script crafted by Frank Woods, who had earlier been one of the first film reviewers with the trade paper the *New York Dramatic Mirror*. Dixon described him as "a man of wisdom, not a child."[4]

Kinemacolor ceased operations at its Hollywood studio in June 1913, with *The Clansman* still uncompleted and, basically, abandoned. There is no indication of how far along the film was in production or even if any footage had actually been shot. In the meantime, D.W. Griffith had quit the American Biograph Company, where he had made his directorial debut in 1908, and signed a contract with Harry Aitken, who owned a number of film exchanges and had very grandiose plans to be a major producer. After Griffith and Aitken had made four films together in 1914, the pair decided it was time to make a "special" film.

D.W. Griffith was most familiar with *The Clansman* and its author, not only because of his Southern background, but also because he and his wife, Linda Arvidson, had appeared for two and a half months in the 1906 touring production of *The One Woman*, earning, respectively, $75.00 and $35.00 a week. Dixon had fired the couple after hiring a new leading man at half of Griffith's salary, but there was apparently no animosity between the two men. Many years later, Griffith wrote to Dixon, "I often recall the days of m' youth when I was a ham actor and toured the country in your play."[5] Furthering Griffith's interest were positive comments from a friend, Austin Webb, who had appeared as Gus in *The Clansman,* and also from Claire MacDowell, who had toured with the play and had been a longtime member of Griffith's stock company at American Biograph. Finally, there was corroborative support from Frank Woods, who had left Kinemacolor and was now story editor for the Harry Aitken interests. Much later, in a highly questionable autobiography, Griffith was to write, "*The Clansman* had been a terrible frost as a stage play."[6]

At an initial meeting, Griffith told Aitken, Woods, and Dixon that his version of *The Clansman* "will be worth a hundred of the other movies"[7] and that it would cost an unprecedented $40,000 to produce. Dixon weighed in with an announcement that he wanted $25,000 for the screen rights. In that same autobiography, Griffith maintained that Dixon wanted cash up front because he knew just how bad his stage play was. Ultimately, Dixon settled for a $2,000 advance and 25 percent of the gross profits (which would quickly make him a millionaire).[8] Harry Aitken's brother, Roy, remembered Dixon as "florid and energetic," emphasizing at the meeting the need for many scenes in the film depicting the Klan.[9]

The Kinemacolor studios in Hollywood were taken over by the Aitken/Griffith faction, later becoming known as the Fine Arts Studio, and *The Clansman* went into production on Independence Day 1914. The start of shooting on *The Clansman* represented the start of the most financially successful period in Dixon's life, but he was not around to see it happen. While Griffith filmed in Los Angeles and its environs, Dixon stayed in New York, after providing Griffith with a trunkful of books from his library.

The bulk of the film was shot at the Sunset Boulevard studio, with the majority of the exterior scenes shot on an adjacent lot. The brief shot of cotton fields was filmed not in the South but in Calexico, while the sequence of Mae Marsh as Flora running away from Gus and jumping off the cliff was taken at Big Bear Lake. The battle scenes were filmed at what was then known as Universal Field and is now Forest Lawn Cemetery in Burbank.[10] On November 13, 1914, *Variety* reported that production on *The Birth of a Nation* was completed, although obviously editing was not.

The Birth of a Nation is as much the story of two families, the Camerons and the Stonemans, as it is about the Civil War, Reconstruction, or the Klan. However, the second subtitle in the film, and the first to deal specifically with the plot, provides a clear understanding of where Dixon (and obviously also Griffith) placed the blame not only for slavery but also for the Civil War: "The bringing of the African to America planted the first seed of disunion." A preacher is seen blessing the slaves, while another scene depicts the meeting of a group of abolitionists, one of whom, played by Jennie Lee (later to be seen in blackface as the faithful mammy), is greatly moved by the plight of the Negro slaves.

The casting of Jennie Lee in these two roles is quite deliberate on Griffith's part. At times in the film, he would appear to be enjoying a private joke over parallel castings. For example, George Siegmann plays the leader of the Confederate soldiers who rescue Piedmont from attack by a renegade Negro band, and later he is seen as Silas Lynch, who seeks to destroy "white" Piedmont. Robert Harron portrays Austin Stoneman's younger son and later plays a Negro soldier who arrests Dr. Cameron and arranges his humiliation.

The Stoneman sons, Phil and Tod, visit the Cameron family in Piedmont, South Carolina, where Tod and Duke Cameron become chums, Phil and Ben Cameron renew their friendship, Phil falls in love with Margaret Cameron, and Ben sees a photograph of Elsie Stoneman, which he snatches away from Phil. With startling speed, the Civil War overwhelms the two families, with the sons of each in uniform. A gang of guerillas invades Piedmont, but the Cameron parents and their home are saved by Confederate troops. Tod Stoneman and the two younger Cameron boys, Duke and Wade, are killed on the battlefield. Atlanta is burned and Sherman marches to the sea. After leading a charge against a Union trench, Ben Cameron, known as "the Little Colonel," is wounded and sent to a military hospital in Washington, D.C. Two scenes on the battlefield are lifted from descriptions in the novel *The Clansman*: Ben Cameron's giving water to a wounded Union soldier (p. 7) and his ramming of the Confederate flag into the mouth of a Union cannon (p. 8).

In Washington, D.C., while under sentence of death as a guerilla, he is nursed by Elsie Stoneman. When his mother comes to visit him, Elsie takes her to see Lincoln, who pardons Ben. He returns to his nearly ruined home, while Elsie, Margaret, and Phil Stoneman attend Ford's Theatre on the night of Lincoln's assassination. "Our best friend is gone," laments Dr. Cameron afterward. "What will become of us now?"

As in the novel, dialogue spoken by Elsie Stoneman in subtitle form is "lifted" without acknowledgment from Walt Whitman's *Specimen Days and Collect* (1882–83), in which the poet wrote of his time as a hospital nurse in Washington, D.C. Dixon also borrows Whitman's description of Lincoln's death and of John Wilkes Booth's appearance at Ford's Theatre. Frances Oakes, who was the first to identify this borrowing, points out that Dixon was obviously unfamiliar with wartime life in the nation's capital.[11] Thus, we have the amusing spectacle of Whitman impersonated by Lillian Gish. I am sure the gay poet would have approved of his reincarnation in drag.

Austin Stoneman and his allies are now in command of the future of the South. "You are the greatest power in America," mulatto housekeeper Lydia Brown tells Stoneman. As in the novel (p. 91), Stoneman is identified as "the uncrowned king." Southern whites are disenfranchised and the South Carolina legislature is dominated by Negroes, while Austin Stoneman travels to Piedmont with Elsie and Phil, along with mulatto Silas Lynch, who is elected lieutenant governor. Although Stoneman at this point in the film is the dominant figure in the future of the South, he will be displaced by Silas Lynch, who plays a far more prominent role on screen than he does in either the novel or the play.

A renegade Negro named Gus is attracted to the younger Cameron daughter, Flora, "the little sister," and follows her to a spring, where he confronts her. Flora runs away in terror, leaps off a cliff, and is killed, but not before revealing Gus's name to Ben Cameron. Unlike the lovesick Gus of the play, he is shown here as a lumbering, slavering brute, more animal than human as he chases after Flora. At the same time, Griffith is keen to point out that he is not emblematic of the Negro race, with a title identifying him as "Gus, the renegade, a product of the vicious doctrines spread by the carpetbaggers." Just as in the play, Gus is also a victim of society.

Meanwhile, Ben Cameron has conceived the idea of the Ku Klux Klan, Elsie Stoneman has distanced herself from him because of his membership therein, and Dr. Cameron has been arrested when

Klan uniforms are discovered in his home. Griffith personalizes the Klan. It is no longer a national Southern institution, but rather a local affair created by Ben Cameron. There is something almost "folksy" about Griffith's Klan. One might well imagine the men getting together with their womenfolk and organizing square dances and barbecues.

Dr. Cameron is rescued by his faithful Negro servants, along with Phil Stoneman, who kills a Negro in the process. Phil and the Camerons take refuge in the cabin of two Union veterans, while Elsie Stoneman is forcibly detained by Silas Lynch, who reveals his desire to marry her. When Austin Stoneman (who is identified as in favor of interracial marriage, at least in principal) discovers Lynch's plans for his daughter, he is also held captive. The Klan rides to the rescue of both groups, and the film proper ends with two honeymooning couples, Elsie and Ben, and Margaret and Phil, at the seashore. As in his next film, *Intolerance*, Griffith could not refrain from brief allegorical scenes with which to end, and harm somewhat, *The Birth of a Nation*. Here the God of War dissolves into Jesus Christ as a title asks, "Dare we dream of a golden day when the bestial War shall rule no more. But instead—the gentle Prince in the Hall of Brotherly Love in the City of Peace." It is as if Griffith has suddenly changed course; he turns *The Birth of a Nation* from an epic historical drama into a treatise against war.

Missing from extant prints of the film, but apparently there originally, are scenes of the mass deportation of African Americans, with a title stating, "Lincoln's plan of restoring negroes to Africa was dreamed of only, never carried out," or perhaps more simply announcing, "Lincoln's solution." It might well be argued that this one title that may or may not have been originally present is the only example of racial theory put forward by Griffith. While the racial stereotyping in *The Birth of a Nation* is obviously distasteful from a modern perspective, it is not particularly out of step with the era in which the film was made.

There have long been suggestions that the Ku Klux Klan holds a print of *The Birth of a Nation* with this lost ending; when I was associate archivist with the American Film Institute in the early 1970s, I tried to contact Imperial Wizard Robert M. Shelton, but he would neither confirm nor deny such a claim.

To play the pivotal role of Elsie Stoneman, Griffith selected Lillian Gish, who had been on screen with him since 1912. Blanche Sweet, Griffith's most prominent leading lady of the time, had assumed that she would have the coveted role, and when she learned otherwise, she left Griffith's employ to work for a new entrant into filmmaking, Cecil B. DeMille. To play opposite Lillian in the role of Ben Cameron, the Little Colonel, Griffith chose Henry B. Walthall. The nickname "the Little Colonel" was used because Walthall was a somewhat diminutive actor in his midthirties, whereas in the novel, Ben Cameron is described as tall and a dozen years younger than Walthall. Other major roles—there is no emphasis in the film on stars as such—were played by Mae Marsh (Flora Cameron), Miriam Cooper (Margaret Cameron), Robert Harron (Tod Stoneman), and Elmer Clifton (Phil Stoneman), all of whom were well-considered leading players with potentially lengthy careers ahead. In reality, Elmer Clifton became a director, and Robert Harron died under tragic circumstance in 1920. Major character actors Ralph Lewis (Austin Stoneman), Mary Alden (Lydia Brown), George Siegmann (Silas Lynch), Walter Long (Gus), Josephine Crowell (Mrs. Cameron), Spottiswoode Aitken (Dr. Cameron), and Jennie Lee (the faithful mammy) completed the cast.

The Birth of a Nation is remarkable for the number of future stars in roles that can be described as little more than extras: Elmo Lincoln (who was to be the screen's first Tarzan), Eugene Pallette, Bessie Love, Alma Rubens, Pauline Starke, and Wallace Reid (a future matinee idol who, as blacksmith Jeff, loses his shirt in a fight scene that is almost homoerotic). There is also a large contingent of future directors here, including Joseph Henabery (as Abraham Lincoln), Raoul Walsh (as John Wilkes Booth), John Ford (as one of the Klansmen), David Butler (as one of the group with Jeff the blacksmith), and perhaps even Erich von Stroheim.

Aside from those already mentioned as playing historical roles, character actor Donald Crisp appears as General Ulysses S. Grant, and English actor Howard Gaye plays General Robert E. Lee. Gaye was to follow his performance as Southern hero Lee with the role of Jesus Christ in *Intolerance*, presumably appropriate casting by a Southern director. Dixon was particularly pleased with Joseph Henabery's performance as his presidential hero, writing, "My gratitude and congratulations on your Lincoln—a simple, dignified, superbly effective piece of work. I thank you."[12]

With *The Birth of a Nation*, wrote critic and poet Vachel Lindsay, Griffith "not only hurled upon the world the careers of twenty or thirty stars who have gone on ever since, he again asserted all the philosophy of history written in blood upon the old stars and bars. Every title had the old Southern violence, sentimentality, lack of precision, out-of-focus romanticism. Every photograph had the reality of the South which it is so difficult to put into words."[13] To Vachel Lindsay, there was no question about sources. Everything "bad" in the film was credited to Thomas Dixon, and everything "good" to D.W. Griffith.[14]

There has been much speculation as to whether Griffith used Dixon's play as the source material for *The Birth of a Nation* or whether he used the novel of *The Clansman*, along with elements from *The Leopard's Spots*. The reality is that the play of *The Clansman* was the primary basis for the film, but the production also contains elements from the *Clansman* novel. An obvious example is the character of Phil Stoneman, who is in the novel but not in the play. The character of Flora is in *The Leopard's Spots*, but she is also in the *Clansman* play, replacing the character of Marion Lenoir in the *Clansman* novel. Thus, she comes to *The Birth of a Nation* quite obviously from the play and not *The Leopard's Spots*. It was, of course, impossible for Dixon to identify or document his sources in either the novel or the play, but Griffith makes extensive use of footnoting in his subtitles, in particular relying upon Woodrow Wilson's *History of the American People*. While the accuracy of some of Griffith's "sources" has been discredited in recent years as questionable, there should be no doubt that to Griffith, Dixon, and everyone else of their generation, these texts were considered definitive. Neither Griffith nor Dixon should be excoriated for using them, but rather the original writers should be criticized for their sloppy scholarship.

All conjecture regarding source material for *The Birth of a Nation* is, in large part, irrelevant in that the film is very obviously the work of one man—D.W. Griffith. Dixon provided a basic storyline, but nothing more. Griffith's development of the play, with obvious and significant help from Frank Woods, is what makes *The Birth of a Nation* the masterpiece—racist or otherwise—that it is. It is pointless for any ardent supporter of Thomas Dixon to argue differently. The mere fact that *The Birth of a Nation* opens prior to the Civil War and includes, in graphic detail, that bloody conflict, while *The Clansman*, both novel and play, opens immediately after the end of hostilities, is proof positive of Griffith's auteurship. You cannot adapt what Dixon did not write.

According to Lillian Gish (and there are of course major flaws in her story),

> Mr. Griffith did not need the Dixon book. His intention was to tell his version of the War between the States. But he evidently lacked the confidence to start production on a twelve-reel film without an established book as a basis for his story. After the film was completed and he had shown it to the so-called author, Dixon said: "This isn't my book at all." But Mr. Griffith was glad to use Dixon's name on the film as author, for, as he told me, "The public hates you if it thinks you wrote, directed, and produced the entire film yourself. It is the quickest way to make enemies."[15]

In structure, also, *The Birth of a Nation* differs substantially from Dixon's play. The characters are better developed, even though this is a silent film reliant upon titles. The historical tableaux add much to the historical narrative and were obviously impossible to include in the play. One title, "War's Peace," followed by a shot of the dead on the battlefield, captures with quiet simplicity the futility of the Civil War—and all wars. One of the most insignificant and yet the most moving of all shots in the film shows the arms of the sister and mother reaching out to Ben Cameron in embrace and welcoming him home. Not one spoken word in the play has as much dramatic impact as this mute scene. *The Birth of a Nation* does not contain as much material on Abraham Lincoln and his assassination as does the novel, but what is here makes its point decisively and emotionally. Even the story of the founding of the Ku Klux Klan makes sense to those not familiar with the organization, whereas the play—perhaps because it is so heavily geared to a Southern audience—does little to explain the origin of the Klan. It is just there and taken for granted as the obvious, immediate solution to the Negro problem.

In *The Birth of a Nation*, Ben Cameron watches as two white children cover themselves with a sheet and terrify four black children. There is a title, "The Inspiration," followed by another title, "The Result. The Ku Klux Klan, the organization that saved the South from the anarchy of black rule, but not without the shedding of more blood than at Gettysburg, according to Judge Tourgee of the carpet-baggers" (i.e., Albion Winegar Tourgée, writing in 1880).

Above all, Griffith displays an admirable understanding of the need for suspense. He builds far more slowly and carefully to a climax. Rather than have an ending reliant only upon the saving of Elsie Stoneman from Silas Lynch, Griffith makes her but one of the central characters in jeopardy. In fact, in *The Birth of a Nation*, everyone the audience has come to know and love is in danger. The Cameron family and Phil Stoneman, surrounded in the cabin of the Union veterans, are also in need of a last-minute rescue. Indeed, one title from Griffith, "The former enemies of North and South are united again in common defence of their Aryan birthright," puts across Dixon's argument for national white unity far better than does anything he wrote in novel or play form.

At least one scholar has argued that *The Birth of a Nation* may never have escaped its origins,[16] but this is true only in one aspect, and that is the use of white actors in blackface to play all the prominent and perhaps all the minor Negro roles. "I didn't think anything about it," said Miriam Cooper, who played Margaret Cameron;[17] she had earlier appeared in blackface herself, playing "Topsy" characters in a number of Southern dramas produced by the Kalem Company. Griffith claimed, perhaps with reason, that there were no African American actors available to play these parts, and so he adopted the theatrical tradition of whites in blackface. But *The Birth of a Nation* is not theatre, and what may arguably work behind the proscenium arch does not work on screen. From a distance in the theatre, an audience may have some difficulty in distinguishing blackface from black; but on film, a white actor in blackface is precisely that—a caricature, leading to either grimaces or outrage from an audience. Much of the potential racist power of *The Birth of a Nation* is, in fact, lost because the Negroes here are too close to comic parody.

There is only one identifiable African American in the cast, and that is Madame Sul-te-Wan, playing a Negro woman who abuses Dr. Cameron as he is paraded before his former slaves. "I'm going to let you do all the dirty work in *The Clansman*," Griffith told her.[18] Madame Sul-te-Wan, who sometimes claimed to be the grandmother of Dorothy Dandridge, was a longtime friend of D.W. Griffith, and at his memorial service in Hollywood, there is footage of her, visibly distraught, being led from the building.

With *The Birth of a Nation*, D.W. Griffith proved himself master of *his* craft, whereas with the play of *The Clansman*, Dixon showed himself to be still a mere amateur. The aftermath of the making of *The Birth of a Nation*—the sheer anger of the African American and liberal forces—evidences Griffith's power of presentation. Dixon played with the emotions primarily of Southern audiences with his play. Griffith aroused a nation in both praise and outrage. Both men demonstrated once and for all that propaganda could now reach far beyond the printed page. As a team, the one providing the idea, the other the creative genius, they were unique in American history up to this time and, ultimately, far beyond.

Once Griffith had completed *The Birth of a Nation*, Thomas Dixon took over as its primary promoter. As *The Clansman*, the film was first screened in preview form at the Loring Opera House in Riverside, California, on January 1 and 2, 1915. There was one afternoon and one evening performance per day, with admission prices at twenty and thirty cents. The official premiere of the film, still titled *The Clansman*, took place at Clune's Auditorium in downtown Los Angeles on February 8, 1915. Prior to the Los Angeles engagement, Griffith took 120,000 feet of film to New York, at which time it was presumably screened for Thomas Dixon. *Variety* (January 29, 1915) reported that the film would "be chopped down to five or six reels." But within a week, the trade paper announced a length of twelve reels.

From its running time, if nothing else, it is obvious that both Griffith and Dixon knew the film was unique in the history of the American motion picture up to that time (although the Italian epics *Cabiria* and *Quo Vadis?* were of similar lengths, and I am assured by actress Blanche Sweet that she and D.W. Griffith saw the latter together in New York).[19] An enthusiastic Dixon contacted Woodrow Wilson, and *The Clansman* became the first film to be screened at the White House on February 18, 1915. Upon viewing the production, Woodrow Wilson made the comment, although exactly when or where is unknown, "It is like writing history with Lightning. And my only regret is that it is all so terribly true."

Wilson and Thomas Dixon are far closer in racial philosophy than most liberal biographers of the president might have one believe. Like Dixon, Wilson could not "overcome the heritage of his youth" in the South.[20] He believed that blacks held an inferior position in society, and as president of Princeton University from 1902 to 1910, he did not welcome African American students. In his 1902 *History of the American People*, described by one critic as "an admirable balance between extreme Northern and Southern views,"[21] Wilson displayed his blatant prejudice—very close to that of Dixon—against immigrants from southern and eastern Europe. It may be, as one biographer has argued, that "it was not that his intentions in regard to the blacks were odious but that circumstances forced him to do what must often seem odious things."[22] Nevertheless, under Woodrow Wilson's presidency, Republican blacks in government positions were replaced by white Democrats, and for the first time since the Civil War, government departments were segregated.

Woodrow Wilson may have stepped back from his initial enthusiasm for *The Birth of a Nation*, but there should be no doubt that he *did* admire the film and that the views expressed therein were as much his as they were Dixon's and Griffith's.

Following the White House screening, Dixon was able to arrange a second presentation a day later for members of the Supreme Court after Chief Justice Edward D. White had confirmed to him that he had been a member of the Ku Klux Klan and Dixon, in turn, had assured White that the film told the true story of the Klan.

It was Dixon who at some undetermined time—probably February 1915—suggested the change of name from *The Clansman* to *The Birth of a Nation*,[23] and under that title on March 3, 1915, the film opened at New York's Liberty Theatre, where it remained until January 2, 1916.

African American together with liberal opposition to the film quickly mounted. There were privately printed pamphlets denouncing the film, such as the four-page, carefully worded commentary by Francis J. Grimke, published in Washington, D.C., on October 30, 1915, in which he wrote of "an attempt to give respectability to a band of lawbreakers and murderers known as the Ku Klux Klan." An editorial writer in the *New York Globe* (April 6, 1915) wrote, "To make a few dirty dollars men are willing to pander to depraved tastes and to foment a race antipathy that is the most sinister and dangerous feature of American life." Four days later, both Dixon and Griffith responded, with the former pointing out that three representative New York clergymen did not suggest a single change or cut to the film and had given it high praise.[24] Dixon continued, "I am not attacking the negro of today. I am recording faithfully the history of fifty years ago. I portray three negroes faithful unto death to every want and two victim negroes, misled by white scoundrels. Is it a crime to present a bad black, seeing we have so many bad white ones?"

Typical of liberal response was Francis Hackett's essay in the *New Republic*, which concluded, "Whatever happened during Reconstruction, this film is aggressively vicious and defamatory. It is spiritual assassination. It degrades the censors that passed it and the white race that endures it."[25] Thanks largely to the endorsement by Woodrow Wilson and the implied approval of the Supreme Court, censorship was never really an issue for *The Birth of a Nation*. Mayor James Curley of Boston tried, without success, to ban the film, and there were protests on its presentation at the Tremont Theatre there, but not the riots that are often reported in modern accounts. On a local level, the NAACP agitated throughout the United States for cuts, and some minor ones were made (notably a scene of white women being molested by Negroes and the final sequence depicting the ultimate solution to the Negro problem). During the eight-month 1915 and four-month 1916 runs of the film in Chicago, no children were permitted to attend any screening. Only in Ohio was the film banned completely, after Republican Governor Frank B. Willis put pressure on the Ohio Board of Film Censors, but the ban was lifted in 1917. In the *Crisis* (May 1915), W.E.B. Du Bois argued that the entire second half of the film should be suppressed, but Booker T. Washington did little to support Negro opposition to *The Birth of a Nation*.

For the African American community, *The Birth of a Nation* served as a wake-up call and very much helped consolidate the activities of the NAACP. Another legacy of *The Birth of a Nation* that cannot be disputed, even if Griffith and Dixon were nothing more than innocent bystanders as it happened, was what is sometimes described as the Klan revival, but which might more accurately be identified as the creation of the modern Ku Klux Klan.

Neither Dixon nor Griffith deserves credit or condemnation for the new Klan. That honor goes to Alabama-born William Joseph Simmons, a born-again Christian who appears to have been obsessed with the notion of fraternal orders, many of which were little more than drinking clubs. For Simmons, the Ku Klux Klan was the ultimate fraternal organization.

Simmons might not even have been a footnote in American history had it not been for the April 27, 1915, murder of fourteen-year-old Mary Phagan in Marietta, Georgia, and the subsequent arrest of Leo M. Frank, a New York Jew, for the crime. On August 16, 1915, Frank was seized from his prison cell and lynched by a group of one hundred men, who described themselves as the Knights of Mary Phagan.[26] Two months later, the Knights gathered on Stone Mountain, outside of Atlanta, and burned a huge cross.

As the American film industry became Jewish-controlled, it steered clear of films, excepting comedies, with major Jewish themes or characters. It was not until 1947 and *Gentleman's Agreement* that Hollywood made a major feature film on the subject of anti-Semitism, and then the producer was the only non-Jewish head of a major studio, Darryl F. Zanuck. The fear of those in the industry was that by drawing attention to themselves and their religion they might arouse undeserved criticism or, worse, censorship of their releases by a still largely anti-Semitic American population.

However, in 1915, there were more Gentiles than Jews active in the industry, and self-preservation was less a concern. Two films dealt contemporaneously with the arrest and trial of Leo M. Frank. The first was *Leo M. Frank (Showing Life in Jail) and Governor Slaton*, produced by Hal Reid, the father of matinee idol Wallace Reid, and featuring an appearance by Frank's mother. The other was a five-reel reenactment, *The Frank Case*, directed by Russian-Jewish George K. Rolands. The actual lynching was not filmed, but Pathé News photographed the body hanging from a tree, and Gaumont News shot the site and the crowds.

The lynching of Leo M. Frank was a catalyst for Simmons's applying to the state of Georgia for a charter for the Knights of the

Ku Klux Klan. On Thanksgiving evening, Simmons and his supporters gathered on Stone Mountain and ignited a sixteen-foot cross.
Only fifteen Klan members were present that evening, but a few
days later, on December 6, 1915, *The Birth of a Nation* received its
Atlanta premiere, with posters depicting a robed Klansman on a
rearing horse. Simmons and his followers in Klan attire rode on
horseback in front of the theatre, the crowd waiting to enter began
cheering, and the new Klan was firmly established with Simmons
as its Imperial Wizard.

A group of enterprising Buffalo, New York, businessmen took
segments from *The Birth of a Nation* early in 1916 and reedited
them into a three-reel production, *In the Clutches of the Ku-Klux-
Klan*. To counteract the influence of *The Birth of a Nation* and the
new Klan, producer W.H. Clifford announced plans for *The Black
Boomerang*, founded on the prophecy of Thomas Jefferson: "When
I realize God Is Just, I Tremble for the Future of My Race." In
1920, African American filmmaker Oscar Micheaux released *Within
Our Gates*, which dealt with both lynching and racial conflict and
may have been influenced by the Leo M. Frank case.

Neither Dixon nor Griffith accepted any responsibility for the
establishment of the modern Klan. Griffith claimed to have known
nothing of what happened in Atlanta following the local premiere.
In 1928, he told *Collier's* magazine,

> I've been accused of having made *The Birth of a Nation* as
> propaganda for the Klan. What's more, throughout the
> years I have been constantly asked to explain the relation-
> ship between that picture and the Klan. That accusation
> seemed foolish to me; so did the question. But, if Simmons
> actually used *The Birth of a Nation* to raise membership
> in the Klan, as he says he did, running his Klan advertising
> simultaneously with advertising of the picture, I can see
> how many persons may have been confused.
>
> I had no more idea that *The Birth of a Nation* might
> be used to revive the old Klan than I might have had that

Intolerance would revive the ancient persecution of the Huguenots.

A terrific power lies in the motion picture. It's a power that is only too leanly recognized in these days. I'm constantly amazed and sometimes almost terrified by it.[27]

That powerful image and message that *The Birth of a Nation* evokes has not diminished with the passing years. Writing in 1997, an African American student at the University of California at Berkeley commented, in an oratorical style that Dixon would have admired, "Wilson, Dixon and Griffith and their large fraternity of racist intellectuals had supplied a fabulous history, a white history, which portrayed the white as the forever normal, forever real, the race responsible for the order of the world, the race which was the destiny of the species, the true subject of world history and its civilizations."[28]

5

THE FALL OF A NATION

Thomas Dixon must have been very much cognizant of his contribution to the success of *The Birth of a Nation*. Without his storyline,
there would have been no film. As a novelist, Dixon knew the value
of the script as much as any modern screenwriter. At the same time,
he was aware that it was Griffith who was receiving the public
acclamation, and only in the condemnation from African American and liberal voices was Dixon awarded equal prominence. From
a modern perspective, it is perhaps difficult to believe, but it would
seem somewhat obvious that, among contemporary filmmakers,
Dixon was to a considerable extent responsible for the success of
The Birth of a Nation. Cecil B. DeMille, who was at the beginning
of his career at this time, felt that Dixon's literary contribution to
the film was highly important. In his autobiography, he writes:
"Griffith was not a dramatist. He could take Thomas Dixon's story
of *The Clansman* and, through the magic of his direction and camera work, make it into the still thrilling *Birth of a Nation*. But when
he followed that with his own original story of *Intolerance*, magnificent in conception and studded with unforgettable scenes, audiences left the theater simply bewildered."[1] The notion that
Intolerance does not work as a motion picture is as incredible as

the suggestion that Griffith was not a dramatist, but what DeMille writes is, in all probability, what the majority of his fellow film-makers believed at the time.

Dixon had proved his worth to Griffith as a promoter. He was now determined to demonstrate that he could be equally as important a producer and director as the creator of *The Birth of a Nation*. D.W. Griffith was at best only a partial auteur. As screenwriter, producer, and director of a new film, Thomas Dixon would truly warrant such a description.

Following completion of *The Birth of a Nation*, D.W. Griffith embarked on what was to be his most ambitious production, *Intolerance*, an epic drama on the theme of the title, with stories drawn from four periods of history. It was, and is, suggested by some critics that *Intolerance* was its director's attempt at atonement for perceived racial intolerance in *The Birth of a Nation*. However, neither Griffith nor Thomas Dixon was aware of anything for which they needed to atone. As Griffith wrote to the British film journal *Sight and Sound* (spring 1947), "My picturization of history as it happens requires . . . no apology, no defence, no 'explanations.'"

Griffith's new film preached peace. For his first production, Dixon seized on a major political theme of the day, "preparedness." The majority of Americans were opposed to any intervention in the war in Europe, but a small and growing group of prominent citizens, including most notably Theodore Roosevelt, argued that what was happening across the Atlantic was a wake-up call for the country. Armed intervention in favor of Britain and her allies was one point of view, but more explicitly, Roosevelt and his supporters believed strongly that the United States was underprepared for war, that there was a need to get ready for an attack on the United States by Germany. The most influential book on the subject was Hudson Maxim's *Defenseless America*, published by Hearst's International Library in 1915, and it became the basis for a major motion picture, *The Battle Cry of Peace*, produced by J. Stuart Blackton, cofounder of the Vitagraph Company of America and, coincidentally, an Oyster Bay neighbor of Theodore Roosevelt.

THE FALL OF A NATION

The Battle Cry of Peace was first shown publicly at New York's Vitagraph Theatre on August 6, 1915, and among those applauding the epic along with a speech denouncing the popular song "I Didn't Raise My Boy to Be a Soldier," by Captain Jack Crawford, poet scout of the Grand Army of the Republic, was Thomas Dixon. The latter was obviously a strong supporter of the preparedness movement, and he was certainly influenced by The Battle Cry of Peace, elements of which can be found in his first production.

Once he had determined the theme of his first independent film, Dixon considered it only appropriate to advise President Wilson of his plans and to elicit his support. The president, a strong advocate of neutrality in the European conflict, was anything but supportive: "I must frankly say to you that I am sorry after reading the synopsis of your new enterprise, because I think the thing a great mistake. There is no need to stir the nation up in favor of national defense. It is already soberly and earnestly aware of its possible perils and of its duty, and I should deeply regret seeing any sort of excitement stirred in so grave a matter."[2]

Undeterred by Wilson's response, unwilling to recognize as did the American president what a worldwide conflict might mean for the United States, as witness the bloodshed of the Civil War, and bolstered by the fame of The Birth of a Nation, Dixon decided to title his production The Fall of a Nation. When J. Stuart Blackton produced The Battle Cry of Peace, he was still a British citizen, and pacifist and pro-German elements in the United States claimed that his film had been funded by the British Embassy in Washington, D.C. In later years, Dixon admitted that he had been visited in 1915 by Cecil Chesterton, described as "an agent of the British Government." When Chesterton asked Dixon if America would come to the aid of "the mother land," the latter responded, "Nothing is more certain. . . . My soul answered with a cry of joyous kinship. Millions of Americans feel this."[3]

Dixon must surely have been sympathetic to the arguments put forward by Cecil Chesterton, the brother of novelist and writer G.K. Chesterton, since the former had already praised The Birth of

91

a Nation and its "author": "When Mr. Dixon says that a Mulatto citizenship is too high a price to pay even for Emancipation, I know that if I were an American I should say the same. All that I can say as an Englishman, and I hope as a patriot, is that, conscious as I am of the many and heavy sins upon my country's record, I pray God that she may never have to pay for them as the American republic has paid for Negro slavery."[4]

In the summer of 1915, the author took up residence in Hollywood, initially leasing for one year a house at 7018 Hawthorne Avenue. He formed the National Drama Corporation to produce the film, and Cleveland Moffett was paid $400 to collaborate on an initial screenplay, although he received no credit on the released film. Contemporaneous with preparation of a screenplay, Dixon also wrote a novelization, subtitled *A Sequel to "The Birth of a Nation"* and published in June 1916, to coincide with the first screenings of the film.

The National Drama Corporation was incorporated on July 28, 1915, with working capital of $150,000 (primarily loaned by Dixon) and under the trusteeship of Dixon, William R. Perkins, and Lindsey Hopkins. Dixon was named general manager and director of the corporation in March 1916 at a salary of $300 a week, rising to $500 a week once *The Fall of a Nation* was produced. Dixon transferred to the corporation the motion picture rights to various of his novels. The National Drama Corporation exploited, through licensing to other producers and distributors, three other titles: *The One Woman, The Foolish Virgin,* and *Comrades.*

Production on *The Fall of a Nation* began in September 1915 at an unidentified rental studio in Los Angeles, but in January 1916, the company began filming at Dixon's own studio, complete with a laboratory, built on a former orange grove at Sunset Boulevard and Western Avenue in Hollywood. The facility boasted both an open and a glass-enclosed stage, together with a life-size reproduction of a New York street. It was Dixon's intention to utilize the lot for later productions, but after completion of *The Fall of a Nation*, the studio was sold to William Fox and became the Fox Western Avenue Studio.

Perhaps with the notion that the story and the production were bigger than any one individual, Dixon hired no prominent film players; leading lady Lorraine Huling and leading men Percy Standing and Arthur Shirley have left no mark on film history. "They are not recognized stars—not yet at least—but in each can be found that indefinable quality through which the picture on the screen may become a mirror of the mind," explained the author.[5] Dixon was presumably unable to persuade any of Griffith's leading players from *The Birth of a Nation* to participate in his venture. William C. Thompson, who also headed the film laboratory, was the principal cinematographer, and two minor directors, Bartley Cushing and George L. Sargent, served as Dixon's assistants. Where Dixon proved to be a master showman, if not a master filmmaker, was in hiring Victor Herbert, responsible for such popular operettas as *Babes in Toyland* and *Naughty Marietta*, to compose an original score for *The Fall of a Nation*. While serious composers had worked on a number of foreign film scores and at least one classical composer, Walter Cleveland Simon, had written scores for a couple of American short subjects, this was the first time that a major composer was involved in an American feature film. Obviously, Dixon was aware of the tremendous emotive power of Joseph Carl Breil's partially composed and partially adapted score for *The Birth of a Nation*. Further, he realized the prominence that the participation of a composer such as Victor Herbert could guarantee his film. Dixon's screenplay was now a libretto, and *The Fall of a Nation* was touted as "cinema grand opera." Victor Herbert boasted to the *New York Times* (May 3, 1916), "For the first time in the history of American pictorial drama, a complete accompanying score will be played that has never been heard anywhere else. . . . In brief, the musical programme will not be a mosaic or patchwork of bits of Wagner, Grieg, Verdi, Bizet, and others, but will be strictly new, as individually written to each particular scene." The composer worked initially from Dixon's scenario and then revised the score to synchronize with the edited film. Herbert's colleague Harold Sanford rehearsed the musicians.

Victor Herbert's score for *The Fall of a Nation* has survived, and it is a stirring achievement, strong and powerful, evoking images in the mind that are perhaps more vigorous than those actually filmed. Contemporary critics praised the score. In a sharply negative review of the film in *Photoplay* (August 1916), Julian Johnson wrote, "In the opening episodes, where the picture prelude was leading up to the founding of the American republic, Mr. Herbert displayed true Beethoven genius, introducing faint suggestions of the themes of the various American national airs, and in the battle scenes the jargon and dissonance was so masterful that it almost hypnotized the audience into the belief that the picture was thrilling. It was the music which thrilled and awakened the flagging interest."

Victor Herbert's involvement in a preparedness film is actually somewhat odd. The composer was at the time president of the Friends of Irish Freedom, prominent in many Hibernian associations, and a keen supporter of Irish rebellion against British rule. To Dixon, Germans were the enemies. To Herbert and other professional Irish Americans, Germans were England's enemies and Ireland's friends. At one point, the composer drafted a letter to Dixon, warning, "England is our danger, not Germany."[6] At Herbert's express request, Dixon did not identify the American invaders as German, although their nationality is patently obvious.

The Fall of a Nation does not survive, but thanks to contemporary reviews and, primarily, the novel, we have a fairly clear vision of its content. While some 362 pages in length, the novel is printed double-spaced and is therefore a relatively short work—particularly for Thomas Dixon. The book begins with a note to the reader: "This novel is not a rehash of the idea of foreign conquest of America based on the accidents of war. It is a study of the origin, meaning and destiny of American Democracy by one who believes that the time is ripe in this country for a revival of the principles on which our Republic was founded."

A twelve-page prologue documents America's founding as a result of Europe's woes and American history, with a strong emphasis on the Monroe doctrine. The first pilgrims are denounced as invaders, who terrorize, rob, and murder the Native Americans, a theme that Dixon embraces in later novels. A rather ridiculous subtitle in the film has it, "First they fell upon their knees, then upon the aborigines." (Dixon uses this same wording in his 1903 novel *The One Woman*.) It must have been very difficult for Dixon, but he manages to ignore totally the Civil War, although he does quote, without attribution, Lincoln's words: "Government of the people by the people and for the people shall not perish from the earth." Dixon reminds, "Eternal vigilance is the price of liberty today as yesterday and forever" (p. 12).

Explaining the use of the prologue in the film, Dixon said, "The motion picture is the finest vehicle of historical exposition ever devised. I can teach more history in fifteen minutes of motion pictures than in six months of the library or the classroom. I have tried to show what America means to us, namely the polyglot nationalities of which we are composed. A rapid survey of nearly 400 years of history serves the purpose and leads up to the story of *The Fall of a Nation* proper which tells what these polyglot peoples did when threatened by the extinction of the national life."[7]

The central characters in *The Fall of a Nation* are New York Congressman John Vassar, a young man who has introduced a bill advocating a strong army and navy; his neighbor, Virginia Holland, leader of the Modern Feminist Movement; and New York millionaire Charles Waldron, who finances Holland's activities. Both Vassar and Waldron are in love with Holland. Vassar's bill is defeated, thanks to the lobbying efforts of six hundred chartered peace societies, the United Women Voters of America, and socialists who "had once more swamped the American labor unions with their missionaries" (p. 157).

After two years of war in Europe, the pope arranges an armistice, and a newly formed Parliament of Man meets at the Hague. Japan influences the exclusion of China, and the minor republics of South America, together with the entire African continent, are also excluded. American feminists cheer the election of Queen Wilhelmina of the Netherlands as presiding officer of the assembly, which partitions China and divides Africa among the imperial powers, with only the United States and Switzerland objecting.

When the American president argues that "the Monroe doctrine shall . . . be affirmed as the second basic principle on which the Federation of the World shall be established" (pp. 185–86), only Brazil supports the motion. As foolish Americans celebrate a great peace jubilee, explosions rock New York and soldiers in dull brown uniforms march down Broadway. The Imperial Confederation, headed by Charles Waldron, now identified as Prince Karl von Waldron, has taken over America. Enemy submarines destroy the Pacific Fleet as it tries to pass through the Panama Canal, and the president and his cabinet are arrested. Washington, Philadelphia, Boston, Chicago, and St. Louis are occupied.

The battle scenes were filmed at a cost of thirty-one thousand dollars, and Dixon utilized the same Hollywood location—then called Universal Field and now the site of Forest Lawn Cemetery in Burbank—where Griffith had shot the battle sequences for *The Birth of a Nation*. Dixon wrote to Victor Herbert on November 21, 1915: "We are putting on the screen now the most thrilling battle the world has ever seen. Our setting looking down on sunlit slopes piled with dead, and dying and charging thousands, framed between black frowning hills wreathed with exploding shells, is something words *can not* convey. Believe me when I tell you that our battle scenes will make *The Birth of a Nation* look like 30 cents compared to a million dollars."

Chapter after chapter documents the looting of New York, the rape of its women, and the murder of its men by citizens of an unidentified country who wear Germanic-style uniforms and have strong Germanic names. Contemporary reports on the film indicate that characters strongly resembling pacifists William Jennings Bryan and Henry Ford were shown, with flowers in their hands, approaching the enemy and subsequently facing humiliation. Vassar joins with the remaining leaders, taking refuge on Long Island, in the fight for freedom. Virginia Holland is taken under Waldron's protection, and he determines to make her "the leader of a new woman's party [the Woman's Imperial Legion of Honor] to proclaim the blessings of the imperial and aristocratic form of government" (p. 318). Holland agrees, while secretly working to build up an army of women, the Daughters of Jael, who will retake America. The novel concludes on the first anniversary of America's subjugation as these million strong, young, and beautiful Daughters of Jael, aided by Vassar's secret army and using steel knives, attack and kill the enemy. Vassar takes Holland in his arms, declaring, "You have lifted a fallen nation from the dust!" (p. 359).

It is not known whether the Daughters of Jael played the same role on screen as in the novel. On December 10, 1915, Dixon wrote to Victor Herbert, "I can tell you now that I have decided to make a different use of the Daughters of Jael from the one in the novel and in the first version of the play. The Daughters of Jael will not be an organization for assassination but for cooperation with our army. They will act as spies and decoys, they prolong the banquet until the men can effect the uprising."

Concurrently with the New York presentation of *The Fall of a Nation*, producer Thomas H. Ince released his antiwar melodrama *Civilization*. While the two films are diametrically opposed in ideology, both pointedly make use of the female population. Dixon has them as warlike liberators, and Ince has them as messengers of peace.

The similarity between the Klan in *The Birth of a Nation*, riding to the rescue of the South, and the Daughters of Jael, with their "white-robed girl riders" (p. 359), riding to the rescue of the entire United States, is blatantly obvious. "It is a new Ku Klux Klan," wrote the *New York Evening Sun* (June 7, 1916), noting "Mr. Dixon's uncanny genius for stirring up a ruction. *The Clansman* stirred old embers of prejudice into fire and *The Fall of a Nation* is bound to create something of that sort of effect." At the same time, Dixon uses the novel (and presumably the film) not only to emphasize that only a united nation can fight oppression by the conqueror but also to indict racism, be it the attitude of Europe and Japan toward Africa and China, the ethnic cleansing of Native Americans by the first European settlers, or the attitude of modern twentieth-century Americans toward outsiders. When Virginia Holland's father denounces Jews and foreigners, he is reminded by his daughter that John Vassar, whom he admires, is of Polish extraction, and thus his argument is blunted. It is as if the father represents the old American racism and Virginia Holland a new, more tolerant society.

Dixon was a fervent foe of anti-Semitism. In his journals from the 1930s, he urged that Americans be "elevated to [the] happy innocence of a little child [who] doesn't ask if [you are] a Jew or a Catholic." In 1905, he wrote:

> The Jew has not been assimilated into our civil and social life because of his money—but for a very different reason. The Jew belongs to our race, the same great division of humanity. The Semitic group of the white race is, all in all, the greatest evolved in history. Their children have ever led the vanguard of human progress and achievements. . . . Our prejudice against the Jew is not because of his inferiority, but because of his genius. We are afraid of him, we Gentiles who meet him in the arena of life, get licked and then make faces at him. The truth is the Jew had achieved a noble civilization—had his poets, prophets, priests and kings—when our Germanic ancestors were still in the woods cracking cocoanuts and hickory-nuts with monkeys. We have assimilated the Jew because his daughter is beautiful and his son strong in mind and body![8]

Two years earlier, Dixon had made some interesting comments on racial prejudice:

> Race prejudice is of two kinds. One is a mean thing. This is the prejudice which proceeds from fear of another race's

superior powers or abilities. Such is the prejudice against the Jew. It exists simply because the Jewish race is the most persistent, powerful, commercially successful race that the world has ever produced. Thousands of them have been assimilated by America and thousands more will be assimilated. Millions of them may be swallowed by our Germanic race, and that will not change your complexion—but you can't swallow a single nigger without changing your complexion.[9]

It is an extraordinary comment not only because of the incredible racist remark in the last sentence, but also because it is remindful of what did happen to German Jews who were not assimilated but swallowed up in concentration camps.

In his 1924 novel *The Black Hood*, Dixon compares a Jewish merchant to a modern Klansman, noting "the Jew's fine Christlike face in startling contrast to the beast beside him," and when the Klansman strikes the merchant, Dixon's outraged hero cries out, "God chose a Jewish girl to be the mother of Jesus Christ, the Savior of the world and *you* strike a Jew!" (p. 164). The filmmaker must have taken great pleasure in his humiliating parody of Henry Ford, in view of the automaker's rabid anti-Semitism.

The Jewish merchant of *The Black Hood* had earlier appeared in less defined form as the character Sam Nickaroshinski in *The Traitor*. Here he is depicted as a sympathizer with the oppressed people of the South, pressing one hundred dollars into the hand of the Ku Klux Klan leader as he heads off for imprisonment in the North. As Walter Benn Michaels has noted, Dixon's Jew is "a negrophobic American hero, a supporter of the Klan."[10]

The author's views on Native Americans are best expressed by the leading female character in his last novel, *The Flaming Sword*: "We have assimilated the Indians. . . . I once thought that we had exterminated them. We have not. . . . The Indian has no trace of Negro blood in him. The attempt to associate him with the Negro is infamous. This was a white man's country when we came here"

(p. 234). If someone like Thomas Dixon could display such toler-ance toward Native Americans, it is small wonder that in the 1920s and 1930s many African Americans would pass themselves off as Native Americans.

The Fall of a Nation begins in the present, presumably 1916, and ends about 1919. It can thus be defined as science fiction, a genre not usually associated with Thomas Dixon. Woman suffrage is a fact and, as presented here, is to a large extent the cause not only of the foreign conquest but also of its eventual overthrow. Virginia Holland, whether in pacifist or warrior guise, is a strong woman, compared on screen and in contemporary reviews to Joan of Arc. (Among the books in Dixon's library was Kate E. Carpenter's *The Story of Joan of Arc for Boys and Girls,* published in 1902.) If nothing else, Dixon's attitude toward female emancipation is con-fused and confusing; but then, this is a work of science fiction, and not set in its writer's own world with his own philosophy.

Immediately prior to the film's premiere, Dixon spoke at length about the film and the power of the cinema to present spectacle:

> Six pictures of the quality of *The Birth of a Nation* might be displayed in New York at the same time and there would be an audience for every one of them. . . . There is not the slightest danger of overproduction of dramas with a big idea handled in a big way. We need only to conceive them.
>
> No one questions for a moment the superiority of the cinema for the presentation of spectacles, but spec-tacular effects are not the end and aim of a producer who understands the psychology of an audience and strives to interest the mind and reach the emotions. If a stage play, or a screenplay, or a novel misses the human note it is a failure in the larger sense. I really believe that the biggest things in *The Fall of a Nation* are the smallest things, the scenes in which a smile and a tear are com-bined. I would sacrifice any part of the picture rather

than three minutes of heart-gripping action that should make an audience weep. One must be made to feel personal griefs and joys before he can be held by a story of epic scope.[11]

The film opened in downtown Los Angeles at Clune's Auditorium in May 1916. Then, just as *The Birth of a Nation* had opened at New York's Liberty Theatre, so did *The Fall of a Nation*—on June 6, 1916. (Dixon tried unsuccessfully to book his film into the Metropolitan Opera House.) The initial presentation took three hours, with three intermissions, and concluded with a short speech by its maker. Following the twelve-minute prologue, the first act was titled "A Nation Falls," the second act "The Heel of the Conqueror," and the third act "The Uprising." The trade press was enthusiastic. Lynde Denig in the *Moving Picture World* (June 24, 1916) noted, "Mr. Dixon chose a tremendous national theme and treated it with keen regard for the importance of trivial personal affairs in the lives of those who constitute the nation" and went on to praise the juxtaposition of humor and satire in the story with tragedy. Joshua Lowe in *Variety* (June 9, 1916) complained, "There is a wealth of fine filmmaking here, so much so that the main criticism is its abundance." The critic for *Motion Picture News* (June 24, 1916) was thrilled by the battle scenes but wondered why John Vassar and company would take refuge on Long Island rather than somewhere more distant, say, the Rocky Mountains or the Great Lakes; he also criticized the antiquated painted backdrops for some of the interior scenes.

The *New York Times* (June 7, 1916) wrote of "an unbridled photoplay of the battle, murder and sudden death species, much of it graphic and exciting, some of it quite absurd, and all of it undeniably entertaining. . . . And, like all big spectacular pictures, it must face the eternal question, 'Is it as good as *The Birth of a Nation*?' It has not yet been possible to answer this in the affirmative."

The Fall of a Nation played at the Liberty Theatre through July 15 and was then released on a road-show basis by V-L-S-E, a distribution entity owned by Vitagraph, producer of *The Battle Cry of Peace* and a company that recognized the commercial potential of preparedness films; it already had a second one, *Womanhood, the Glory of a Nation*, in preparation. The first presentation of *The Fall of a Nation* after New York was at the Illinois Theatre in Chicago. Despite the prominent use of Victor Herbert's name, the film garnered little enthusiasm from the city's German and Irish immigrants and closed within two weeks. Ultimately, *The Fall of a Nation* netted a healthy profit of $120,000 for its producer.

The Fall of a Nation was also screened in neutral European countries. A German film executive, Franz Seldte, who would later be Hitler's minister of labor, saw the film in Switzerland and commented, "I know the sentimental slush. A nation turned beast attacks free America, torturing women and cutting off children's hands. . . . The very word 'America' fills me with dumb fury. They've invented a new doctrine over there; America for the Americans . . . all that damned hypocrisy about world peace, freedom and justice from the very fellows who wiped out the whole gifted race of Indians with powder and lead so they could settle in their nest themselves."[12] The final sentiment was not that far removed from Dixon's own views.

Perhaps as a sop to Victor Herbert, and certainly in response to critical commentary, Dixon vehemently denied that his film was anti-German. Under the unintentionally amusing headline, "Dixon Denies Race Prejudice," the filmmaker told the *Moving Picture World* (June 24, 1916): "It is alleged that the large number of German faces in the hosts of the invading army and in the cast of *The Fall of a Nation* convicts the author of cherishing anti-German prejudices. On the contrary, I chose these men because they were out of work and hungry. Five hundred Germans, many of them reservists, applied to me for work in the battle scenes of the picture, and I was glad to give it to them. They represented fairly well the varying types of the imperial federation of Northern Europe which I imagined to be attacking America."

Dixon's attitude toward Germany was to undergo massive

rethinking after World War I. The intense animosity that he had expressed toward Germany in *The Fall of a Nation* seemed to disappear. In a 1937 entry in his journal, he noted, somewhat inaccurately in that Italy had fought on the side of the allies, "Italians & Germans were very badly treated after the war—hence Mussolini & Hitler." Later in 1937, he opined, "Most Italians & Germans don't like Military Dictatorship but they feel its [*sic*] more secure than anarchy."

Concurrently with the film's critical reception, the novel was being examined by reviewers. The *New York Times* (June 18, 1916) was kind, writing, "If the author's style glows and flames in uncurbed opulence, still more does the matter of the tale open the reader's eyes with wonder as the author pours out with reckless prodigality the treasures of his imagination." Less enthusiastic was the *Boston Transcript* (June 14, 1916): "It would be difficult to discover anything more futile and foolish than *The Fall of a Nation*, even in the midst of an epoch that produces many futile and foolish books. . . . But it need hoodwink none of us into believing it to be a propagandist tract against pacifism. It is nothing but a story, and a very poor story at that. It is exactly the sort of story to be expected of the author of *The Clansman* and *The Foolish Virgin*."

Critics might ridicule *The Fall of a Nation*, *The Clansman*, and *The Foolish Virgin*, but the first two had already been filmed to great popular acclaim, and within a year *The Foolish Virgin* was to appear in the first of its two screen adaptations.

6

THE FOOLISH VIRGIN AND THE NEW WOMAN

The Fall of a Nation provides some indication of its author's views—though somewhat confused—on women. Despite Dixon's claim that "there is a strong feminist element"[1] in *The Fall of a Nation*, feminists basically are worthy only of ridicule there; women perhaps are too easily swayed to be allowed the right to vote. Women can be, and are, strong, but only in supportive roles. Feminine wiles can serve a useful purpose, such as bringing down the enemy. A Joan of Arc–like figure can arise and can gain respect, but only if her purpose is male-approved. For example, in Dixon's 1929 novel, *The Sun Virgin*, there are two strong women, Teresa, around whom the love story revolves and who disguises herself as a man to join Francisco Pizarro's 1532 invasion of Peru, and the title character. Dixon admired novelist Gertrude Atherton, an exponent of the New Woman, and he was also supportive of Carrie Chapman Catt, president of the International American Woman Suffrage Association and a leading figure in the campaign for adoption of the Nineteenth Amendment.

Yet his views on feminism were fairly antiquated well into the 1920s, the era of the flapper. In his 1925 novel, *The Love Com-*

plex, Dixon has his central character, Dr. Alan Holt, say of his sweetheart, Donna, "I don't want her to be my equal! I want her to be my girl. Dependent on my love. It's old-fashioned stuff, maybe. But we have a long way to go before we outgrow it" (p. 43).

Dixon provides his closest examination of the modern woman in his 1915 novel, *The Foolish Virgin: A Romance of Today*. His heroine, Mary Adams, is a New York schoolteacher, "an old-fashioned girl" who dreams of finding the perfect husband. She explains to her friend, artist Jane Anderson:

> I don't believe in women working for money. I don't believe God ever meant us to work when he made us women. He made us women for something more wonderful. I don't see anything good or glorious in the fact that half the torment of humanity you see down there pouring through the street from those factories and offices is made up of women. They are wage-earners—so much the worse. They are forcing the scale of wages for men lower and lower. They are paying for it in weakened bodies and sickly, hopeless children. We should not shout for joy; we should cry. God never meant for woman to be a wage-earner! (p. 6)

At the New York Public Library, Mary Adams meets Jim Anthony, who has become a criminal as a result of his upbringing in the New York tenements. The two quickly fall in love, marry, and head for North Carolina in search of Jim's mother, from whom he was separated as an infant. The mother is now an insane drunkard, living in a hut. Not recognizing her son, she tries to murder him for the valuables she finds in his luggage. When Mary learns that her husband is a burglar, she leaves him and is taken in by the local doctor. Pregnant, Mary is terrified that her son will inherit Jim's traits, but she is reassured by the physician: "only *your* mind can reach the soul of this child. . . . *Your* mind will be the ever-brooding, enfolding spirit forming and fashioning character" (p. 318).

Jim reforms, returns the items he has stolen, and with the doctor's help, builds a new home for the bride. Eighteen months after the birth of her child, Mary and Jim are reunited, and he tells her, "I'm going to work for you, live for you and die for you—whether you stay with me or not. I've got the right to do that, you know" (p. 352). "Mary should have ended in the poor-house and Jim in jail. Such an ending might have saved the book from a little of its absurdity—if anything could," commented P.G. Hulbert Jr. in the *Bookman* (January 1916).

There is a vague hint of eugenics in *The Foolish Virgin* as the doctor discusses the birth of her child with Mary Adams, but it really is nothing more than the silliness of Thomas Dixon in believing that only a woman can determine the character of an unborn child. He argues that only the most obvious physical traits are inherited from the father: "He is merely a supernumerary who steps on the stage for a moment and speaks one word announcing the arrival of the queen. The queen is the mother. She plays the star role in the drama of Heredity" (p. 313). Yet, from a modern, New Age perspective, perhaps there is some validity to Dixon's philosophy of birth. If smoking, drinking, and drugs can harm an unborn child, why cannot good thoughts, good deeds, and the like play a positive role? Mary Adams's son will be a fine young man because, as the doctor points out to his mother, "You are to think only beautiful thoughts, see beautiful things, dream beautiful dreams, hear beautiful music" (p. 317).

At the same time, a woman cannot abrogate responsibility for the selection of her child's father:

I am telling you that he is the father of your son—that he has rights which you cannot deny him; that when you gave yourself to him in the first impulse of love a deed was done which Almighty God can never undo. Your tragic blunder was the rush into marriage with a man about whose character you knew so little. It's the timid, shrinking, home-loving girl that makes this mistake. You must face it now. You are responsible as deeply and truly as the man who married you. That he happened at that moment to be a brute and a criminal is no more his fault than yours. It was *your* business to *know* before you made him the father of your child. (p. 344)

Dixon's heroine is not only foolish but also unrealistic, forgetful of reality, and dreaming of her prince charming. Jim Anthony is hardly a knight in shining armor, and the marriage is totally illogical. Marry in haste, repent at leisure, or at least for a year and a half, seems to be the message that Dixon is offering. It is not Jim Anthony who is the hero here, or even the friendly neighborhood doctor, but rather the South. The South has a regenerative effect on Jim and helps cure him of the ills—that is, crime—that he developed in New York. Dixon had written earlier on the unpleasantness of city life compared to rural life, not necessarily in the South. He developed a 1902 essay, "From the Horrors of City Life," published in *World's Work,* into the 1905 philosophical volume *The Life Worth Living: A Personal Experience.* Here, he writes of his family's New York home, "just a nineteen-foot slit in a block of scorched mud with a brownstone veneer in front. Our children were penned in its narrow prison walls through the long winters, and forbidden to walk on the grass in the cold, dreary spring. The doctor came to see us every week" (p. 6). In conclusion, Dixon notes, "The acme of living cannot be attained in the city. In the city we are spendthrifts. We give, give and never receive. I believe that man's full growth will be best reached by spending one-third of his time in town and two-thirds in touch with Nature" (pp. 137–38).

As F. Garvin Davenport Jr. has noted, "Industrialism and capitalism had created the evils of the northern city."[2] As much as England is a garden to its citizens, so, to Dixon, is the South a garden, in which tranquillity and innocence are blended together. It is the "ark of the covenant of American ideals" (*The Leopard's Spots*, p. 334). To paraphrase Davenport, the Negro and industrialism are linked by their darkness, and they will destroy the white harmony of both the North and the South.

Dixon was not the only novelist of the period to find dramatic appeal in the Southern branch of the Appalachian mountain chain. *The Foolish Virgin* reaches its climax in the Great Smoky Mountains of North Carolina, close to the city of Asheville. Another contemporary author, John Fox Jr., wrote a series of novels set in the Kentucky mountains, including *The Trail of the Lonesome Pine*, *The Little Shepherd of Kingdom Come*, and *A Knight of the Cumberland*, all beautifully illustrated by F.C. Yohn and all emphasizing the romantic.

The Foolish Virgin was silly enough to be popular, and the screen rights were acquired by the Clara Kimball Young Film Corporation as the second starring vehicle for the star. "I have sold the rights to *The Foolish Virgin* only because I feel that Clara Kimball Young is the best fitted to present my book in screen form," disingenuously explained Dixon to *Motion Picture News* (July 29, 1916), ignoring the substantial, but undisclosed, sum of money paid for the rights by Young's business manager and company president, Lewis J. Selznick. Clara Kimball Young (1890–1960) was a somewhat buxom leading lady, equally adept at both drama and comedy, who had been on screen since 1912 and was at the height of her fame in that decade. She was often referred to as the "Dark Madonna," noted for the depth and intensity of her eyes. The actress was already at work on the first film for her new company, an adaptation of the Robert W. Chambers novel *The Common Law*, along with director Albert Capellani and leading man Conway Tearle, when the three began filming *The Foolish Virgin* in August 1916. The primary achievement of the filmmakers was in telling the story with a minimum of subtitles.

The storyline was ideal for a leading lady of the popularity of Clara Kimball Young, and the actress delivered a well-praised performance. "Miss Young brings out the varying moods and shades of character called for by the role, with a sureness of touch expected from an actress of her reputation," wrote William Ressman

Andrews in the trade paper *Motion Picture News* (December 30, 1916). To *Exhibitor's Trade Review* (December 23, 1916), the production was "a sterling attraction." Noting the fame of both its star and its source novel, the *New York Dramatic Mirror* (December 23, 1916) suggested the film might be advertised simply as "Clara Kimball Young in *The Foolish Virgin*." When *The Foolish Virgin* opened at Tally's Broadway Theatre in Los Angeles, the *Evening Express* (January 6, 1917) commented upon its star's "superlative beauty and dramatic gifts."

The Foolish Virgin was remade in 1924 as a vehicle for Elaine Hammerstein, who had earlier starred on stage in several of her producer-father Arthur's musicals. George W. Hill was the director, and Robert Frazer was the thief-husband, now renamed Jim Owens. Aside from renaming a central character, the new version of *The Foolish Virgin* also added a forest fire, through which Jim dashes to reach his wife and child. Contemporary reviews indicate that Jim is no longer a thief and that his marriage to Mary Adams rescues her from a scheming lawyer. "It should please the average audience," commented *Variety* (December 10, 1924), while *Photoplay* (February 1925) wrote, "The story is silly, uninteresting, tiresome." The latter was a statement that must surely have hurt Thomas Dixon, watching from New York as his novels and his screen adaptations were losing popular appeal.

Both screen versions provided opportunity for the actress playing the role of Jim's mother. In 1916, it was Catherine Proctor, who is primarily associated with the stage and was to make only one other silent film appearance. In 1924, it was the superb leading-lady-turned-character-actress Gladys Brockwell. Anyone who has seen Brockwell as Nancy Sikes in the 1922 screen adaptation of *Oliver Twist* must be certain that her characterization here will have put to shame that of Elaine Hammerstein.

As a footnote to *The Foolish Virgin*, one should not ignore *The Way of a Man* and *The Love Complex*, both of which have as their central themes the role of women—the New Woman—in modern society. *The Love Complex*, published in 1925 by Boni and Liveright, covers some of the same territory as *The Foolish Virgin* and may well have been based in part on Dixon's scenario for his 1923 film *The Mark of the Beast*. Here, a young doctor, Alan Holt, decides to spend two years in extensive research into the new science of psychology before considering marriage to his fiancée, Donna Sherwood. She becomes infatuated with a con man named Wallis Banning, whom Holt knows to be a crook but whom Donna believes to be a government agent. Holt explains it to Donna: "Your interest in this man is one of the simplest illusions of the Unconscious Mind produced by your father's image. Your father was the first man in both your conscious and unconscious life. You idealize him. You meet a man who suggests his personality and because you loved your father, you imagine that you love him" (p. 91).

Donna and Banning elope, and en route to an isolated roadhouse in the Catskills, they are married. At the roadhouse, run by a decidedly strange couple, Hilda and Louis Grey, Donna discovers Banning's criminality. They fight, and Banning tears off Donna's clothes, but she escapes to the bedroom and bolts the door. Holt arrives and considers killing Banning but is saved the trouble when the latter is knifed by Hilda Grey. Donna urges Holt, as a doctor, to save Banning's life, but he dies, conveniently, just before the operation. Donna is now free to marry Holt, and Hilda throws herself off a cliff.

It is all wildly melodramatic, and while Donna displays some strength of character as she is stripped nude by Banning—disarming and defeating him with the gleam of hatred in her eyes—she is basically a weak woman:

> She drew her figure to its full height without shame, without fear and held his gaze in a steady stare of hate. Her eyes were bloodshot from the strain of the struggle, but they gleamed with a deadly light.
>
> He felt disarmed and defeated. He was not only defeated. He was afraid of her.

"Mr. Dixon's novel is hand-made melodrama, seasoned with a few dashes of pseudo-science and Freudianism," reported Herschel Brickell in *Literary Review* (August 15, 1925). "It is not a novel for discriminating readers, who insist upon an intelligent handling of plot and character. Its people are mere dummies, and at no point does the story rise above the level of the good old ten-twenty-thirty [cent] thrillers." The theme is the matter of real love versus the sexual urge, the misery that infatuation can cause—be it Donna's infatuation for Holt that permits her to wait too long for him or the sheer passion of her infatuation for the brash and eager Banning. Unfortunately, Dixon's telling is as weak as his plot, and Will Cuppy in the *New York Tribune* (July 26, 1925) was correct in saying, "As a study of love at first sight versus love that has 'ripened' it is probably one of the worst."

The Way of a Man: A Story of the New Woman is dedicated somewhat cheekily by Dixon to Dorothy Dix, with neither her approval nor her foreknowledge. Dorothy Dix was the pseudonym of Elizabeth Meriwether Gilmer, a journalist famous for her column of advice to the lovelorn. "She is one of the characters in the book— oh, just a minor character who lends excellent atmosphere by reason of her sweetness and goodness."[3] The central character in *The Way of a Man* is also a journalist, Ellen West, a New Woman whose views are expressed in her column in the *New Era Magazine*. She falls in love with the boyish Ralph Manning but rejects his marriage proposal: "I demand and I will have the poetry of love—or I will have nothing. I loathe the kept woman—wife or mistress. I refuse to use my sex for economic purposes. Marriage is a trade in which a woman practices the art of sex allurement to make a living off men. I don't have to stoop to such a trade. I have one" (p. 86).

Manning is determined to behave as he and Thomas Dixon understand a gentleman should and to marry Ellen. Still Ellen argues: "I will not sell my sex for my keep, either in the bonds of matrimony or the bonds of the kept woman outside of marriage. I will not be a parasite. I will not obey any man who walks this earth. If I must be the mother of men, I will be their equal at least. I will be freed from conventional slavery (pp. 108–9).

Ultimately, it is Ellen who seduces Manning. She takes him to a log cottage, perched over a stream in the mountains beyond Nyack. After he has cleaned himself up from the journey, Manning enters the living room and finds that Ellen has removed "her corsets and slipped into a dark, blood-red negligee trimmed in black fur" (p. 150). She takes him in her arms: "Our position here to-night is an advance in morality—not a lapse. We seek the reality, not the shadow. We scorn the letter of an outgrown ritualism. The murmur of the brook beneath our cabin is our wedding march. . . . The mist of the fall is my bridal veil" (pp. 154, 155).

Ellen quickly discovers that a nonbinding, nonlegal marriage can have its disadvantages. She becomes jealous of Manning's quick rise to success and his larger income than hers, and she is even more jealous of the women who hang around and flirt with him. The situation comes to a climax with the arrival of Ellen's young niece, Rose O'Neil, who is a miniature version of Ellen. Manning falls in love with her, and eventually Ellen is forced to accept their relationship. In fact, she arranges that the couple will marry. When Ellen reveals her former association with Manning to her father, he threatens to shoot the young man, but Ellen suddenly accepts the advances of millionaire sportsman and newspaperman Edwin Brown. Brown buys the *New Era Magazine* for his new wife. It is no longer the organ of radical feminism and becomes a successful business venture. Ellen finds time to write her editorials at her desk in the nursery, where her young son pulls at her skirts.

Aside from the basic feminist premise and its ultimate collapse, *The Way of a Man* is relatively free of typical Dixon preachment. It is also surprisingly modern, almost trashy at times. It is little wonder that the *Dial* (March 22, 1919) complained, "Mr. Dixon is a sensation-monger, knowing only the vulgarly violent emotions, striving always to lash the reader into some state of passion. Violent and luscious adjectives pursue each other across the page, where mechanical emotions rumble along through a paste-board world to their stereotyped conclusions."

The author is not unkind in his description of Ellen and her rebellion against society. From a modern perspective, Ellen's stand on feminism has appeal, and Manning seems rather weak and un-worldly in his initial rejection of a sexual, nonbinding affair. Manning's weakness is further emphasized by a sudden nervous breakdown after he has taken time off work to write a play, the manuscript for which is typed by Rose. Manning somewhat proves the theory that the boy-next-door type belongs next door, rather than in a sultry affair. Also within the novel, as a guest at a party Ellen West throws in the opening chapters, is a poet named Lloyd Bridges, described as effeminate, "a long-haired man [who] could never appeal to a real woman" (p. 7). Bridges is, arguably, the only gay character to be found in any of Dixon's novels, although James Zebulon Wright points out to me that the author was neither "anti-gay" nor "homophobic."[4]

Gossip columnist Louella Parsons interviewed Dixon in January 1919, and the author assured her, "I believe in women's suffrage. This [*The Way of a Man*] is based on woman's economic independence. It deals with the sex problem as related to the new woman, the woman who goes out in the world and earns her own living and carves her own career—whether or not marriage is practical for the breadwinning female. . . . This story is not what I believe. . . . I am merely telling it as it happened."[5] Dixon described the storyline, telling Parsons that it would be his third film production for the company he had initially organized to produce *The One Woman*. "It has been written with the screen in mind, and will be put on the screen after it has been put on the market as a book." At least one reviewer, in the *Boston Transcript* (March 1, 1919), was aware of a potential ulterior motive behind the text: "Like all his novels, it is crude in manner, flamboyant in style, exaggerated in its attempt to bring forth the realities of life, and the veriest melodrama in its construction. The glare of the footlights is upon its every scene, the unreality of the motion picture scene is evident on its every page." *The Way of a Man* is ideally suited to silent screen melodrama, and Dixon sold the film rights to producer Joseph M. Schenck on September 12, 1919.[6] The producer obviously intended *The Way of a Man* as a vehicle for his actress-wife Norma Talmadge—and it would be have been a good one—but nothing came of the project.

7

DIXON ON SOCIALISM

As early as June 8, 1903, at a meeting of the American Booksellers Association in New York, Thomas Dixon warned that while the Negro was a menace to one element of America's strength, socialism was an enemy to another element. "It attacks first the family, the stronghold of individuality, and the bulwark upon which our civilization rests, and then the fibre of the individual himself." Continuing on the same theme, in his first novel, Dixon noted, "Two great questions shadow the future of the American people, the conflict between Labor and Capital, and the conflict between the African and the Anglo-Saxon race" (*The Leopard's Spots*, p. 334). The latter conflict he declared to be the most dangerous, and thus it became the subject of his two best-known works, *The Leopard's Spots* and *The Clansman*.

The title of Thomas Dixon's 1903 novel, *The One Woman: A Story of Modern Utopia*, might suggest that its primary topic is feminism. In reality, while the feminist views of one of the two central women here play a strong part in the storyline, the theme is socialism and the danger it represents to the social order. The main character is the Reverend Frank Gordon of New York's Pilgrim Congregational Church. He is a charismatic figure, who preaches socialism to a large and generally supportive congregation. He argues his views with his closest friend, Wall Street banker and millionaire Mark Overman, who tells him:

> This maggot of Socialism in your brain . . . is the mark of mental and moral breakdown, the fleeing from self-reliant individual life into the herd for help. You call it "brotherhood," the "solidarity of the race." Sentimental mush. It's a stampede back to the animal herd out of which a powerful manhood has been evolved. . . . Socialism takes the temper out of the steel fiber of character. It makes a man flabby. It is the earmark of racial degeneracy. The man of letters who is poisoned by it never writes another line worth reading; the preacher who tampers with it ends a materialist or atheist; the philanthropist bitten by it, from just a plain fool, develops a madman; while the home-builder turns free-lover and rake under its teachings. (pp. 32–33)

Gordon's wife Ruth is afraid of socialism: "It seems to open gulfs between us. You read and read, while I can only wait and love" (p. 26). While Ruth is waiting and loving, Gordon meets and falls in love with Kate Ransom, a new member of his congregation, who gives him a million dollars with which to build a new church but who refuses to promise to obey him at their wedding ceremony, following Gordon's divorce from Ruth. Overman warns him that "Women, savages and children are inferior and immature forms of evolution. But they are going to prove more than a match for you" (p. 169). Ultimately, it is Overman who destroys Gordon when Kate falls in love with him. Gordon kills Overman in a fight over the woman. With Kate testifying against him, Gordon is sentenced to die, but the ever-faithful Ruth rushes to the governor, her former sweetheart who is still in love with her, and obtains a pardon. There is a race by train to the prison just as the execution is to take place, a race that must surely have influenced D.W. Griffith in his last-

Thomas Dixon with his family: wife Harriet (Bussey) and children Thomas III (known as Junior), Louise, and Gordon. Courtesy of Duke University.

Above, Publicity flyer for original stage production of *The Clansman.* From the author's collection. *Below,* The Klansmen in the original stage production of *The Clansman.* From the author's collection.

Above, The Klansmen in *The Birth of a Nation* (1915). From the author's collection. *Below,* Mae Marsh as Flora, "the Little Sister," in *The Birth of a Nation.* From the author's collection.

Original program for *The Fall of a Nation* (1916). From the
author's collection.

Above, Valda Valkyrien as Elena Worth in *Bolshevism on Trial* (1919). From the author's collection. *Below,* The U.S. Marines to the rescue in *Bolshevism on Trial*. From the author's collection.

Left, Ex-governor Carteret meets with Major Norton: "You are a maniac to-night." One of John Cassel's illustrations from *The Sins of the Father: A Romance of the South* (1912) shows the remarkable similarity in appearance between the fictional character Norton and Thomas Dixon. From the author's collection. *Below,* Jane Novak as the title character in *Thelma* (1922). Courtesy of the Academy of Motion Picture Arts and Sciences.

Above, Madelyn Clare and Warner Richmond in *The Mark of the Beast* (1923). Courtesy of the British Film Institute. *Below,* Gladys Brockwell (left), Robert Frazer, and Elaine Hammerstein in *The Foolish Virgin* (1924). Courtesy of the British Film Institute.

Above, Madelyn Clare, the second Mrs. Thomas Dixon. Courtesy of the British Film Institute. *Left,* Thomas Dixon in later years. Courtesy of Duke University.

minute rescue of the boy from the gallows in *Intolerance*. The similarity is quite remarkable.

The character of Frank Gordon is very obviously based on Thomas Dixon himself. Gordon is six feet four, with broad shoulders, blond hair, steel gray eyes, a strong aquiline nose, and a frank, serious face. Dixon was six feet three and a half, with a commanding yet gaunt physique, jet black hair, a serious face, and piercing brown eyes. Gordon's hair turns prematurely gray in the course of the novel, as did Dixon's after the 1907 Wall Street crash. While preaching at the Twenty-third Street Baptist Church in New York, Dixon, like Gordon, came into conflict with the church elders. Some of the hard-luck stories that appear as fiction in *The One Woman* are repeated as fact in Dixon's autobiography, *Southern Horizons*.

There was even a Kate Ransom in Dixon's life at that time—a young woman in the congregation who had fallen in love with him but with whom Dixon always denied having a relationship.[1] "The passages describing the life of a city preacher carry weight by a sense of personal experience," noted a reviewer in the *American Monthly Review of Reviews* (November 1903).

It was the author's claim that the novel was based on the life of the Reverend George D. Herron, a socialist preacher and personal friend of Dixon's, who fell in love with a member of his congregation, divorced his wife, and married the other woman. According to Dixon, the later marriage was a marriage by proclamation.[2] Obviously, Dixon borrows from his own career, with elements in *The One Woman* duplicating aspects of its author's own life as he left the Twenty-third Street Baptist Church to found the People's Church. The notion of a benefactor providing one million dollars to found a new church is not as unlikely as it may seem; when John D. Rockefeller heard of Dixon's plans for a "Church of the People," he offered to give the young preacher a half million dollars if Dixon could raise an equal amount. As a Baptist, Rockefeller was a friend and supporter of Dixon, but it seems unlikely that he formed the basis for the character of Mark Overman.

Dixon might have been writing of himself in the 1890s, or at least the Thomas Dixon of his imagination, when he described Gordon: "An idealist and dreamer, in love with life, colour, form, music and beauty, he had the dash and brilliancy, the warmth and enthusiasm of a born leader of men. The impulsive champion of the people, the friend of the weak, he had become the patriot prophet of a larger democracy" (p. 5).

"The One Woman" is a phrase of which Dixon was extremely fond. He used it as the title of chapter 6 in The Leopard's Spots and later had one of the leading characters refer to "the One Woman, the only woman in the world to me."

From a modern perspective, The One Woman is a difficult novel to appreciate as its author intended, because Dixon's preacher-hero makes such a fine argument for socialism that one is hard-pressed to understand its ultimate rejection. Frank Gordon is a good man, sharing his income with the poor, arguing, "The aim of Socialism is to bring to pass this dream of heaven on earth" (p. 34). The Christianity that Gordon preaches is the Christianity of Christ, tolerant toward all except perhaps the Catholic Church, which is not identified by name but certainly attacked here: "Theology is a science, religion a life. The one is a fact, the other an analysis after the fact. The stage-coach yielded to the limited, the sailing craft to the ocean greyhound, but we are told that the only age that ever knew the truth, or had the right to express it, was the age which burned witches, executed dumb animals as criminals, whipped church bells for heresy, held chemistry a black art and electricity a manifestation of the devil" (p. 123).

The biggest argument against socialism is that it will destroy the monogamous family. Yet when it does, in the beautiful and physical form of Kate Ransom, one wonders not at the outrage of it but that Gordon's wife is so pathetic that she clings to her husband when she should have kicked him out of the door; and one wonders why she does not marry her childhood sweetheart, who, after all, is now governor of the state of New York. When Kate Ransom speaks up to Gordon, saying, "I claim my rights as your equal," women at the end of the nineteenth century should have been cheering, just as would women at the start of the twenty-first century. Dixon's sole complaint against socialism would appear to be that it results in sexual license. As Edward Clark Marsh wrote in the *Bookman* (October 1903), "Socialism, with Mr. Dixon, means sexual license and the disruption of the family."

One can scarcely question Gordon's view that "in America we had but two classes, the masses and the asses." Even his attack on New Yorkers has a satisfying ring to it, relevant as it is today to vast portions of the United States and its inhabitants:

> Of all the little things on this earth a little New Yorker is the smallest. I've met ignorance in the South, sullen pig-headedness in New England; I've measured the boundless cheek of the West, my native hearth; but for self-satisfied stupidity, for littleness in the world of morals, I have seen nothing on earth, or under it, quite so small as a well-to-do New Yorker. He has little brains, or culture, and only the rudiments of common sense, but, being from New York, he assumes everything. Of God's big world, outside Wall Street, Broadway, Fifth Avenue, Central Park and Coney Island, he knows nothing; for he neither reads nor travels; and yet pronounces instant judgment on world movements of human thought and society. (p. 80)

(Dixon had similar comments to make about New York in his 1896 text *The Failure of Protestantism in New York and Its Causes*. The above commentary pretty much appears, in a shorter version, on page 17 of that book.)

Yes, the problem with *The One Woman* is that Thomas Dixon is too good an orator, and he has created Frank Gordon in his image. If Frank Gordon is unsophisticated, then the world would be a better place without the sophistication of capitalism. Perhaps Dixon held a more independent view of socialism than can be determined. If, in regard to homosexuality, the Catholic Church can hate the sin and love the sinner, then perhaps Dixon could hate socialism but love the socialist. Certainly, Dixon had a high regard for socialist and labor leader Eugene V. Debs, of whom he wrote: "Men called him Socialist, Anarchist, Firebrand. But there was a *divine* fire, a Christ spirit in the man that held our people. I cared nothing for his politics. I loved him. When they put him in prison for resisting the World War, every man in the penitentiary with whom he came in contact, from the warden to the lowest convict, felt Christ in him and spoke his name with reverence."[3]

Dixon's ambivalence toward socialism may well be influenced by his obvious opposition to the evils of Northern industrialism (for which, read capitalism) and by his belief that African Americans and industrialism (capitalism) are somehow interlinked, as F. Garvin Davenport Jr. has suggested, by their darkness and their tendency to destroy white harmony.[4] It is a theme that can be found as early as *The Leopard's Spots* and General Worth's mills, which "employ 2,000 hands down there, and consume hundreds of bales of cotton a day" but have not one Negro employee.

The One Woman was Dixon's second novel, and following upon the well-publicized *The Leopard's Spots*, it could not help but be the subject of much discussion, both negative and positive. It may be nothing more than romantic melodrama, coupled with social commentary, but *The One Woman* represented far more than popular reading matter. Typical of the reviews in praise of the book is the following in the *Philadelphia Public Ledger* (August 16, 1903):

> It is doubtful if any book of the year has excited quite the amount of controversy that has been accorded *The One Woman*. It murders Socialism with the same animalism with which the hero kills his friend. It paints in colors that are not to be mistaken the consequences of the too rapid social evil. The action is terrifically and breathlessly rapid. You will read it over and over in whole or piecemeal. You will be enraptured and angered. You will

think about it and dream about it. You will praise it and condemn it, admire and despise it. And after all you will decide that it is a great book.

The One Woman was one of the best-selling novels of the year, and according to its publisher, "No book published in recent times has received such a torrent of savage abuse from unknown critics and such enthusiastic praise from the leaders of thought. The reviews of *The One Woman* printed during the first month of its life would fill a volume of 1000 closely printed pages."[5]

In 1931, the Otis Publishing Corporation published Thomas Dixon's *Companions*, advertised as "a story of the new idea of marriage." The novel was actually far from new, being nothing more than a recycling of *The One Woman* with a change of character names. In *Companions*, Rev. Frank Gordon becomes Rev. John Lockwood, his wife Ruth becomes Mary, Mark Overman is rechristened Dan Slocum, and Kate Ransom is now Grace Barnard. Conveniently, the list of Dixon's books opposite the title page of *Companions* fails to reference *The One Woman*. The comment by the minister that "the World War has made a new map of the earth" (p. 111) is just about the only acknowledgment of the passing years since 1903, although Dixon does add a hint of sex with reference to a School of Human Relationships, replacing the old-fashioned Sunday School. Here, "Love affairs between boys and girls of thirteen, fourteen and fifteen years of age became the order of the day" (p. 200), and there is "full instruction in birth control" (p. 201). The message is the same, "Socialism and Communism are the greatest delusions that ever bewildered the mind of poet or sentimentalist" (p. 29), and, unfortunately, so is the writing style. The novel represents outmoded writing for the jazz age, let alone the age of depression.

As early as 1906, Dixon had published a dramatic version of *The One Woman*, evidence that it was ideal for screen adaptation not so much because of the antisocialist theme but because it offered two good roles for women and one for a man. The play, which differed somewhat in storyline from the novel, opened in Norfolk, Virginia, in 1906 and toured the South with relative success through 1907. In January 1918, the Mastercraft Photo-Play Corporation was formed in New York, with Dr. F. Eugene Farnsworth as president and director general, E.R. Sherburne as treasurer, and Isaac Wolper as general manager. The company had the set purpose of bringing the works of Thomas Dixon to the screen. "It is the intention of the Mastercraft Photo-Play Corporation to work with the author, the same as Mr. Griffith and I worked with *The Birth of a Nation*, and this is the chief reason why I am becoming affiliated with this newly formed organization," explained Dixon.[6]

In reality, Mastercraft was producing *The One Woman* under license from the National Drama Corporation, which had previously contracted with an entity called the Society Players Film Company to produce the film. Dixon was given the title of director general of *The One Woman*, although he received no such credit in publicity releases, and a salary of three hundred dollars per week for the nine weeks of production.

Despite plans to begin production within four to five weeks and a grandiose scheme to build a fifty-acre studio in Boston and an equally large studio in California, it was not until mid-February of 1918 that a director was announced for Mastercraft's first production, *The One Woman*, and arrangements were made to film at the Paralta Studio on Melrose Avenue in Los Angeles (and now part of the Paramount lot). The chosen director was thirty-two-year-old Reginald Barker, previously associated with producer Thomas H. Ince, who had been responsible for first-rate productions starring William S. Hart and Charles Ray. There were endless delays as the screenplay by Harry Chandlee and E. Richard Schayer was completed and approved by all concerned, most notably Dixon. Production was further delayed because the leading man, W. Lawson Butt, was unavailable, away on location for a Louise Glaum feature. Shooting eventually commenced in May 1918 and was completed by late June.

The actresses selected for the film production were Clara Williams (as Kate) and Adda Gleason (as Ruth), both of whom were reliable performers but lacking any major talent. W. Lawson Butt, the British stage actor who was chosen to play Frank Gordon, was large and domineering in appearance but certainly no great presence in terms of either good looks or screen image. As the company explained it, "Mastercraft does not exploit stars in connection with any of its pictures, but concentrates on the story."[7] Or perhaps more accurately, Mastercraft did not want to spend any money on a star name, arguing that Thomas Dixon was the "star."

The storyline closely follows that of the novel, except that on screen Gordon and Kate Ransom are not legally married; she is his common-law wife. In the novel, a "churchless clergyman" who has become a socialist performs a wedding ceremony, and Kate, against Gordon's wishes, wears a conventional wedding gown. According to the *Moving Picture World* (December 7, 1918), "The last scene shows him [Gordon] kneeling at his wife's feet and embracing the children. In a moment of righteous indignation the forgiving woman called him a common cur. It would be interesting to know the son's opinion of his father if the boy grows up and learns the truth."

Film historian Kevin Brownlow boasts in *Behind the Mask of Innocence* of having seen an original 35mm nitrate print of *The One Woman* in the private archives of a British film collector. While praising the director but not the direction as "brilliant," Brownlow describes *The One Woman* as "essentially a silent talkie." He derides a scene in the film that is not in the novel, in which the minister uses an analogy with chickens in order to attack socialism: "Full brothers, yet ready to fight at the drop of a hat, why? Both want the same pullet! Man, too, is a fighting animal, and when Socialism comes to pass, the EAGLE will light in the barnyard—and then—good night roosters!"[8]

On my behalf, Kevin Brownlow contacted the collector. The latter had a copy of my 1992 study *Nitrate Won't Wait: A History of Film Preservation in the United States* but had obviously paid little attention to it, in that he could no longer locate the print and assumed that the film had decomposed.

Based on contemporary reviews of the production, it would appear that a train wreck in the novel, whose primary function is to demonstrate the selflessness of Gordon's wife Ruth, was too expensive to shoot. Perhaps Dixon considered it out of place on screen, and its presence on the printed page seems almost pointless.

The *Moving Picture World* quite rightly pointed out that it was sex and not socialism that was the foundation of *The One Woman*. The Kate Ransom character is played as a screen vampire. The subject matter is as much free love as political belief. However, as another trade paper, *Motion Picture News* (November 30, 1918), commented, "It will divide people into two distinct factions: those who oppose Socialism, will enjoy it; those who favor it, will be highly offended by it." The journal went on to suggest that exhibitors might get a socialist of their acquaintance to write "a scathing and denouncing letter to a newspaper while you are showing *The One Woman*. It will certainly bring replies in favor of your picture and there you will have a storm of public opinion centering around your picture."

Similarly, *Variety* (September 20, 1918) noted, "The picture is certain to give satisfaction with any audience, but the volume of profit to be derived from it is dependent upon the ingenuity exercised in persuading a few prominent, long-haired socialists in rising on their hind legs to protest against the photoplay as not in keeping with the socialistic teachings."

Despite a promise that *The One Woman* was the "first in a series of special productions . . . which will be taken from the best of Mr. Dixon's literary works,"[9] Mastercraft made no other films and appears to have been absorbed by Paralta, with which it shared office space in New York. The film netted a profit of twenty-one thousand dollars. *The One Woman* was the first in a trilogy by Dixon on the subject of socialism. The second novel, *Comrades*, deals, more accurately, with communism and was ripe for screen adaptation in 1919.

8

THE RED SCARE

The One Woman is generally described by critics as the first in a trilogy of novels dealing with socialism, followed by *Comrades* in 1909 and *The Root of Evil* in 1911. The veracity of the claim of the three novels to an antisocialist bias is somewhat in doubt. *Comrades* is more appropriately identified as a treatise against communism, while *The Root of Evil* throws completely into question Dixon's supposed opposition to socialism. The novel is better identified as an attack on capitalism, and there are many passages that might well be regarded as appropriate to the early years of the twenty-first century rather than the early years of the twentieth. At one point, the central character makes a statement that could easily be lifted from a modern newspaper editorial: "But the Napoleons of finance to-day will be wearing stripes in Sing Sing to-morrow. We are merely passing through a period of transition which brings suffering and confusion. The end is sure, because evil carries within itself the seed of death. A despotism of money cannot be fastened on the people of America" (p. 118).

Published in 1911 and dedicated to Dixon's father, *The Root of Evil* tells the story of a young Southern lawyer, James Stuart, as he rises to prominence in New York. His childhood sweetheart,

Nan Primrose, marries millionaire John C. Calhoun Bivens, whom Stuart knew and protected at the university and who has a healthy respect for the lawyer. To Dixon, Bivens represents the worst type of American: "the little razor-back scion of poor white trash from the South" (p. 14). Stuart fights the trusts that have developed in the United States but fails to realize that his fight is being maneuvered by banking interests that stand to gain through the collapse of various industrial entities. A secondary plot involves the altruistic Dr. Henry Woodman, who cares for the poor of the city and fights the takeover of his drug company by Bivens and whose daughter will eventually marry Stuart. It is Woodman who makes most of the finest speeches in the polemic on capitalism. He argues with Bivens's plan to take over his business:

> You have closed mills instead of opening them, thrown out of work thousands, lowered the price paid for raw material bringing ruin to its producers, increased the price charged for your products to the ruin of the consumer, and saddled millions of fictitious debts on the backs of their children yet unborn. Combine, yes, but why not pay the people whose wages you have stolen as well as the owners whose mills you have closed? If combination is so extremely profitable, it should bring some benefit to the millions who are consumers—not merely make millionaires out of a few men. Who is bearing the burden of this enormous increase of fictitious wealth? The people. The price of living has been increasing steadily with the organization of each industry into a trust. Where will it end? (p. 52)

Consistently, Dixon renounces the notion of wealth and power. As James Stuart explains to Nan Primrose, "Not a single great man whose words have moulded the world was rich. The combined fortunes of Darwin, Mozart, Shakespeare, Raphael, Aristotle, Socrates, Mohammed, and Buddha weren't equal to the possession of even

the smallest and most insignificant members of our mob of six thousand millionaires—six thousand nobodies" (p. 387).

It has been argued by some critics that Woodman's theft of
jewelry from Bivens is the result of the doctor's support of socialism. Thus, Dixon is claiming that socialism leads to crime. But this
is hardly a valid argument in view of the general tone of the entire
novel, the fact that socialism is never identified as such, and
Woodman's subsequent trial and easy escape from punishment
thanks to a sympathetic judiciary. Stuart's passionate courtroom
plea on Woodman's behalf is still moving almost a century after it
was written:

> I speak to-day, your honour, in behalf of the man who
> crouches by my side overwhelmed with shame and grief
> and conscious dishonour because he took a paltry pack-
> age of jewellery from a man who has never added one
> penny to the wealth of the world and yet has somehow
> gotten possession of one hundred million dollars from
> those who could not defend themselves from his strength
> and cunning. . . .
>
> Morals are relative things. They are based on the
> experiences and faith of the generations which express
> them. Men were once hanged for daring to express an
> opinion contrary to that held by their parish priest. . . .
>
> I am not excusing crime. I am crying for the equality
> of man before the law. The English people beheaded their
> king because he imposed taxes without the consent of
> their parliament.
>
> The millionaire who demands vengeance against this
> broken man to-day has an income greater than the com-
> bined crowned heads of Europe and wields a scepter
> mightier than tzar or emperor. . . .
>
> A burglar breaks into a store and robs the safe. A
> mighty man of money breaks into the management of a
> corporation which owns an iron mill employing thou-

sands. He shuts down the plant, throws one thousand people into want, passes the dividend, drives the stock down to a few cents on the dollar, buys it for a song from the ruined holders, starts up the mill again and *makes* five million! That is to say, he broke into a mill and robbed the safe of five millions. We send the burglar to the penitentiary and hail the manipulator of this stock as a Napoleon of Finance. . . .

An enraged Italian stabs his enemy to death. The act is murder. This man corners wheat. Puts up the price of bread a cent a loaf and kills ten thousand children already half-starved from insufficient food. We electrocute the Italian and print pictures of the wheat speculator in our magazines as an example of Success.

In other words, the theft of five thousand dollars is grand larceny. The theft of five millions, stained with human blood, is a triumph of business genius. (pp. 308–11)

For six pages, Thomas Dixon, through his mouthpiece James Stuart, presents one of the most noble, impressive, and invigorating speeches against capitalism. Slavery is denounced alongside polygamy, famine, and the plague as a universal scourge that the world has outgrown as it has created a new and nobler God. Earlier in the novel, Dixon turned his attention to political corruption, noting that a New York police captain, leading a battalion of officers intent on brutally breaking up a left-wing demonstration, was "reputed to be a millionaire, though his salary had never been more than enough to support his wife and children" (p. 222). If nothing else, *The Root of Evil* almost compensates for the worst excesses of racism to be found elsewhere in Dixon's writings. If *The Clansman* is a novel for a century ago, one that deserves only oblivion, then *The Root of Evil* is a novel for today and for all the ages.

In comparison, *Comrades*, first published in 1909, is trivial in style; the writing appears as rushed as the novel's conclusion. The characters are not sufficiently drawn, particularly the socialist leaders, and both the hero and the heroine are relatively unappealing. One is amused, as presumably Dixon intended, by the problems the socialists or communists create for themselves, along with the disparaging comments on many of the more pathetic followers of socialism, but there is little here for a reader with a serious interest in the issues. As the *New York Times* (February 6, 1909) stated, "Although there is a good deal of mere talk in the story, it sweeps along with a nervous rush, starred with superlatives, and enjoying constantly a high emotional temperature. Mr. Dixon makes his characters do surprising stunts. They develop unexpected and illogical traits without warning, turn summersaults of temperament, and do whatever is necessary to keep the story moving according to the author's plan." Others, including R.E. Bisbee in *Arena* (July 1909), were outraged by the trivialization of the socialist movement: "In his story of social adventure he [Dixon] conjures up an absurd situation, builds a mighty man of straw, and then thrashes it with all the enthusiasm of a Don Quixote charging a windmill. No man, not even an irresponsible Dixon, has any right, just for the sake of creating a sensation, to so falsify a great social movement as has this irrational teller of tales."

The initial image confronting a modern reader on the cover of the first edition of *Comrades* is what appears to be a swastika, or more precisely, eleven swastikas walking across the front of the novel as if footsteps leading—where? Are they indicative of welfare and well-being, as exemplified originally by the symbol and also by socialism, or is there a hidden, and obviously confused, meaning?

For *Comrades*, Dixon leaves New York and the South for a new location, San Francisco, where live Colonel Worth, his guardian Elena, and his son Norman. The novel opens with the news of Dewey's destruction of the Spanish fleet in July 1898. Colonel Worth is relatively tolerant of socialists: "I don't deny their right to speak their message. What I can't understand is how the people who have been hounded from the tyrant-ridden countries of the old world and found shelter and protection beneath our flag should turn thus to curse the hand that shields them" (p. 4).

Colonel Worth has no objection to Elena and Norman's attending a socialist gathering. As Norman becomes more and more absorbed with socialism and its young, beautiful, charismatic leader, Barbara Bozenta, the colonel allows him to hold a socialist gathering at his country house on the outskirts of Berkeley on July 4. However, when Norman lowers the Stars and Stripes and hoists the Red Flag, the colonel takes immediate action, cancels the party, and orders Norman from his home.

However, at Elena's insistence, Norman is allowed to return, and the colonel secretly provides the million dollars needed to purchase the island of Ventura, off the coast of Santa Barbara, and "establish the ideal Commonwealth of Man." The colonel realizes that the project, like socialism, is doomed to failure and that he will easily recoup his investment in the island. With Norman as head of the island's executive council, the project quickly becomes a farce as the thousands of socialists on the island are unwilling to take on any hard work, some of the women turn to prostitution, and others in the group deal their own summary justice. Sadly, Norman is forced to admit that liberty has degenerated into license and that only law, power, and authority, rejected under the old system, can restore stability.

Norman is forced out of office by Comrades Herman and Catherine Wolf, the powerful leaders of the socialist movement in San Francisco. First, they disarm all citizens, and then Norman is assigned to work in the stable. The sergeant of the guard is told to give him thirty-nine lashes if he causes trouble. Freedom of speech is denied and a communist workforce created: "At the end of two months of Wolf's merciless rule the efficiency of labor had so decreased, it was necessary to lengthen the number of hours from eight to nine. As every inducement to efficiency of labor had been removed there was no incentive to any man to do more than he must" (p. 284).

When Norman invents a dredge for mining gold from the beach(!), the invention is seized by the state (i.e., Wolf). Next, Wolf abandons Catherine in favor of Barbara: "It is the essence of Socialism. In my next proclamation I shall declare for the freedom of love. Every great Socialist has preached this. Marriage and the family form the taproot out of which the whole system of capitalism grew. The system can never be destroyed until the family is annihilated" (p. 293).

A prescient Thomas Dixon creates a Stalinist figure in Wolf, who eventually declares:

> From to-day the State of Ventura enters upon the reign of pure Communism which is the only logical end of Socialism. All private property is hereby abolished. The claim of husband to the person of his wife as his own can no longer be tolerated. Love is free from all chains. Marriage will hereafter be celebrated by a simple declaration before a representative of the State, and it shall cease to bind at the will of either party. Complete freedom in the sex-relationship is left to the judgment and taste of a race of equally developed men and women. The State will interfere, when necessary, to regulate the birth-rate and maintain the limits of efficient population. (pp. 310–11)

Secretly, Norman is able to get a message to his father and to the governor of California. In the space of the last two pages, a company of troops arrive on the island, Colonel Worth frees his son, and the red ensign of socialism is hauled down and replaced by the Stars and Stripes. "It is beautiful, isn't it Governor!" are the final words of Norman and of the novel (p. 319).

As with *The Clansman*, the speed with which Dixon concludes the story is quite incredible. No loose ends are tied up. Wolf's fate is unknown. And what of Norman, who is loved by both Elena, who disappears from the novel once the hero arrives on Ventura, and Barbara? The comments on the poor of San Francisco sound suspiciously similar to those of the Reverend Frank Gordon in *The One Woman*. The advocacy of socialism by Norman and Barbara carries as much weight as the colonel's remarks in opposition. Nei-

ther side has much to offer. "Class must perish and Man be glori-
fied" is the vain cry of the socialists (p. 68). The colonel declares
that "Socialism has no patent on the hope of universal peace," adding, apropos the Civil War, "All the Negroes on this earth are not
worth the blood and tears of one year of that struggle" (p. 78).
(Not surprisingly, Colonel Worth is a Southerner, a soldier of the
Confederacy.)

As Brian R. McGee has pointed out, the attempt to create a
socialist colony fails miserably "because socialist precepts are incom-
patible with human nature."[1] Thus it might very loosely be argued
that, superficially, *Comrades* is similar to the two most famous of
George Orwell's novels, *1984* and *Animal Farm*. And, like Dixon's
work, the George Orwell novels have also been filmed—the latter as
an animated feature—in relatively unsuccessful adaptations.

Comrades is, in fact, a parody of the real-life attempt by novelist and socialist politician Upton Sinclair to create a utopian, socialist, self-supporting community, although Sinclair's vision was
far less radical than Dixon's concept. Acting upon the argument
for a cooperative venture by Charlotte Perkins Gilman, Sinclair
acquired a former boys' school at Englewood, New Jersey, within
an hour's journey from New York. Here, in 1906, he created the
Helicon Home Colony, with fifty or sixty members, including children, all middle-class intellectuals, and among them was future
novelist Sinclair Lewis. The venture was relatively conservative and
relatively successful, despite efforts by the popular press to expose
it as "Upton Sinclair's love-nest." The *New York Times* and other
publications ridiculed the swimming pool, bowling alley, and theatre of the wannabe socialists and questioned the racist and anti-
Semitic aspects of the project. An arson fire destroyed Helicon Hall
in March 1907, and Sinclair never revived the experiment.

Dixon dramatized *Comrades* as *The Red Dawn*, under which
title the play opened at New York's Thirty-ninth Street Theatre on
August 6, 1919. Aside from the setting and the communist theme,
there is not much of the novel left. The central character is now
named John Duncan (played by Averill Harris), an idealist whose

island colony will "prove to the world an ideal of social democracy." Opposed to Duncan is Richard Stanton (played by De Witt Jennings), who welcomes a delegate from the Central Soviet of Northern Europe to the island. "Life is just about what readers of the National Civic Federation Review might expect it to be in any average community under socialist control," sarcastically commented the *New Republic* (August 20, 1919). "There is discontent, some starvation, a good deal of violence—distrust, misery, mutiny, suspicion and rioting."

In a carnival setting, Duncan is relieved of office in a bloodless coup. "Now the red flower blooms tonight!" declares Stanton. "Now for the Red Republic!" As the second-act curtain falls, Duncan addresses the audience: "This sort of thing can be done in Hungary and Russia. We'll see if it can be done with the brand of men who marched with Pershing!"

Stanton advises Duncan that he is involved in the overthrow of the government of the United States, that Negroes, "crazed with the denial of equality, are rioting even as we speak." The African Americans have learned to fight in their own regiments on the battlefields of France. It is all very much as Thomas Dixon was to write two decades later in *The Flaming Sword*. But while the communists succeed in the later novel, here they fail because a third character, Simpson, supposedly an ex-convict, is actually "just a humble agent of our secret service office in Washington." The curtain falls, not with the hoisting of the American flag, but with Simpson's removal of "the red bud of revolution" from his lapel and his replacing it with "the bright badge of public detective."

The opening-night audience was highly amused, as was critic Alexander Woollcott in the *New York Times* (August 7, 1919). However, Woollcott warned that it would be foolish "to let the new play pass on its way with no other record than that of the snickers which greeted its first performance." Offensive in the extreme was "this familiar Dixon touch, this effort to distill all the poisons of hatred and fear" relative to potential black power.

The theatrical production of *The Red Dawn* was linked to

what is defined in U.S. history as the Red Scare, a period in 1919 and 1920 (which some might well argue has lasted through to the present) when government action was taken against those espousing an extreme left-wing, pro-Russian, or Bolshevik cause. Two laws passed during World War I, the Espionage Act of 1917 and the Sedition Act of 1918, formed the basis for a federal campaign not simply against radicalism but also against any criticism or even questioning of the United States. The spread of Bolshevism, culminating in the Russian Revolution, alarmed many Americans. Despite a membership of little more than 150,000, the American Communist Party was considered a grave threat to American society. The Washington, D.C., home of Attorney General A. (Alexander) Mitchell Palmer, who had earlier been alien property custodian, was bombed, and on November 7, 1919, he launched what became known as the Palmer Raids, the brutal and invasive rounding up and deporting of hundreds of enemy aliens, including Emma Goldman. Two months later, in January 1920, Palmer organized the arrest of more than 4,000 alleged communists throughout the United States. (Running the "alien radical" division of Palmer's Bureau of Investigation was the young J. Edgar Hoover.)

It was an extraordinary phenomenon in modern American history, described by historian Robert K. Murray as "a concrete example of what happens to a democratic nation and its people when faith and reason are supplanted with fear." Despite what one might suspect, the Ku Klux Klan was no instigator but rather a product of the Red Scare. The latter helped expand the power and influence of the Klan as "its claims concerning the radicalism of the Negro, Jew, Catholic, laborer, and foreigner carried considerable weight."[2]

The American film industry's attitude toward Russia had primarily been one of support for its peasants and opposition to the czarist policies. Following the October 1917 revolution, the position of the motion picture industry changed to one of attack. Social unrest, coupled with major strikes in the American steel and coal industries, must have disturbed studio executives in an industry as yet immune from labor disputes. There was also fear that the film industry might be subject to government scrutiny in regard to its political stance, as was to happen later in the McCarthy era. In a foretaste of that period, Charlie Chaplin in particular was a subject of major suspicion, so much so that he was forced to assure *Variety* (November 14, 1919), "I am absolutely cold on the Bolshevism theme; neither am I interested in Socialism."

In January 1920, a committee of government and film industry representatives was formed "to combat Bolshevism and to teach Americanization through the medium of the picture." Even earlier, the industry had commenced production of a series of feature films addressing the danger of communism, prominent among which are *The Undercurrent* (1919), *The Red Viper* (1919), *The Volcano* (1919), *Dangerous Hours* (1920), *The Great Shadow* (1920), and *Lifting Shadows* (1920). It was Thomas Dixon who provided the source material for what is not only one of the first of the Red Scare films but also the most important, *Bolshevism on Trial*, released in April 1919.

In that it was based on a 1909 novel, *Comrades*, and in that it preceded major government action against Bolsheviks in the United States, *Bolshevism on Trial* and its author, Thomas Dixon, might well be considered prescient, if not instrumental in forming public opinion against homegrown Bolshevism. As in the majority of Dixon's early films, the players are relatively unimportant, and the only credit following the main title indicates Thomas Dixon as the original author of the novel upon which the film is based (although the actual screenplay was the work of the uncredited Harry Chandlee).

One of the first productions from a new company, the Mayflower Photoplay Corp., not known to have been directly associated with Dixon, *Bolshevism on Trial* went into production in late October or early November 1918 under the working title of *Red Republic*. Company president Isaac Wolper rented space at the New York studios of star Norma Talmadge, located at 318 East Forty-eighth Street. The film was originally to have starred Madelyn Clare in the role of Barbara Bozenta, but she was replaced by Pinna Nesbit. Clare was to reappear in Dixon's life as the star of *The Mark of the Beast* and as his second wife.

Interesting casting in the role of Saka, who is enlisted by Norman Worth's father to keep an eye on him, is Chief Standing Bear. Born on the Pine Ridge Reservation in 1865, Standing Bear claimed to be the "first real Indian" to appear on the American stage, and *Bolshevism on Trial* marked his screen debut.

The storyline was transferred from California, with most of the action filmed at the Royal Poinciana Hotel in Palm Beach, Florida, identified as an island off the Florida coast. (Initial plans called for the film to be shot on St. Simons Island off the coast of Georgia.) The city in which the principals live and in which the first communist meeting takes place is not identified but is presumably not San Francisco—more probably New York.

The film, of necessity, truncates the novel considerably, with the planned purchase of the island revealed in the first scene, Elena now the legitimate sister of Norman, and the socialist gathering at the colonel's home dropped, along with Norman's invention of the dredge. For reasons unknown, Herman Wolf becomes Herman Wolff. The film moves along at a fast and entertaining pace. There is much humor here in the antics of the new socialists as they argue over their rooms, "everybody delightfully equal." Norman suffers little at the hands of Herman Wolff, and the coast guard arrives in plenty of time to save him from being shot and Barbara Bozenta from being forced into marriage with Wolff. The pair return "to the land of laws and decency," and the Stars and Stripes replace the Red Flag as in the novel.

The direction of Harley Knoles (who was subsequently to enjoy a career in England) is not particularly creative, but neither is it inefficient. There are no scenes of the debauchery associated with free love and socialism, but the film did, apparently, contain scenes of nude female bathing, subsequently cut. Despite the hectic storyline, the performers avoid melodramatics. There is a natural sincerity, in particular, to the performances of Robert Frazer as

Norman and Jim Savage as his chauffeur, Tom Mooney. The film also marks the last screen appearance by Valda Valkyrien, as Elena. A famous beauty in her native Denmark, the actress was named in 1914 as "The Most Beautiful Woman of Her Race," an Aryan designation that must have appealed to Dixon. The one memorable performance is by Leslie Stowe, as the villainous, beetle-browed Herman Wolff. He is described as "Power without conscience," and this is a powerful role. There are those who might claim there is a Jewish, and thus anti-Semitic, quality to the characterization, but this is not correct, and certainly Thomas Dixon would have fought any such implication. There might be a large number of stereotypical Bolshevik types with long beards visible in the audience at the initial meeting of the comrades, but anti-Semitism is not an issue here.

The film was greeted most favorably by the critics. Edward Weitzel in the *Moving Picture World* (May 3, 1919) described it as "an entertaining and frequently amusing satire on the false doctrine which has wrecked Russia's social system." According to Peter Milne in *Motion Picture News* (April 19, 1919), "*Bolshevism on Trial* damns red-handed anarchy and, it is of special interest to note, gives the honest socialist a square deal. In other words, the picture attacks no political party in this country, but gives a merciless and at the same time dramatic exposé of the activities of disorganized government as report has it existing in Russia today." Even the distinguished critic Julian Johnson, writing in *Photoplay* (July 1919), was impressed:

> Instead of a hastily thrown-together argument against red lawlessness, or a timid bolstering up of some of its gentlest tenets, I found a powerful, well-knit, indubitably true and biting satire. . . . Here, Dixon got a lot of argument and a lot of drama. I think that his finale is hasty, movieish and inconclusive, but the excellence of the body of his story, his exhibition of the stream of human nature running one way and the vain current of impractical ide-

alism struggling in the other direction—this is so simply, logically and even humorously set forth that until he comes to his last reel I do not hesitate in calling the contrivance an absolutely masterful photoplay, one which may be seen with profit, not by the non-comprehending juvenile, perhaps, but certainly by adult audiences everywhere.

A president-to-be was also impressed. Calvin Coolidge, then governor of Massachusetts, wrote to Charles R. Rogers, New England manager for distributor Select, "I think the idea of the film, *Bolshevism on Trial*, is very timely. We surely need to educate our people along the lines that your picture depicts. I hope it will be very successful."[3]

Not content with favorable reviews, *Bolshevism on Trial*'s distributor advised exhibitors to promote the film as an attack on socialism, suggesting that red flags might be displayed at the theatre and soldiers hired to tear them down. There was considerable criticism of the promotional ploy, so much so that Select was forced to assure the public that *Bolshevism on Trial* "is not a propaganda picture, and is not directed against Socialism. . . . The production is designed purely for entertainment. Select has circulated no advertisement or publicity, either directly or indirectly, advising methods which might create a riot, or which are opposed to the orderly procedure of American communities, and recognized as such by the Federal Government."

Dixon and the Mayflower Photoplay Corp. did contemplate a second production together, but one not based on a work by Dixon. On October 21, 1919, he and Mayflower signed an agreement with Walter Hackett for the exclusive motion picture rights to his play *The Invisible Foe*, for the sum of five thousand dollars.[4] California-born Walter Hackett (1874–1940) spent most of his life in the United Kingdom but was the author of some twenty-one plays produced on the New York stage between 1908 and 1937. *The Invisible Foe* opened at the Harris Theatre, New York, on December 30, 1918, and featured Percy Marmont, a British actor who became a leading man in American silent films, and Flora MacDonald, who had been the second female lead in *The Fall of a Nation*.

The three-act comedy had a spiritualistic theme and involved an uncle who returns from the dead to identify a villain in his family. It was poorly received by the critics, and it is difficult to understand why the plot might have appealed to Thomas Dixon. In any event, neither Dixon nor Mayflower completed the film, although there is a possibility that it was eventually produced by director Emile Chautard and starred a minor actress named Lucy Cotton. A 1922 film titled *Whispering Shadows* appears to be based on *The Invisible Foe*, although its actual release date is undetermined.

Ominously for Thomas Dixon's film career, *Bolshevism on Trial* was relatively unsuccessful. The public did not want propaganda, even as entertaining as this. A year after its initial release, the film was reissued, slightly edited and retitled. The most major change was the renaming of the central female character from the "foreign" Barbara Bozenta to the "American" Barbara Alden. The new title, *Shattered Dreams*,[5] might well serve as a description of Dixon's later film career.

9

MISCEGENATION

One twentieth-century novelist for whom Thomas Dixon had great admiration was Gertrude Atherton (1857–1947). The appeal might seem odd in that Atherton's novels were noted for their eroticism, most notably her 1923 best-seller *Black Oxen*, and the writer was highly praised for her promotion of the New Woman. But Atherton was also a racist, as is very clear from her 1900 novel *Senator North*. Like Dixon, Atherton found inspiration in a real-life individual, Senator Eugene Hale of Maine, and, as Dixon would do repeatedly, Atherton warned of the danger of miscegenation. In *Senator North*, a principal character, Harriet Walker, is the daughter of a white man and an octoroon; she possesses all the stereotypes of the Negro and is advised never to smile, "for her wide grin 'was the fatuous grin of the Negro.'"[1] *Senator North* was part of Thomas Dixon's library along with another of Gertrude Atherton's novels, *The Conqueror* (1902), in which she displayed almost childlike hero worship for Alexander Hamilton.

The reality in the South before, during, and after the Civil War is that perhaps as much as 80 percent of the Negro population had mixed blood. The Southern plantation owners considered themselves white aristocracy and as such believed they had a God-given right to take advantage of their black female slaves. It is very clear that the "poor white trash" had little, if any, responsibility for the problem of miscegenation. It did not start with Thomas Jefferson and it did not end with Reconstruction.

Thomas Dixon had studied Isaac Taylor's *The Origin of the Aryans* (published in 1898 by Charles Scribner in the contemporary science series), but he preached racial purity with both a passion and an illogicality that smacks of psychosis. The three immigrant groups that produced his family—the English, the Germans and the French—were the prime examples of the master races. To this group he added the basic Aryan countries, but then his thinking becomes decidedly muddled. Like Adolph Hitler, Dixon despised the Slavic races, the Africans, and the African Americans. The ethnic group now identified as Hispanic was not a part of Dixon's worldwide Aryan nation. Portugal made the cut, as did, curiously, Japan and Turkey in the 1930s. Dixon described his alliance as the "Christian Commonwealth,"[2] but the Jews were equally admitted to membership, as were Native Americans and the great pre-Spanish civilizations of South and Central America, the Aztecs, the Incas, and the Mayans.

Dixon's admiration for the non-Aryans and non-Christians appears based on respect for their racial purity—Jews, for example, did not generally marry outside of their own people. He looked upon the Native Americans and the other very early settlers of this hemisphere as representative of a noble people with praiseworthy cultural traditions. All these groups married their own kind—members of their own tribe—and here is an obvious example of Dixon's obsession with the threat of interracial marriage.

It is no accident that in the 1920s and 1930s, African Americans would often attempt to "pass" as Native Americans. A 1930 feature film, *The Silent Enemy*, which supposedly documented and consisted entirely of a cast of the Chetoga tribe of Native Americans, included African Americans in leading roles, unbeknownst to its producer. Earlier, African Americans had "passed" as Hawaiians, and a popular song of around 1916 has a Negro woman shouting at her boyfriend, appearing on stage in a Hawaiian band, "They May Call You Hawaiian on Broadway, But You're Just a Plain Nigger to Me."

Dixon's views on miscegenation are made profoundly clear in his first novel, *The Leopard's Spots*, in which the book's only educated black, George Harris, seeks to marry the daughter of his white friend, the Honorable Everett Lowell. Lowell is the stereotypical, almost laughable, white liberal, supportive of the African American cause—provided no Negro seeks to be his son-in-law. As the Reverend Durham warns, "One drop of negro blood makes a negro. It kinks the hair, flattens the nose, thickens the lip, puts out the light of intellect, and lights the fires of brutal passions" (p. 242). In *The Clansman*, Harris is replaced by Silas Lynch, although his desire to marry the white and virginal Elsie Stoneman is not verbalized until the play of *The Clansman* and *The Birth of a Nation*, in both of which it is a crucial element.

Charles Gaston, the hero of *The Leopard's Spots,* is very much aware that there are more Negroes in the United States than inhabitants in Mexico, the third republic of the world: "Amalgamation simply meant Africanization. The big nostrils, flat nose, massive jaw, protruding lip and kinky hair will register their animal marks over the proudest intellect and the rarest beauty of any other race. The rule that had no exception was that one drop of negro blood makes a negro" (p. 388). The fixation is with the physical rather than the intellectual. It is the "ugliness" of the Negro that is to be feared, not his lack of intelligence, which obviously, even if Dixon does not wish to acknowledge it, can be corrected. Physical appearance has no connection with brainpower; in fact, from a modern perspective the opposite is true, as illustrated by the phrase "dumb blonde."

The power and the wile of Lydia Brown, Austin Stoneman's mulatto housekeeper-mistress, prove that Dixon does not understand the characters he has created. She is strong and domineering as much because of her Negro mother as her white father. Yet again, it is an issue not of intellect but of appearance. Lydia Brown is a mulatto or a mongrel, and while the mongrel dog may always be less desirable than the pedigreed, its intelligence, its faithfulness, and its love may be equal or superior to that of the most wanted of breeds.

The Birth of a Nation does an admirable job in consolidating and presenting in vivid terms Dixon's basic philosophy on miscegenation. The character of Lydia Brown is more amply defined here than in The Clansman. Mary Alden, giving one of the worst performances in the film, plays her as a vamplike character; Lydia Brown is the Civil War version of Theda Bara as seen if not in blackface, at least in passing-for-white-face. Lynch's lust for Elsie Stoneman is more vividly outlined, with emphasis not only on his desire for a white woman but also on the political power and advancement that will be the result of such a marriage. Silas Lynch is very much a white politician in the making. The implication is that miscegenation will breed a new brand of politician, as lawless as those sitting in the South Carolina legislature and as dangerous and self-obsessed as Austin Stoneman.

Dixon preached the purity of the white race, just as the largely forgotten Sutton E. Griggs preached the purity of the Negro race. The African American Griggs (1872–1933) was, like Dixon, a clergyman who took to writing novels. In 1905, he published The Hindered Hand; or, The Reign of the Repressionist through his own company, Orion, in Nashville, Tennessee. There he sought to present an African American view of the South. One chapter in the book, chapter 31, discusses a book that, though unnamed, is obviously The Leopard's Spots, "the work of a rather conspicuous Southern man, who had set himself the task of turning the entire Negro population out of America" (p. 206). Like Dixon, Griggs is opposed to interracial marriage. His central character, Ensal Ellwood, asks, "Fellow Negroes, for the sake of world interests, it is my hope that you will maintain your ambition for racial purity" (p. 196). One of the most tragic sequences in the novel concerns the courtroom revelation that a woman who has passed herself off as white is, in reality, a descendant of Negroes. The woman is subsequently ridi-

146

culed and insulted. Sutton E. Griggs presents a view of the South and its treatment of the Negro that is as lurid and outrageous as any to be found in the novels of Thomas Dixon, but, sadly, Griggs is a writer without power or authority.

Dixon and Griggs are not the only major Southern writers to have considered the topic of miscegenation. Mark Twain (born in Florida, Missouri) used the subject of miscegenation as the background for *The Tragedy of Pudd'nhead Wilson and the Comedy of Those Extraordinary Twins* (American Publishing Company, 1894). Here, Roxy, a Mulatto slave woman, switches her son, Tom, with David, the son of her owner, Percy Driscoll. Tom is vicious and a murderer, for which his mother blames his black blood, and a convoluted plotline has Tom selling his mother to a Louisville sugar planter. As Dixon did so often, Twain borrows elements from another of his novels, *The Prince and the Pauper* (1881); and also like Dixon, he presents his story with a strong sense of tragic irony. Mark Twain had also written movingly of slavery in the November 1874 issue of *Atlantic Monthly*, in "The True Story," where an old slave woman is separated from her son at auction and reunited with him during the Civil War.

The theme of miscegenation is present in several of Dixon's novels, and it is central to *The Sins of the Father: A Romance of the South*, published in 1912 by D. Appleton and Company and based on an earlier stage production. The title is obviously taken from the phrase "the sins of the fathers," which appears in the Book of Common Prayer and is a paraphrase of Exodus 20:5— "I the Lord thy God am a jealous God, and visit the sins of the fathers upon the children unto the third and fourth generation of them that hate me." The book is dedicated to Randolph Shotwell of North Carolina,[3] but, for obvious reasons, Dixon stresses (in a "To the Reader" note) that the central character of Major Daniel Norton is not based on Shotwell but on "a distinguished citizen of the far South, with whom I was intimately acquainted for many years." In fact, the illustrations in the novel by John Cassel depict Norton as looking remarkably like a young Thomas Dixon.

Major Daniel Norton is introduced as a typical Dixon hero, who fought valiantly for the Southern cause in the Civil War, edits a North Carolina newspaper, and is the local leader of the Ku Klux Klan. He protects from Klan attack a middle-aged farmer, Bob Peeler, who plans to marry his mulatto housekeeper, and through Peeler, Norton meets the mulatto's daughter, Cleo: "As he looked in to her eyes he fancied that he saw a young leopardess from an African jungle looking at him through the lithe, graceful form of a Southern woman" (p. 25).

Despite having a wife and a newborn son, Norton begins a sexual relationship with Cleo. Ultimately, the affair leads to the death of Norton's wife and Cleo's entering Norton's household as his son's nanny. As Norton's wife faces the tragedy of her husband's infidelity, a doctor explains: "this is a living fact which the white women of the south must face. These hundreds of thousands of a mixed race are not accidents. She must know that this racial degradation is not merely a thing of to-day, but the heritage of two hundred years of sin and sorrow!" (p. 122).

Throughout the text, the white characters ponder the racial issue. The Negro is indispensable to the South, but "Isn't the price we pay too great? Is his labor worth more than the purity of our racial stock? Shall we improve the breed of men or degrade it? Is any progress that degrades the breed of men progress at all? Is it not retrogression? Can we afford it?" (p. 166). Norton argues with a white Southerner, sympathetic to the Negro cause: "The negro is the lowest of all human forms, four thousand years below the standard of the pioneer white Aryan who discovered this continent and peopled it with a race of empire builders. The gradual mixture of our blood with his can only result in the extinction of National character—a calamity so appalling the mind of every patriot refuses to accept for a moment its possibility" (p. 201).[4]

On a personal level, with Cleo insinuated into his household, because his son, Tom, looks on her as a mother figure, Norton sees only "the thing he hated—the mongrel breed of a degraded nation" (p. 196). Cleo is sent away, but writes to Norton that she is pregnant with his child. The major arranges for the child's education and upbringing, and Cleo again forces her way, through Tom, into Norton's household. Tragedy, of course, strikes with the arrival in the household of Cleo's daughter, Helen, with whom Tom falls in love. Despite the best efforts of Norton, the couple is secretly married. Norton reveals that Cleo has Negro blood first to Helen, who makes plans to leave immediately for Europe—"The one thing I've always loathed was the touch of a negro" (p. 381)—and then to Tom, who, at first, refuses to give up Helen despite her "tainted" blood. He accuses his father of prejudice, but the major responds,

> Prejudices! You know as well as I that the white man's instinct of racial purity is not prejudice, but God's first law of life—the instinct of self-preservation! The lion does not mate with the jackal! (p. 401)

> Born of a single black progenitor, she is still a negress. Change every black skin in America to-morrow to the white of a lily and we'd yet have ten million negroes— ten million negroes whose blood relatives are living in Africa the life of a savage. (pp. 401–2)

> A pint of ink can make black gallons of water. The barriers once down, ten million negroes can poison the source of life and character for a hundred million whites. (p. 403)

> Nothing is surer than the South will maintain the purity of her home! It's as fixed as her faith in God!" (p. 405)

The reader is quickly ahead of Dixon in determining the outcome here. Father and son pledge a suicide pact. Norton first shoots his son and then kills himself. But the bullet only grazes Tom, and as he recovers, Cleo admits that Helen is not her child. Her daughter died at birth, and she adopted Helen, who was born of white parents. It is all very unsatisfactory and obvious, but from a moralistic viewpoint (if such is possible in a novel like this), Norton had to pay the price for his initial infidelity with Cleo, from which stemmed the tragedy of *The Sins of the Father*. "No life built on a lie could endure" (p. 372).

The novel does deal in part with Southern politics and the power of the Klan and its leaders to influence voting. Further, Dixon provides what he obviously considers to be examples of Negro humor—"there are some scenes of real darky humor," reported *Literary Digest* (May 4, 1912)—in conversations between Norton's two black servants. It is through the servants that the reader first learns of the possibility that Helen is not Cleo's child.

Reviewers were not overly impressed. Margaret Sherwood in *Atlantic Monthly* (November 1912) complained, "Some of the historical background puts a strain upon one's credulity; and the tale betrays, perhaps, too much of our love of continued climax of effect." The *New York Times* (April 21, 1912) commented, "In the author of *The Sins of the Father* we detect a tendency to treat very sensationally all those ills which the South has been heir to since the days of Reconstruction."

Miscegenation is, of course, a prominent issue in Dixon's Reconstruction trilogy and also, thereby, in *The Birth of a Nation*. Aside from the latter, the only film associated with Dixon in which it plays a major role is the William Fox production of *Wing Toy*, released in January 1921. It is not the issue of white-black marriage under discussion in the film, but rather white-yellow marriage.

The title character in *Wing Toy* is adopted as a baby by a Chinese laundryman; at the age of sixteen she is to be forced into marriage with the proprietor of a Chinese gambling den, when she is discovered to be the daughter of the district attorney and thus free to marry a white American cub reporter who has fallen in love with her. The story was provided by a popular novelist of the day, Pearl Doles Bell, and Dixon may have been persuaded to write the screenplay in part because of the success of D.W. Griffith's 1919 drama *Broken Blossoms*. Based on a Thomas Burke story, "The

Chink and the Child," *Broken Blossoms* also involves white-yellow miscegenation: a young English girl, Lucy, played by Lillian Gish, finds safety and platonic affection from a Chinese merchant in London's East End, played by Richard Barthelmess. (In recent years, it has been suggested that the relationship between Lucy and her Chinese protector may not have been as innocent as suggested and that pedophilia might also be an issue here. Similarly, the age of Wing Toy does not preclude the same conclusion.)

Just as Chinese Americans were disturbed by *Broken Blossoms*, so was the community far from happy with *Wing Toy*. The title character was played by Shirley Mason, a new star with William Fox who was following in the more famous footsteps of her sister, Viola Dana. The cub reporter hero was portrayed by Raymond McKee; and all the Chinese roles were essayed by white American actors. "None of the principals entirely look the parts of Orientals, but this is not essential to carry the illusion," explained the *Moving Picture World* (February 12, 1921). The only hint at authenticity was the filming of most of the exterior scenes in Los Angeles's Chinatown. According to *Motion Picture News* (January 15, 1921), *Wing Toy* was "one of the most correctly staged pictures ever offered to an exhibitor."

Initially titled *Chin Toy*, the film went into production in December 1920 and was completed only a couple of weeks prior to its release. It must have been somewhat galling to Thomas Dixon to know that a film for which he was merely the screenwriter was being shot at the studio he had built for the production of *The Fall of a Nation*. Dixon's contribution to the film was barely recognized by the critics, and *Wing Toy* was dismissed by all as a "more or less simple melodrama,"[5] "pleasant and agreeable in tone."[6]

10

JOURNEYMAN FILMMAKER

The 1920s began not too auspiciously for Thomas Dixon with the bankruptcy on February 8, 1921, of the National Drama Corporation, with which Dixon had been closely associated since production of *The Fall of a Nation*. The corporation had controlled motion picture rights to various of Dixon's novels and as late as April 1920 had authorized investment of ten thousand dollars in production on stage and film of two more of the author's works, *A Man of the People* and *The Reckoning*. The corporation had high hopes for the former, which had opened on the stage in Chicago in July 1920 but failed to find an audience.

Dixon's problems with National were further compounded by a nasty lawsuit involving his son-in-law, William C. Burns. The husband of Dixon's only daughter, Louise, Burns had little obvious rapport with the film industry, having been previously associated with the plumbing business in Griffen, Georgia. Nevertheless, Dixon paid for his travel to Los Angeles, and Burns was hired by the National Drama Corporation in January 1916, eventually becoming the corporation's general manager. Burns lived with his father-in-law in New York from July 1916 through October 1917 and assumed the position of assistant business manager of the corporation.

He became secretary and a director of the corporation on July 1, 1917, and in July 1918 was given a salary of six thousand dollars a year. While the corporation floundered, Burns began purchasing outstanding notes and bonds at five cents on the dollar, knowing them to be worth twenty cents on the dollar.

Burns left the corporation on August 1, 1919. He and Dixon had become estranged when Dixon discovered what his son-in-law had been doing in violation of his duties as an officer of the corporation. Dixon maintained that Burns was unfaithful to the corporation, made every effort to ruin it, and finally succeeded in forcing National into bankruptcy. Although Dixon blamed his son-in-law, the trustee in bankruptcy, Thorne Baker, blamed Dixon, alleging malfeasance and misfeasance. The outcome of the legal action is unclear, but it appears to have been settled out of court.

Despite the problems with National, the 1920s were to prove Dixon's most prolific decade as a filmmaker. He wrote screenplays for ten feature films; wrote, directed, and produced an eleventh; and had one of his most popular novels, *The Foolish Virgin*, adapted once again for the screen. (The 1921 text by John Emerson and Anita Loos, *How to Write Photoplays*, was added to Dixon's library, joining an earlier volume on screenwriting from 1913, *The Technique of the Photoplay*, by Epes W. Sargent.) At the same time, aside from the previously discussed *Wing Toy*, none of the films provided Dixon with an opportunity to offer much, if any, social commentary. They are all average program pictures, which received little critical recognition on initial release—none of Dixon's films after *The Fall of a Nation* were reviewed in the *New York Times*—and made no impact on the public conscience.[1] It might be argued that these films are of interest primarily because they are indicative of Dixon's acceptance by the film industry and are proof of his capability as a screenwriter on any topic.

What is perhaps most remarkable about them is that all the scripts were written outside of Hollywood. Early in 1920, following the death from polio the previous year of his son Jordan, Thomas Dixon decided to return to his New York home at 867 Riverside

Drive, while also maintaining an office for the Thomas Dixon Corporation at 43 West Thirty-seventh Street. From those two addresses, Dixon created his various screenplays of the 1920s.

The first two under discussion, *Where Men Are Men* and *Bring Him In*, are Westerns produced by the Vitagraph Company of America. The final couple of the decade, *The Trail Rider* and *The Gentle Cyclone*, also Westerns, feature popular Western star Buck Jones and are directed by W.S. Van Dyke, who was to achieve prominence in the 1930s with his work on such major MGM features as *Trader Horn* (1931), *Tarzan the Ape Man* (1932), *The Thin Man* (1934), *San Francisco* (1936), and *Marie Antoinette* (1938). *Photoplay* (August 1926) described Dixon's last film of the 1920s, *The Gentle Cyclone*, as "flat," adding, "The plot is developed in the most obvious manner possible and without sufficient material for a feature length photoplay. Buck Jones is his usual self. Nothing is outstanding throughout the picture except Buck has three charming young ladies supporting him."

The storylines of all four Dixon-scripted Westerns provide but one indication that the author was able to insinuate any of his own opinions into the scenarios, all of which are based on stories by others. The genre is, arguably, close in style to some of Dixon's novels; an obituary in the *Fayetteville (N.C.) Observer* (April 4, 1946) observed in Dixon's books "a pattern of violence which at its best was spine tingling and which at its worst was reminiscent of the hack western."

Variety praised both of the Dixon-scripted Buck Jones vehicles as superior in storyline to other efforts by the cowboy star. And with regard to Vitagraph's *Where Men Are Men*, which was directed by and starred William Duncan as a gold prospector forced to clear himself of the murder of his partner, *Variety* (September 23, 1921) wrote, "For a western picture, this is comparatively interesting." The second Vitagraph production, *Bring Him In*, directed by and starring Earle Williams as a fugitive from the Canadian Northwest Mounted Police, was also recommended by *Variety* (November 4, 1921) as "a splendid program picture." Its chief recommendation for those seeking a unique Thomas Dixon touch in the storyline is the addition of a half-breed, who has no connection to the plot but is introduced as someone abusing the heroine, Fritzi Ridgeway, and thus available to receive an appropriate beating from hero Williams. It is a small but telling and subtle indictment of miscegenation.

The remainder of Dixon's scripts of the 1920s written at the request of others were for melodramas, beginning with *Thelma*, released in November 1922 and based on an antiquated 1887 novel, *Thelma, a Norwegian Princess,* by Marie Corelli. The latter was the pseudonym of Mary Mackay, an English novelist whose earlier popularity eclipsed that of Thomas Dixon in that her novels were the reading matter of choice by women on both sides of the Atlantic. (Dixon never achieved great success in Europe.) She died in 1924, and the bulk of her novels were written in the late 1800s and early twentieth century. Her best-known work, *The Sorrows of Satan* (1895), was filmed in 1917 and 1926. *Thelma* was first filmed in 1916 under the title *A Modern Thelma*. It was Marie Corelli's name and not Dixon's that the distributor, F.B.O., used to promote the film.

Thelma is the story of an old-fashioned Norwegian girl, played here by Jane Novak, who discovers love in London, marrying Sir Philip Errington, but experiences hatred both in her native village and in London after her marriage because of the jealousy of others. Dixon's adaptation was faithful to the novel, and at least one trade paper, *Motion Picture News* (December 2, 1922), described the film as "a splendid screen version of Marie Corelli's popular novel." *Variety* (December 1, 1922) was less enthusiastic, complaining of a slow tempo and noting only "a couple of brief thrills, but they do not linger in the memory." *Photoplay* (February 1923) described *Thelma* as "beautiful scenically, and with Jane Novak looking her best," but complained about Dixon's updating of the storyline: "There are times when it seems garish and sentimental in a sloppy way."

Following completion of *Thelma*, Dixon decided to return to production with *The Mark of the Beast*, which he produced, directed, and scripted from his own original and unpublished story.[2] (It is obvious, however, that the film contains major elements borrowed from *The Foolish Virgin*, and one wonders why the owners of the screen rights to the latter did not consider a lawsuit for plagiarism.) The title is borrowed from a 1916 novel by Reginald Wright Kauffman (published by the Macaulay Company), a copy of which was owned by Dixon. In September 1922, Dixon engaged space at New York's Tilford Studios, located at 344 West Forty-fourth Street, and created Thomas Dixon Productions, financing for which was provided, in large part, by William A. White, Arthur S. Bandler, and Oscar F. Grab. The timing was good in that United Artists had just announced the reissue of *The Birth of a Nation*, prominently advertised as "founded on Thomas Dixon's story *The Clansman.*"

Described as a drama of the subconscious and with only five characters, *The Mark of the Beast* was characterized by its author as appealing to the intelligence rather than bombarding the emotions.[3] The story concerns itself with psychoanalysis and the potential of the subconscious mind to direct action. As such, *The Mark of the Beast* is unique among silent films. While a handful of silent productions feature psychologists and psychiatrists, psychoanalysis was not a major screen subject until the 1940s with *Lady in the Dark* (1944), which was, of course, based on a Broadway musical, and *The Dark Mirror* (1946).

The central character in *The Mark of the Beast* is psychologist David Hale, who is engaged to Ann Page and fascinated by her problems with sleepwalking. She is influenced to marry a thief named Donald Duncan, despite his being of "obviously lower type," because of his resemblance to her deceased father. When Duncan takes her to a cabin in the mountains, she discovers the true nature of the beast as he attacks her. Hale follows the couple to the cabin, out of professional interest in the relationship, and rescues Ann. The latter is subsequently free to marry Hale after Duncan's mother, who conveniently also occupies the cabin and has not seen her son in ten or twelve years, stabs and kills him in an effort to steal jewelry that he has also previously stolen. As one critic unkindly noted, the mother's subconscious mind would surely have identified Duncan as having at least some resemblance to her son. (Unfortunately, because the film is no longer extant and a detailed synopsis does not survive, the best descriptions available must come from contemporary reviews.)

Producers Security announced plans to release the film in March 1923,[4] but *The Mark of the Beast* was eventually put into distribution by a somewhat more prominent enterprise, W.W. Hodkinson (a company headed by the original founder of Paramount Pictures) in June 1923. The film was either five or six reels in length—contemporary reports vary—with a running time of sixty or sixty-five minutes. Dixon maintained that any story could be told in five reels, ignoring the fact that *The Birth of a Nation* was twelve reels in length and could not have been told in less. And despite the brevity of *The Mark of the Beast*, *Variety* claimed it was fifteen minutes too long.

Dixon introduced the film to a receptive audience composed of members of the Authors' League of America at a special screening at New York's Town Hall on June 1, 1923. However, there was little enthusiasm from critics or the public when *The Mark of the Beast* was screened commercially. "It is an author's challenge to 'machine-made' pictures," commented *Photoplay* (August 1923). "The 'machine' wins. A lot of pretentious bunk about psycho-analysis. Poor story, poor continuity, poor casting, poor direction—Poor public!" One trade publication advocated that the film be screened "for intelligent audiences," which is perhaps why *The Mark of the Beast* did not receive a public New York presentation until November 13, 1923, when it played at Loew's Theatre. At that time, *Variety* (November 15, 1923) took a look at the film and branded it "a mediocre composition. . . . Both cheaply produced and but averagely acted."

The Mark of the Beast received relatively favorable reviews in the two major weekly film publications, *Moving Picture World* and

Motion Picture News, and they are worthy of quoting at some length. In *Moving Picture World* (June 16, 1923), C.S. Sewell commented:

> Mr. Dixon's connection with the show business has stood him in good stead in making this picture, for, although he described it as a drama of the subconscious mind and has built up his theme on the working of this apparently uncontrollable force which causes the woman in question against her own judgment to throw over a refined man for one of obviously lower type who turns out to be a burglar; he has appealed to the intellect through the emotions. The result is a picture that while it will interest higher class patrons from its psychological side has plenty of thrills and punch scenes to hold its own with the average audience.

In an editorial, the trade paper *Motion Picture News* (June 16, 1923), which seemed a long-term supporter of Dixon, praised the film: "There is not a scene of wasted footage in the entire picture. What is told carries a spontaneity of action and a compactness which heightens the plot and gives it vigor." In the same issue, reviewer Laurence Reid wrote:

> With all the hue and cry being raised concerning the usual distortion of an author's story during its development on the screen, and the superfluous length of the average photoplay, Thomas Dixon, who wrote *The Birth of a Nation*, has been prompted to write, adapt, direct and edit his own picture, *The Mark of the Beast*, the theme of which deals with the sub-conscious mind in controlling thought and action. The author deserves commendation in his treatment of the story—which will appeal to the intelligentsia even if he loses contact with his theme.
> A tale based upon the idea of psychoanalysis cannot be expected to be clearly defined. It's a subject which has

no limitations. Confining to terms of action show [*sic*] up its shortcomings. Where the praise enters it should be given for the compact scenes which carry not a single detail of superfluous footage—and the exceptionally good acting. Whether the picture will stimulate a desire on the part of picturegoers to see it is problematical. There isn't so much entertainment in it judging it purely upon its theme. . . .

The actions of the characters are given psycho-analytical explanations in the captions—which, while brief and to the point, nevertheless, are incapable of fully expressing the idea behind them. Errors of omission and commission must be expected in any treatment of such a subject. Mr. Dixon is much better in his dramatic execution of it since it is built like a play and sweeps forward with a real crescendo of events which culminate in a tense climax. The characters are sharply drawn. The scenes carry much suspense. And it is compact with interesting sequences. The spectator will not learn much of psycho-analysis from it. And he won't have any sympathy with a mother who stabs her own son. Nevertheless, he will follow the idea and execution of it with the strictest attention.

The cast of *The Mark of the Beast* was far from distinguished. Numbering only five, it was headed by Robert Ellis in the role of Dr. David Hale, with Warner Richmond as Donald Duncan and Gustav von Seyffertitz and Helen Ware as his parents, John and Jane. All had been active on screen since the previous decade, but, with the exception of von Seyffertitz, a character actor noted for the brilliance of his villainous performances, none had evoked any major interest from either audiences or producers. The same might well be written of Madelyn Clare, the actress playing Ann Page, but her importance was ultimately not in reference to the film industry but to the life and career of Thomas Dixon.

Born Madelyn Donovan in Cleveland, Ohio, Madelyn Clare

was orphaned at the age of six and brought up by relatives in New York. She had no need of a job but was introduced by a theatrical costume designer friend to producer and actor Benjamin Chapin, who was noted for his impersonations of Abraham Lincoln. Chapin hired Madelyn to play Nancy Hanks Lincoln in a series of short subjects on the life of Lincoln that he was producing in 1916 and which were subsequently screened in feature-length form, in 1917, under the title *The Lincoln Cycle*. She was never a film star or even a leading lady, but Madelyn Clare played second female leads in eight films prior to *The Mark of the Beast*: *All Woman* (1918), *The Hidden Truth* (1919), *The Misleading Widow* (1919), *The Discarded Woman* (1920), *If Only Women Knew* (1921), *The Supreme Passion* (1921), *False Fronts* (1922), and *Young America* (1922). All of Madelyn Clare's films were produced in the New York area; she never worked in Hollywood, and as far as can be ascertained, she never appeared on the legitimate stage.

She may very well have met Thomas Dixon during production of *Bolshevism on Trial*. He was obviously aware of her as an actress, if not somewhat more intimately, prior to production of *The Mark of the Beast*. With the completion of production, Madelyn Donovan decided her career as an actress was over, and she devoted the remainder of her life to Thomas Dixon, serving as his researcher, confidante, and mistress.

If *The Mark of the Beast* is important as the only film that Thomas Dixon directed as well as wrote and produced, it is equally important for bringing Madelyn Donovan openly into his life. Years later, she commented to Dixon biographer Raymond Cook that *The Mark of the Beast* was "too advanced psychologically for its time and that it would fail at the box office."[5]

After *The Mark of the Beast* and the release of the second screen adaptation of *The Foolish Virgin*, with which Dixon was not involved, the writer's final contributions of the 1920s to the motion picture were all screenplays for productions of the William Fox Corporation. Although the films were released between 1924 and 1926, it seems probable that they were all written in 1924 and that Dixon was briefly under contract to Fox. One can only conjecture about the relationship between the two men. Fox was a coarse, vulgar, crude studio head, ambitious and vindictive, with German Jewish parents, who grew up in a tenement on New York's lower east side. There seems little for Dixon to admire here; but, like Dixon, Fox lived in New York, keeping himself three thousand miles away from the center of filmmaking, and it may be that the two men socialized. There is always the possibility that the two became business friends when Fox took over Dixon's Hollywood studio after production of *The Fall of a Nation.*

The first of the Dixon-written Fox productions to be released was *The Painted Lady*, in which Dorothy Mackaill stars as an ex-convict, imprisoned for a crime committed by her sister, who takes to prostitution in the South Seas and is eventually rescued from her sordid life and the villain by a sailor played by George O'Brien. "Not for children" was the opinion of *Photoplay* (December 1924). *The Painted Lady* was followed by *The Great Diamond Mystery*, which, *Variety* (October 22, 1924) explained, "concerns its simple little self with diamonds, murders, suspicious-looking butlers, plenty of cops, and a number of young men with vari-shaped mustaches who make unscrupulous love to the little heroine." The last was portrayed by Shirley Mason, as a writer of murder mysteries who saves her sweetheart, played by William Collier Jr., from the electric chair. "Illogical gaps are not covered," complained *Photoplay* (January 1925) of Dixon's screenplay.

The Brass Bowl, released in November 1924, was another mystery, with Edmund Lowe in a dual role as a wealthy bachelor and an international crook. "One of the most gripping mystery stories in some time," commented *Photoplay* (January 1925), more in praise of the original novel by Louis Joseph Vance than of Dixon's screenplay. Edmund Lowe also starred in Dixon's next screenplay, *Champion of Lost Causes*, released in January 1925. Based on a Max Brand magazine story, the film features Lowe as an author in search of material at a gambling resort, where he identifies a murderer. *Variety* (April 29, 1925) was fulsome in its praise of Dixon's work: "Corking mystery melodrama with a society element that is presented in compact story form on the screen with sustained suspense throughout." The two Buck Jones Westerns ended Dixon's career as a silent filmmaker, but there were other abortive attempts at film production by him in the 1920s.

Dixon adapted *The Road to Yesterday*, a 1906 play by Beulah Marie Dix and Evelyn Greenleaf Sutherland, for the screen. Its very silly storyline involved a newlywed American couple who are transported back in time to seventeenth-century England when the train on which they are traveling from New York to Chicago is involved in a crash. The religious and occult aspects of the plot may perhaps have intrigued Dixon, but when the film was ultimately produced and directed by Cecil B. DeMille in 1925, Thomas Dixon's name did not appear in the credits; the screenplay was the work of Beulah Marie Dix and DeMille's longtime associate Jeanie Macpherson. The Thomas Dixon script was extant in the mid-1960s when James Zebulon Wright read it, but it cannot now be located.

Julius Tannen, noted on the vaudeville stage for his comic monologues, planned to star in a film version of Dixon's short story "The Torch," with financial backing from banker Robert Lehman. In 1921, Dixon had published *The Man in Gray*, documenting the murderous and fanatical career of John Brown and his 1859 seizure of Harpers Ferry. "The Torch" covered similar territory, arguing, like *The Man in Gray*, that the martyrdom of Brown was largely responsible for the Civil War. A May 31, 1927, contract was drawn up, with Dixon to receive royalties from the net profits of the film and also to serve in the capacity of "assistant producer." Nothing came of the project, and on February 25, 1928, Dixon, alleging breach of contract, filed suit in the New York Supreme Court for five hundred thousand dollars. (Brown's seizure of Harpers Ferry was shown on screen for the first time in D.W. Griffith's 1930 production of *Abraham Lincoln*. As portrayed by Raymond Massey, John Brown was a major, and villainous, character in the 1940 Warner Bros. feature *Santa Fe Trail*, directed by Michael Curtiz and starring Errol Flynn and Olivia de Havilland, a production of which Thomas Dixon would doubtless have approved.)

In 1924, Dixon copyrighted a one-act play, *The Hope of the World*, which was never produced on stage but which is remarkable for its prescience and for the arguments that its author makes against war.[6] Its relevance to the world today, rather than the world of three-quarters of a century ago, is obvious. The set is a recess of the laboratory of Thomas Alva Edison, to which comes a mother, "Symbol of All Motherhood," and her five-year-old son. The mother tells the inventor of a dream she has had in which he has created a bomb that can destroy entire cities. Edison tells her that such a weapon of mass destruction is already extant, "War, Mother, has become a merciless Science. Science has no soul. . . . We Scientists work for the advancement of humanity. But war tears from our hand the discoveries of years and turns them into weapons of death." He continues, "We have allowed the politician to make the Church of God a recruiting station for gathering more food for cannon! He becomes our master. At his command Catholic kills Catholic, Protestant kills Protestant, brother kills brother without question. The politician loves power—war increases his power. He is always at heart a war maker."

The solution, explains Edison, is that "We must teach a new Patriotism—to love our country not *against* the world but because it is a part of God's beautiful world which is all our inheritance! We must teach the Fatherhood of God and the brotherhood of Man! To Europe, Asia, Africa and America." When the Mother asks how it is possible to teach the people who speak so many tongues so quickly, Edison produces his Kinetoscope, introduced in 1893: "We can make them see now. The eye is the door of the soul. Its language is universal. Through it we can speak to Europe, Asia, Africa, America, and every island of the Seas, the same message—and, it's the hope of the world!" Like the wireless, the new-style Kinetoscope will receive images and sound through vibrations of the air—"vibrating waves of love," reconstructing "the thinking of the world." The Mother leaves, intent on creating The Brotherhood of Man, Inc. The glow of a new hope fills her soul, and, with the enthusiasm of a new purpose, she tells Edison, "Thank you, I see now that I have work to do outside the nursery."

Yes, *The Hope of the World* is naive and quaint, but it offers a message of hope that in an ideal world might move millions. It is of its time certainly, like so much of the writings of Thomas Dixon, but in a very positive way, it is for all time and all generations. *The Hope of the World* is extraordinary for the manner in which it holds its reader, or its audience, and provides a message that offsets many of the offensive qualities in Dixon's work.

It would appear that Dixon planned to expand *The Hope of the World* either as a full-length play or as a treatise on the power of the motion picture. A mock-up of the cover for such a book, complete with a publisher, D. Appleton, and a release date of 1924, and the subtitle "The New Language of men—The Motion Picture," survives in the D.W. Griffith Collection at the Museum of Modern Art.

There were also new novels from Dixon that he obviously believed had film potential. In *The Sun Virgin*, published in 1929 by Horace Liveright and dedicated, "with admiration," to Augusto B. Leguia, president of Peru, he told the love story of Alonso de Molina and Teresa, against a background of Francisco Pizarro's 1532 invasion of Peru and capture of the Incan chief Atahualpa. While the novel praises individual Spaniards, including Hernando de Soto, it is as firmly opposed to the Spanish invasion as Dixon was earlier outraged at the treatment by the original European settlers of the American Indians. He writes of the period following the Spanish takeover of Peru, "A brief span of twenty years! And a people who once laughed and danced without a thought of tomorrow hide in caves and curse the sight of a white man" (p. 306). The novel was poorly received by the critics—the best the *New York Herald Tribune* (June 9, 1929) could write was that it "is no end picturesque"—and the spectacular scope and complex historical nature of the story made it virtually impossible to adapt for the screen. The historical background for the novel was obviously provided by William Hickling Prescott's *History of the Conquest of Peru*, originally published in two volumes in 1847 by Harpers. The background material that probably was of equal interest to Dixon was Cecil B. DeMille's 1917 production of *The Woman God Forgot*, whose storyline concerned itself with the landing of Spanish conqueror Hernando Cortez in Mexico and the defeat of Montezuma. DeMille's flamboyant showmanship coupled with the starring of opera-singer-turned-silent-screen-player Geraldine Farrar and matinee idol Wallace Reid had made the film a major commercial success, but no later features had been produced with a similar theme.

11

NATION AFLAME

Thomas Dixon's association with the motion picture effectively ended with the coming of sound. But there was one last foray into film, important not so much because of the production, which was relatively minor, but because it underlined Dixon's determined opposition to the modern Ku Klux Klan. There is some confusion as to exactly what was the author's contribution to *Nation Aflame*. On the film itself and in original publicity, it is promoted as *Nation Aflame* by Thomas Dixon, "Author of *The Birth of a Nation*." There is a collaborative story credit to Oliver Drake and Rex Hale, a screenplay credit to Oliver Drake, and, finally, an additional dialogue credit to William Lively.

Dixon may have made a trip to Los Angeles shortly after *Nation Aflame* was completed, perhaps for promotional purposes or possibly to promote work for himself. One of Dixon's journals contains the cryptic note, "Hollywood & Vine St John W. Stahl, Studio Universal City wed Feb 3 on." Wednesday, February 3, indicates that Dixon was in Los Angeles in 1937. Hollywood and Vine is a famous city intersection but many miles away from Universal City and Universal Studio in the San Fernando Valley. John M. Stahl—we can safely assume the "W" is a mistake—had no known connection with *Nation Aflame*, but he was a prominent Universal director of the period, responsible for such melodramatic women's pictures as *Back Street* (1932), *Imitation of Life* (1934), and *Magnificent Obsession* (1935). *Imitation of Life* concerns itself with miscegenation and the efforts of a light-skinned African American to pass herself off as white. The story may well have intrigued Dixon and perhaps persuaded him to try to pitch some of his novels or a new and unidentified work to the director. Dixon may also have had an entrée to Stahl through his second wife, Madelyn Donovan, in that she and Stahl had made their screen debuts together in 1916 with *The Lincoln Cycle*, she as one of the players, he as the director.

Unfortunately, by this time, Dixon was virtually forgotten by Hollywood, and references to him in contemporary trade papers are just about nonexistent. On June 2, 1934, *Motion Picture Herald* reported that the author of *The Birth of a Nation* was penniless, adding, "Possibly he picked the wrong nation." One of the last news items on Dixon to appear in *Daily Variety* is dated July 18, 1936, and announces that he is to play the role of Abraham Lincoln in his play *The Prairie Lawyer*. As if in clarification of the subject's noncelebrity status, the trade paper added, "Dixon, 72, is also an attorney and novelist." Dixon did not copyright a play with the title of *The Prairie Lawyer*, although it may have been a revised version of his 1920 effort *The Tycoon: An American Drama of the Life of Lincoln* in three acts and an epilogue, also known as *A Man of the People*.

The opposition of Thomas Dixon to any revival of the Klan is evidenced as early as 1907 in *The Traitor*, the final volume of *The Reconstruction Trilogy*, set in the foothills of North Carolina between 1870 and 1872. At the same time, he used the novel's dedication page to affirm his support for the original Klan and its members: "Dedicated to the men of the South Who Suffered Exile, Imprisonment and Death for the Daring Service They Rendered Our Country as Citizens of the Invisible Empire."

The central character is lawyer John Graham, the chief of the local Ku Klux Klan, whose family home has been "stolen" from him by Judge Butler of the U.S. Circuit Court. Graham falls in love with Butler's daughter, Stella, who is also wooed by Steve Hoyle, a fellow lawyer who becomes chief of the new local Klan, established after Graham dissolves the old one as no longer a Southern necessity.

When Judge Butler is murdered at a Klan masquerade party in his home, given by his daughter, Graham is the prime suspect, and Stella sets out to trap him by having him confess to being the Klan chief. At Graham's trial, Steve Hoyle prosecutes him ruthlessly, but thanks to the efforts of an officer of the U.S. Secret Service, the real murderer is revealed to be carpetbagger (and Republican) Alexander Larkin. However, with "a jury composed of one dirty, ignorant white scalawag and eleven coal-black Negroes" (p. 305), Graham has little chance of not being found guilty of conspiracy, fined one thousand dollars, and sentenced to five years at hard labor in the U.S. penitentiary at Albany, New York.

Graham is a victim of the newly signed Conspiracy Act, which, Dixon explains, "made membership in the secret order known as the Ku Klux Klan, or Invisible Empire, a felony, and provided for the trial of its members on the charge of treason, conspiracy and murder. The President was authorized to suspend the writ of *habeas corpus* and proclaim martial law in any county of the Southern States, and use the army and the navy to enforce his authority" (p. 135).

Abruptly, in a matter of two pages, Graham is hastily pardoned, marries Stella, and restores the Inwood mansion, in whose ruins his Klan had gathered. "The council chamber of the Invisible Empire . . . where its High Court of Life and Death was held" (p. 229) is now the Graham family home.

The Klan headed by John Graham is one in "retreat from a field of victory" (p. 54). The new Klan that replaces it is inaugurated by the Black Union League, an undefined organization. The harm it does is little discussed by Dixon, who notes only that "for the first time he [Graham] realized the terrible meaning of the lawless power of the Klan. . . . The new Klan had inaugurated a reign of folly and terror unprecedented in the history of the whole Reconstruction saturnalia" (p. 96). Quickly, Graham steps in, capturing six of Hoyle's new Klansmen, giving them forty lashes, and leaving the "stripe-marked half-naked men gagged and bleeding dangling by their arms from the limbs of the trees" (p. 109) on Hoyle's lawn.

The Klan, old or new, represents romance to Southern womanhood. Stella watches Graham's group march threateningly by her father's home: "The spirit of some daring knight of the middle ages comes back to earth again!" she cries. "Superb! Superb! I could surrender to such a man" (p. 49). She organizes a party, attended by a "crowd of gay masqueraders" (p. 117) in Klan uniform, one of whom kills her father. From knights of honor, the Klan has quickly become nothing more than a group of vapid partygoers.

Reviews were generally negative, with the *New York Times* (August 3, 1907) calling Dixon a yellow journalist and the *Outlook* (August 17, 1907) describing the book as "almost hysterically high-keyed in expression."

Dixon pretty much rewrote *The Traitor* in 1924 under the title of *The Black Hood*. The setting is Independence, North Carolina, in 1871; Judge Butler becomes Judge Graham, his daughter is renamed Claudia, and John Graham becomes John Craig. The unattractive and overweight Steve Hoyle of *The Traitor* now becomes the handsome George Wilkes, who has avoided service in the Civil War and become the wealthiest man in the county.

The ending is considerably different, with Wilkes attempting to manipulate his rival's death by telling the Klan that Craig has revealed his identity to Claudia and thus must be punished by execution. The Klan members fight among themselves, and Craig and Claudia are rescued by federal troops. A colonel of the U.S. troops speaks the last words of the novel: "There's room for just one uniform in this republic and I am wearing it" (p. 336).

The few isolated groups that made up a revived Klan had no political power when *The Traitor* was published, but by 1924, the Klan's influence and strength were substantial—in large part thanks, unwittingly, to Griffith and Dixon's production of *The Birth of a Nation*. The Klan was active in both the South and the North, controlling the political scene in states as varied as Indiana, Maine, Oklahoma, Oregon, and Texas. A year later, in a show of strength, some forty thousand Klansmen were to march down Washington's Pennsylvania Avenue.

In his author's note to *The Black Hood*, Dixon commented that the events of the story were treated in the third volume of *The Reconstruction Trilogy* but added, "The passing of the full half century from 1873 to 1923 has made it possible to see these events in their full perspective and record their significance: The author suggests to the five million members of the new Ku Klux Klan that they read this book. He guarantees to each reader the warning of an old proverb that History will repeat itself."

The novel makes it very plain that the Klan serves no modern purpose. As Craig orders its dissolution, he tells his comrades:

> We rose in a night and seized this dangerous weapon. With mask and revolver we hurled our oppressors from power and sent the negro to school where he must stay for a hundred years of training. Order has been restored. Your legislature has been purged of thieves. A new Governor is in your Capitol. The courts of justice are open. Our work is done. (p. 83)

> The disguise we are using is not a thing to be proud of. It is the badge of an insane, crime-ridden era. Its power is too dangerous to be placed in the hands of any man or group of men in times of peace. . . . I have already been asked by bigots to use it as a weapon of religious persecution. . . . Protestant will demand the extinction of Catholic. Gentile will ask for the persecution of Jews— particularly if they are rivals in business. (p. 84)

The new Klan that arises proves Craig to be correct. The hoods are now black rather than white, a naive symbolism acknowledging the B Western movie genre with the heroes wearing white hats and the villains black. Teenage girls are kidnapped; both whites and Negroes are flogged. One man is castrated because "he had won the woman his enemy had desired" (p. 129). (Again, Dixon embraces sexual imagery.)

If nothing else, *The Black Hood* substantiates that its author has matured as a writer. Like *The Traitor* before it, the novel, despite the Klan subject matter, is basically free of anti-Negro rhetoric. It is devoid of the awkwardness of Dixon's early novels and is as entertaining (and unabashedly lurid) today as it was three-quarters of a century ago. As Herschel Brickell wrote in *Literary Review* (July 5, 1924), Dixon "can tell a story and make it gripping."

Two very different points of view were provided by two of New York's newspapers. "From beginning to end the ultimate purpose of the author is too evident," commented the *New York Times* (June 22, 1924). "He has written a scenario rather than a novel, and it is possible that the moving pictures may be able to supply the characters with the life which they lack in the printed version." However, E.W. Osborn in the *New York World* (June 15, 1924) wrote, "*The Black Hood* is a book of intensely melodramatic quality, one written, we should say, in a good deal of a hurry and not without thought of the films. The best thing about it is the pointed fashion in which it carries rebuke and condemnation to leaders who are promoting recklessly in our present day a revival of the K.K.K. under the worst possible impulses and auspices."

Thomas Dixon had long wanted to produce a film attacking the modern Klan, to be based on *The Traitor*. On December 18, 1922, he wrote to a Mr. Jacoby, who had expressed some interest in financing a screen adaptation:

No successful attack on the modern Ku Klux Klan can be made directly. As yet it has no record. But the attack can be made with resistless power through the historical name and disguise which they have chosen. . . .

In my novel and play *The Traitor*, published 14 years ago, I told the story of the disgraceful downfall of the

Klan through the use of its disguise in times of peace. Every scene in this historical drama of 1871, can be made a two edged sword cutting into the present, in a way that will be beyond successful criticism, even by the Klan itself.

The proposition on which I will base the picture version of *The Traitor* will be:

THAT THE DISGUISE OF A SECRET ORDER IS A REVOLUTIONARY WEAPON WHICH CAN BE WIELDED TO OVERTHROW A GOVERNMENT—BUT THAT ITS USE IN A REPUBLIC IN TIMES OF PEACE CAN ONLY END IN BLOODSHED ANARCHY AND MARTIAL LAW. . . .

I firmly believe that with the present excitement over the modern Klan which will continue for several years *The Traitor* can be made into another sensational success that will rival *The Birth of a Nation*.[1]

Thomas Dixon was to wait another fifteen years—in fact a full thirty years after publication of *The Traitor*—before he could promote an anti-Klan film into production, and his was not to be the first.

Outside of *The Birth of a Nation*, there was no friendly relationship between the modern Ku Klux Klan and the film industry. African American filmmaker Oscar Micheaux depicted the Klan in a far from favorable light in his 1920 production *The Symbol of the Unconquered,* in which the Klan attempts to drive the black hero off the land on which he has discovered oil. In 1921, the newsreel company *Fox News* presented what it claimed to be the only footage in existence of the newly organized Klan, with Imperial Wizard William J. Simmons initiating a new recruit on Stone Mountain. "In Georgia, where Ku Klux Klan parades have been frequent during the last year, certain lawbreakers, both negroes and whites, have been visited by weirdly clad riders and ordered to desist their wrong doings," reported the trade paper *Moving Picture World.*[2]

With *Knight of the Eucharist*, also known as *The Mask of the Ku Klux Klan*, produced in 1922 or possibly earlier, the Knights of Columbus fiercely attacked the Klan as an anti-Catholic organization with footage of its beating of a young Catholic boy. The Klan attempts to close down an Alabama gambling joint in *One Clear Call* (1922), produced by Louis B. Mayer. (The movie magnate claimed to have made his first half million dollars from the distribution rights to *The Birth of a Nation* in New England.) A veteran of the original Klan helps a young boy discover love of God and country in *The Fifth Horseman* (1924). Finally, in 1928, *The Mating Call*, based on a Rex Beach novel, has a Klan leader unsuccessfully plot revenge against his wife's former husband. Of the four feature films with major Klan depictions in the 1920s, two presented the organization favorably and two negatively, which is possibly indicative of the strength of the Klan in American society.

Hollywood had obviously been watching as the modern Ku Klux Klan quickly deteriorated from the prominent political organization that could march triumphantly down Washington's Pennsylvania Avenue on August 5, 1925, to a semi-outlawed, rogue institution. The event that ultimately sparked what might be described as a cycle of hooded legion films was the May 1935 murder of Charles Poole, a Public Lighting Department worker in Detroit, by the so-called Detroit Black Legion, and the revelations at the trial of its activities after Legion executioner Dayton Dean turned state's evidence. The success of the Black Legion was based on its support of Americanism and its opposition to foreigners who threatened the job security of native-born American laborers. With ties to both the Ku Klux Klan and Nazi Germany through the German-American Bund, the Black League operated under a variety of names, including the Christian American Crusaders, Knights of the White Camelia, American Vigilante Intelligence Association, Association of American Gentiles, and Christian American Patriots.[3]

Columbia produced the first film in the cycle with *Legion of Terror*, directed by C.C. Coleman and released in November 1936. Two postal inspectors investigate the activities of the Hooded Legion in the mythical town of Stanfield, Connecticut. After unmasking the leaders of the Hooded Legion, they are congratulated by the chief postal inspector in Washington, D.C., who warns them, and the audience, that because America is a nation of "joiners," its citizens are susceptible to supposed patriot organizations such as the Ku Klux Klan and the Hooded Legion.

Legion of Terror was very much a B picture, with minor players—Bruce Cabot and Marguerite Churchill were the leads—and a minor director. Warner Bros. produced the only A film of the group with *Black Legion,* which was in production concurrently with *Legion of Terror* but not released until January 1937. A reliable studio contract director, Archie Mayo, handled the production and its major studio contract stars, Humphrey Bogart and Ann Sheridan. (Edward G. Robinson was initially to have played the leading role, but he was judged too "foreign-looking.") Bogart plays factory worker Frank Taylor, who, despite his seniority, loses out on promotion to Joe Dombrowski, identified as "a foreigner." As a result, Taylor joins the Black Legion, burns down Dombrowski's chicken farm, and runs him and his family out of town. The Black Legion demands more of Taylor, and eventually, when he is arrested for murder, he reveals the truth of its operations to the court. The film is very obviously influenced by the Detroit murder case, and like *Legion of Terror,* it concludes with a propagandistic speech (this time by the judge).

After release of *Black Legion,* the Ku Klux Klan filed suit against Warner Bros., charging infringement of its insignia and defamation because of a remark asking, "Are we in for another reign of terror by a new Ku Klux Klan?" The Klan lost.[4] Even before release of *Black Legion,* the Maryland State Board of Motion Picture Censors had written, on November 13, 1936, to the Motion Picture Producers and Distributors of America, the body that served as liaison between the industry and the public, to complain of the cycle of films dealing with Ku Klux Klan organizations.[5]

Maurice H. Conn, the head of Conn Pictures Corp., a minor producer of B pictures in Hollywood, had contacted the Production Code Administration, responsible for the industry-sanctioned "censorship" of all American-produced films, with two treatments, one titled *Avenging Angels,* by Rex Hale and Leon d'Usseau, and the other, *Scarlet Legion*, by Rex Hale, in May 1936. The latter was judged "anti-social," with Joseph Breen writing on May 29, 1936, "To suggest a nationwide organization of youths operating under 'bloody oaths' and engaged in 'committing acts of violence and robbery on a wholesale scale,' all of this under the leadership and operation of a killer-gangster, is, in our judgment, thoroughly reprehensible."

Avenging Angels, which was to become *Nation Aflame*, fared somewhat better, with Breen agreeing that the basic story could be developed into a very interesting and worthwhile picture, provided that there would be no reference to definite organizations such as the Knights of Columbus or the Elks and that the victims of the Avenging Angels would definitely not be characterized as Jews, Catholics, or Negroes.

The film eventually went into production in November 1936, with Thomas Dixon now officially credited with the storyline, but with Leon d'Usseau no longer associated with the screenplay. The working title was changed to *My Life Is Yours*. At the request of the Production Code Administration, the Avenging Angels were no longer organized to combat "race and religion" but rather "foreigners." There are, in fact, no African Americans visible anywhere in the production, and considering that one of the major issues is the poverty threatening striking workers, the extras look incredibly well-nourished and well-clothed.

The cast is decidedly second-tier, headed by Noel Madison, usually cast as a small-time villain, as Frank Sandino; the unknown Norma Trelvar as Wynne Adams; former silent leading lady Lila Lee as Mona Burtis; and Arthur Singley as Bob Sherman. The name of Carl Stockdale, who had appeared in the Babylonian story of *Intolerance*, appears in the cast list, but it is impossible to identify him on screen.[6] With Treasure Pictures Corporation now the designated production entity and Television Pictures, Inc., the distributor, Edward Halperin receives credit as producer and his brother, Victor Hugo Halperin, as director. The two are not without interest, having been responsible for an early Carole Lombard vehicle,

Supernatural (1933), and, more importantly, the classic horror film *White Zombie* (1932), starring Bela Lugosi in one of his best screen roles. Immediately prior to *Nation Aflame*, the Halperin brothers had unsuccessfully tried to bring to the screen a modernized version of *Uncle Tom's Cabin*, under the title *Slave of the Sheik*.

The direction of *Nation Aflame* is nothing of which either Halperin brother might be ashamed—they seemed routinely to share producing and directing credits no matter how designated on screen—and the film moves along at a fast, if occasionally melodramatic, pace. It is an exploitation film, and it cannot escape from that labeling. There is an obvious and inescapable cheapness here, but the film does have a gritty, realistic look, reminiscent of some Warner Bros. productions of the period. As with most contemporary B pictures, there is an abundant use of stock footage. The "canned" music is well chosen. The only unfortunate aspect of the production is its use of what is very obviously the Beverly Hills City Hall as the governor's headquarters. The notion that the poor, hungry, and out-of-work would demonstrate outside this particular building is somewhat amusing.

The leading lady, Norma Trelvar, made no other film appearance, but she is exceptionally restrained in her performance and should have done more, despite an unfortunate toothy grin that is reminiscent of Martha Raye at her worst. Where Norma Trelvar came from—she has no stage or radio credits to her name—and where she went remains a mystery.

With its creed of "Pure Americanism," the leaders of the Avenging Angels are provided with some memorable speeches in the film, and one cannot help but believe they came from the pen of Thomas Dixon. They certainly contain all the passion and fervor one might expect from Dixon the preacher. And, as happened in *The One Woman*, the best speeches are those given by characters with opposing (and wrong) views to those of Dixon. Unfortunately, *Nation Aflame* also contains so-called humorous conversations between the trio of Wolfe, Wilson, and Walker that are reminiscent of Dixon's early and pathetic attempts to capture Negro humor on the printed page.

Following a quote from Abraham Lincoln's Gettysburg Address, the film opens as Roland Adams, a one-time mayor and long-time confidence trickster, along with his colleagues Frank Sandino, Wolfe (former silent comedian Snub Pollard), Wilson (Earle Hodgins), and Walker (Si Wills), is run out of town by a group of outraged citizens who have uncovered a land-selling swindle. Regrouping and discussing what they might do next, Sandino suggests they form a secret lodge, whose membership will pay initiation dues as well as the cost of their robes. "Every decent and progressive organization" had been involved in running them out of town, so why not create their own organization? After all, "A mob is bad medicine unless you're on the controlling end." As he explains it, "People everywhere are jealous of the other fellow with his money. Intolerant of his religion. Prejudiced against so-called foreigners. . . . We'll capitalize on jealousy, intolerance and patriotism. We'll form a secret lodge and band our members into a legion of patriotic avengers—The Avenging Angels."

Knowing of the importance of "American names for Americans," Sandino becomes Sands. (The character is apparently of Greek origin, but the Production Code Administration insisted that he not be referred to as "The Greek.") Roland Adams, whose characterization at times suggests an overfamiliarity with W.C. Fields at his weakest, takes the group back to Middleton, where he was mayor until the bootleggers stopped paying him kickbacks and where his daughter, Wynne, has independent means and is engaged to district attorney Bob Sherman.

When Adams arrives at his daughter's home, she is hosting a cocktail party, and Sands takes the opportunity to present his plans to the well-heeled group:

The only way that we can save the youth of our nation is to organize them in one single group. And through them enforce the precepts of one hundred percent Americanism. Corruption in politics must go. Civic virtue and patriotism must be our goal. We must enforce a reverence

178

for our flag and our constitution. And, what is more, protect our American womanhood and guard the sanctity of our homes. We must guarantee that the wealth of America must be shared only by real Americans. [At this point one of the guests asks, "You mean Indians?"—a typical Dixon touch.] To maintain and declare an absolute boycott against foreigners is our only salvation. . . . This nation must rise against these foreign vultures, who even though they slyly become citizens, prey upon our industries and corrupt our government with their insidious propaganda. . . . They'd do anything to control their possible ends. They control our homes, our community relief projects, stores, offices, prices. I ask you are we going to sit back and allow foreigners to take the very bread from the mouths of Americans? The answer is no. Emphatically no.

Despite Sherman's concern that Sands is inciting mob violence, Wynne becomes fascinated with him and actively helps in the establishment of the Avenging Angels, which Sands now claims originated in the days of Julius Caesar. For twenty-five dollars, the citizens of Middleton can now become "true Americans." Sands encourages strikes that can only be broken upon payments to him by the employers. Stock footage suggests mob violence and the burning of property. Sands builds up the Avenging Angels into such a strong political group that it can elect Roland Adams as governor.

Sherman works with newspaper publisher Harry Warren (Alan Cavan) in trying to bring down the Avenging Angels. "Justice needs no mask." Warren has been a good friend to Mona Burtis and her out-of-work husband Dave (Roger Williams), who is a member of the Avenging Angels. He defends foreigners to them, pointing out, "Very few of us are more than once or twice removed from foreigners. I fought in the front lines side by side with this so-called foreigner, but there was no difference in race, color or creed; each gave his life willingly for the preservation of American principles."

179

Dave is persuaded by Sands to help kidnap Warren—"Judas got thirty pieces of silver for his double cross, Dave"—while Mona has no alternative but to keep silent under threat of death. Warren is taken out by the mob into the country, strung up to a tree limb, brutally whipped, and killed.

Warren's killing creates outrage well beyond Middleton. You cannot kill a newspaper publisher and not expect other publishers to become angry, and as Adams points out, "An unfriendly press is the worst enemy we can have." Sherman identifies an anonymous note revealing the location of Warren's body as having been typed on Dave's typewriter. Mona pleads with Sands to save her husband, threatens to kill Sands after he tries to kiss her, and is accidentally shot to death in the subsequent fight over the gun. Dave is later released from jail for lack of evidence and attends Mona's lavish funeral, paid for by Sands and the Avenging Angels.

As hundreds of angry and hungry men and women (or at least as many as a B picture producer can afford) demonstrate outside the governor's mansion, waiting for Adams to sign a relief bill, Sands orders the governor to refuse. Wynne overhears the two men and realizes Sands's duplicity. Adams goes out on the mansion balcony to tell the crowd he will sign the bill, but he is shot down by Dave, acting on orders from Sands. Dave is, in turn, killed by the police. Sherman agrees to run for the governorship after receiving a letter from the president: "Our only salvation rests with those loyal citizens who love the liberty for which our forefathers died. They will not stand idly by while these sinister forces strangle the nation."

A despairing Wynne agrees to help Sherman in his campaign against Sands, sacrificing herself and her reputation, by becoming prominent herself in the Avenging Angels and forming a women's auxiliary. "Our personal affairs are so insignificant beside the service we can render." Deliberately, she spills a drink down her dress at a tryst with Sands, hides at his suggestion in the bedroom, and then reappears, wearing a robe, as he is meeting with leading members of the Avenging Angels.

Rumors about the pair spread, and Wynne does not deny these when confronted by Tommy Franklin (Douglas Walton), the naive, misguided, and overenthusiastic leader of the youth division of the Avenging Angels. "I set you up as an ideal of everything I thought of as fine and clean," he sobs. Wynne spends a night drinking with Sands, ensuring that he is in a drunken and disheveled state when a large group of party leaders and members of the press arrive at her home the following morning. She has failed to "preserve the sanctity of the home," as she promised her supporters. Realizing he has been framed, Sands tries to shoot Wynne, but the police, along with Sherman, arrive, and Sands is shot dead. Sherman has no alternative but to denounce Wynne—"a perfect example of what your Avenging Angels really stand for"—and stands with her as she watches herself and Sands burned in effigy. The couple realizes that no one must ever know of their conspiracy. Sherman asks Wynne to marry him, but she responds, "Not tomorrow, nor tomorrow, nor tomorrow. . . . Your first duty is to them [the people], the state and the country."

However, at Sherman's inaugural parade as governor, he shares a car with the president of the United States (C. Montague Shaw, who deliberately makes no attempt to look like Franklin D. Roosevelt), who tells him, "Your election will drive home more clearly to the people of the nation that theirs is the finest heritage of freedom, democracy and racial and religious tolerance." Wynne watches the parade from the crowded sidewalk, and as the car reaches her, a man in the crowd indicates her presence to the president and he orders the car stopped. The president stands and raises his hat to Wynne, who lifts her veil and blows a kiss to Sherman as he removes his hat. The car moves on, and Wynne disappears into the crowd. It is a surprisingly moving finale, reminiscent of the ending of *Stella Dallas,* where the mother watches through the window as the daughter she cannot acknowledge gets married. There is no need for words here as the president serves almost as a go-between for the two lovers, who perhaps will never share happiness.

There are curious plot developments, not to mention the naming of the publisher after a well-known songwriter of the 1930s. The publisher is a good friend to both Mona and Dave Burtis, and although her betrayal of him is understandable in that there are guns being held to her head, there is no excuse or explanation for Dave's actions. It is equally odd that while the normally law-abiding citizens who have joined the Avenging Angels have no problems with its involvement in torture and killing, they are so obsessed with the immorality of Sands and Wynne. In the late 1800s, the *Christian Index* noted that Southerners were imbued with "a high sense of honor and [the] highest regard for female character,"[7] and this attitude was behind many of the Klan lynchings. Like the Ku Klux Klan before it, the Avenging Angels' "very existence lay in the 'sacred duty' to protect womanhood."[8] Here, the end justifies the means, and despite the eventual downfall of the Avenging Angels, the question remains as to why so many Americans chose to become its members. Intolerance and bigotry will not go away simply because the leaders of the Avenging Angels have been exposed for what they are.

Nation Aflame was screened as early as April 1937 at the Liberty Theatre in Lincoln, Nebraska, but it did not open in New York until October of that same year, playing the lower half of a double bill at the Criterion Theatre. Reviews were generally unfavorable. *Variety* (April 7, 1937) commented on the lack of box-office potential of the leading players and the unoriginality of the storyline. It did, however, note the similarity of the Avenging Angels to the Ku Klux Klan. *Film Daily* (October 20, 1937) complained, "It fails to accomplish much of anything and moves slowly to a foregone conclusion." *Motion Picture Herald* (October 23, 1937) was kinder, noting, "Noel Madison and Lila Lee, both familiar to screen audiences, accentuate the dramatic values." *Motion Picture Daily* (October 27, 1937) found both good and bad in the production: "There is a vein of artificiality, colored with an emotion that rings off key, running through *Nation Aflame*. The production is good, judged by present-day standards, and it bears the mark of being carefully handled."

With the production and release of his last film, Thomas Dixon had come full circle—from *The Birth of a Nation* to *Nation Aflame*, from the glorification of the Ku Klux Klan to the denigration and disrepute of such vigilante organizations. Some of the wrongs of which he was accused after the making of *The Birth of a Nation* are corrected with *Nation Aflame*. But the sad truth is that *The Birth of a Nation* was a major production with a life and reputation of its own long after Dixon had fallen from popularity, whereas *Nation Aflame* was a very minor film with an extremely short lifespan, one that not only is forgotten today but has not even been preserved.

12

THE FINAL YEARS

The stock market crash of 1929, coupled with abortive efforts to develop a mountain retreat called Wildacres near Little Switzerland in western North Carolina, resulted in the loss not only of Dixon's New York home on Riverside Drive (in 1934) but also of the bulk of his fortune. He was philosophical: "I lost my first fortune in the panic of 1907 assisted by the great banker gamblers of Wall Street. The Federal Reserve Act put a period to the era of money squeezing. We never saw the interest on money driven again to 127 per cent. But I still managed to lose mine."[1]

With a certain amount of pride, Dixon noted that by 1934 he had lost $1.25 million. The *New York Times* (April 17, 1934) reported that the author, who now described himself as "penniless," expressed no regret that he had failed to save any of his income. "That I lived this up and lost the rest of it is beside the question," he said. "The point is that I made this money in twenty-seven years." Dixon remained in demand as a speaker. He had campaigned for Franklin Delano Roosevelt in 1932, and the following year, he broadcast on WJZ-New York that "the NRA coal code is a Magna Carta of human rights for the sweat-smeared, begrimed, sodden dwellers of the world beneath the earth." Other aspects of Roosevelt's New

Deal were less appealing to Dixon, in particular the Federal Theatre, which he regarded as Communist-controlled—and to some extent it was. He argued that participation in the Works Progress Administration (WPA) was contingent upon the applicant's membership in the Communist Party. When Roosevelt came up for reelection in 1936, Dixon campaigned for Republican candidate Alf Landon.

Thomas Dixon last received national attention when he appeared in February 1936 at a convention called by Georgia Governor Gene Talmadge and Texan John Henry Kirby and sponsored by the Southern Committee to Uphold the Constitution. As reported in *Time* (February 10, 1936), the author was "still *Ante-Bellum* politically": "Thomas Dixon rose beneath a huge Confederate flag to denounce the New Deal for the Wagner-Costigan anti-lynching bill ('the most brazen attempt to outrage states' rights by placing Federal bayonets at our backs!') and Mrs. Roosevelt for encouraging the Southern Negro to embrace the tenets of collectivist philosophers." A photograph accompanying the news item shows a tired and somewhat disheveled old man, wearing what appears to be a dressing gown rather than the jacket and tie favored by the other delegates.

In the 1930s, Thomas Dixon returned to North Carolina, no longer a famous and popular author but more a relic of a bygone Southern age. In May 1937, Republican judge, and Wake Forest classmate, Isaac M. Meekins assured him of a small but permanent income by appointing him clerk of the Eastern North Carolina District Federal Court. "As Nathaniel Hawthorne found inspiration in the old Customs House of Salem so I hope to enrich my mind in your courts," he told an interviewer.[2] But there was to be only one last published novel, *The Flaming Sword*, and it is generally seen as a critical failure. Published in 1939 by the Monarch Publishing Company of Atlanta, with thirty full-page illustrations by Edward Shenton, *The Flaming Sword* was perhaps not as unsuccessful as was suggested; certainly it went through some four printings in the first two months of publication, June and July. Monarch Publishing was owned by Edward Young Clarke, a white supremacist and local official of the Ku Klux Klan. He disappeared after promising heavily to promote *The Flaming Sword*, and Dixon, apparently, was left with several thousand unsold copies. Despite a lack of publicity, Dixon did receive some favorable reviews.

The *New York Times* (August 20, 1939) wrote, "Mr. Dixon is no doubt sincere and earnest in all intention. But the reader will very probably regard his novel as a nightmare melodrama, and will see in it the expression of a panic fear." The situation in Europe caused the *New York Herald Tribune* (September 17, 1939) to state, "Whatever you may think of the story, it is not as wildly incredible today as it might have seemed a few short weeks ago."

The Flaming Sword is a sequel to *The Clansman* and *The Birth of a Nation*. It also owes much to Dixon's 1919 play *The Red Dawn*. The central character here is Angela Cameron, the daughter of Ben Cameron, "the Little Colonel," and Elsie Stoneman, both of whom are now deceased. It is also a work of science fiction in that it concludes in 1940 with the United States in much the same situation as depicted in *The Fall of a Nation*. Above all, *The Flaming Sword* is a work of extreme racism, in large part because although the period under discussion, 1900–1940, is far closer to our own time than the Civil War and the Reconstruction era, Dixon makes no effort to tone down his opinions of the Negro, and he explains in a foreword, "I have tried in this story to give an authoritative record of the Conflict of Color in America." *Webster's Biographical Dictionary* describes W.E.B. Du Bois as an American educator, editor, and writer. Marcus Garvey, who advocated the return of the Negro to Africa, is identified as a Jamaican Negro agitator. To Dixon, it is Du Bois who is the agitator and Garvey who is the hero. Du Bois has replaced Booker T. Washington, whom Dixon admired, as the African American leader, and therein lies the problem.

Du Bois glorifies Frederick Douglass, a Negro orator who had the audacity to marry a white woman, and as Captain Collier, a Southerner of the old school, explains it, "What the South stands for alone against the world is the integrity of the White Race" (p. 39). Collier explains to the Camerons' aged Negro servant,

Booker T. Washington led the way to a better understanding between us.

This great black man is teaching his race the lessons of industry, thrift, character and sterling manhood. He is teaching them to avoid politics as a pestilence. He is teaching them to demand nothing until they have proven themselves worthy to receive it. He is telling them to do their duty first as good citizens and that their rights will come in due season. He has given to both races new hope and inspiration. (p. 18)

In part 1 of *The Flaming Sword*, Angela Cameron marries but sees her happiness destroyed when a Negro thug enters her home, kills her husband and young son, and viciously rapes her young sister. In part 2, Angela Cameron takes up residence in New York and studies the Negro "problem." In part 3, she works undercover to try and save her country from overthrow by a combined group of Northern Negroes and American Communists. She fails, at least temporarily, and *The Flaming Sword* concludes in 1940 with President Roosevelt and his cabinet under arrest; fires raging in every Northern city; the South fighting to save Atlanta, New Orleans, and San Antonio; the *Soviet Herald* the only newspaper available in New York; and the Soviet Republic of the United States firmly established. Unlike *The Fall of a Nation*, in which the women of America rally to save the country, *The Flaming Sword* ends very abruptly with only the vague hope that democracy will triumph. Angela is reunited with her childhood Piedmont sweetheart, Phil Stephens, and she announces, "We'll just play our parts. It's glorious to be alive and have the chance!" (p. 562).

Much of this very long novel is taken up with Dixon's lecturing the reader. There is certainly some titillation here. Marie Cameron's rape and humiliation are documented in detail: "For another half hour he subjected her to the agony and shame of indescribable sex atrocities until she sank unconscious to the floor" (p. 174). Even more pages are devoted to the killing of the perpetrator,

Dan Hose. He is slowly emasculated, severely whipped—"When the first man tired wielding the lash, another fresh hand seized it until the black body slumped into unconsciousness" (p. 189)—and eventually burned alive. Some calm, white voices are heard protesting the lynching, but basically, Dixon places the blame for both the rape and the killing on W.E.B. Du Bois and articles published in his periodical, *Crisis*.

The novel is convoluted in terms of Angela Cameron's various relationships. In particular, her and Dixon's admiration of a gangster named Tony Murino is curious. Initially, Murino seems to be depicted as a member of the Mafia. He is subsequently identified as an Irish-born bootlegger, who sells only illegally imported alcohol rather than substandard American-produced liquor and therefore gains Dixon's praise. Equally puzzling is the time spent by Angela Cameron with the Rosicrucian Order in San Jose, California. The theosophical doctrine followed by the order would seem to hold little interest for Dixon, although he cannot refrain from pointing out the singular lack of black faces in California, a situation that Angela Cameron finds comforting. "Don't worry, dear," says Angela's guide, "you've left the Black Shadow in Piedmont, South Carolina" (p. 202).

The most extraordinary subplot in *The Flaming Sword* has Angela Cameron hired to promote *The Birth of a Nation*. Neither Griffith nor Dixon is identified as the creator of the production, but Dixon obviously uses his personal knowledge of the film's history as he has his heroine arrange screenings for the president and the Supreme Court. There is surely no other novel in American history in which the heroine finds herself directly concerned with a real-life film featuring her fictional parents.

Dixon's penultimate work of nonfiction, coauthored with Harry M. Daugherty, was *The Inside Story of the Harding Tragedy*, published in 1932 as a rebuttal to his sister May Dixon Thacker's 1930 tome, *The Strange Death of President Harding*. There she argued that scandal had played a role in the passing of Warren G. Harding, a president for whom Dixon had great respect. Two years after the publication of *The Inside Story of the Harding Tragedy*, Dixon published the curious *A Dreamer in Portugal: The Story of Bernarr Macfadden's Mission to Continental Europe*, in which he discusses a colony in Estoril for young boys, created by physical fitness guru Macfadden. "Christopher Columbus first offered to Portugal the mastery of the world," wrote Dixon. "Four hundred years later Bernarr Macfadden renews the offer" (p. 18). It is an eccentric work, which biographer Raymond A. Cook notes has "the literary quality of a paid advertisement"[3] and which, unfortunately, contains a chapter praising Italian Fascist dictator Benito Mussolini. (Dixon had a copy of Macfadden's 1926 study *Rheumatism*, and concurrently with the publication of *A Dreamer in Portugal*, he acquired a copy of Macfadden's *Fasting for Health*. Whether or not Dixon embraced Macfadden's health fads is not known, but ill health was fast approaching.)

The self-proclaimed "father of physical culture" may have an obvious link to his most ardent fan, Charles Atlas, but the relationship to Thomas Dixon is less apparent. Like Dixon, Macfadden was a Southerner—born in Missouri—and like Dixon, he was a rabid anticommunist and initially a supporter and later an opponent of FDR. Dixon's sister May Dixon Thacker also worked as an editor for Macfadden Publications. Because, also like Dixon, Macfadden left no archives, it is doubtful that anyone will ever uncover the connection between the two men.

From 1934 through 1938, Dixon kept a journal—or, more precisely, a collection of jottings, thoughts, aphorisms, and ideas for potential sermons. Typical of much of the material in the journals is the first entry, dated August 26, in which Dixon wrote, "[Jesus'] work was to rise above limitations. We've got to learn to get this power of rising above our limitations—our duty is to see God in every problem—Live in the present . . . everytime we look back to past & glorify it—you're denying good of today."

A year or more later, he wrote, "The full power of God is working thru me for peace, for freedom & spiritual development & The Presence of God is filling every cell of my body. The Presence of God is filling, illumining every corner of my Soul—Finally in 1938 Remind yourself that the whole world is really the self-expressing of the one great mind." On December 1, 1937, Dixon noted:

> You must know what you want to do—you cant [sic] serve God or get you're [sic] life right until you know what you want to do—When you've found out what you want to do—you're ready. It's got to be something sensible—& that you can do—God doesn't pick out a man who can't draw to be a great artist. Always the action of God will be something within your present compass. It will grow & grow but in [a] general way you must know the sort of thing you want to do. . . . The desire to be a success comes from God. . . . Jesus was probably the best company in the world—There was nothing sanctimonious about Him—he taught Freedom & Prosperity—Make 1938 worthwhile—don't let Dec [sic] 31 1938 find you where you are today.

Despite financial limitations, Dixon did find time for visits to Dallas in September 1936 and to New York in November 1937 and January and February 1938. On February 13, 1938, he mused in his journal, "think of the intelligence just here in N.Y.—the subway—the telephone—Radio City etc.—if that same intell [sic] were turned to spiritual development think how we'd advance."

At some time in the 1920s, Dixon had commenced work on an autobiography, to which he assigned two titles: *The Story of a Minister's Son* and *Southern Horizons*. No version exists in complete form, very little space is devoted to his film career, and it is possible that Dixon never actually finished work on the manuscript. As *The Story of a Minister's Son*, a manuscript survives in three volumes in the library of Gardner-Webb University at Boiling Springs, North Carolina. As a 1982 dissertation for New York University, editor Karen Crowe added some supplemental material to the autobiography and published it two years later as *Southern Horizons*. Based on a reading of the published version, it is obvious that Dixon "borrowed" heavily from his own earlier writings. Some of the best phrases in the book can be found in essays and interviews from fifty or sixty years earlier. Even for one obsessed with Southern history and culture, the text is dull. James Zebulon Wright is strongly of the opinion that Thomas Dixon would never have wished for *Southern Horizons* to be published in its extant form and that much of it may have been cobbled together by Madelyn Dixon from various sources, including perhaps her own imagination.[4]

The author did keep abreast of Southern literature. He contacted Margaret Mitchell, praising *Gone with the Wind*, of which he planned to write a study. To his presumed delight, she replied, "I was practically raised on your books, and love them very much."[5] Mitchell also recalled that as a seven-year-old she had dramatized Dixon's *The Traitor*; the clansmen were dressed in their fathers' shirts with the tails cut off.

The demise of Dixon's creative career was perhaps linked to the death of his wife, Harriet, on December 29, 1937. She had served as his secretary and claimed to have transcribed more than five millions words that her husband had written down in longhand using a soft-leaded pencil. Supposedly, she wore out five typewriters in the process of copying his manuscripts. "Her playing on a piano was part of the preparation for all my novels," he told an interviewer. "Stretched on a sofa, I used to listen to her music and work out the plots and characters of my stories."[6]

Harriet Dixon was an understanding and tolerant wife. By an unknown woman, Dixon had an illegitimate son, Phillip Scism, and when the young man married, Dixon and his wife took the couple into the bosom of the family.

Dixon had taken up residence in Raleigh at the Sir Walter Hotel on Fayetteville Street, an affluent establishment viewed as the pulse of political life in North Carolina and the center of sophisticated society.[7] In February 1939, in his rooms at the Sir Walter Hotel, Dixon was stricken by a cerebral hemorrhage. Madelyn

Donovan, Dixon's leading lady in *The Mark of the Beast*, had helped in research on *The Flaming Sword*. After reading the proofs of the new novel, she came to Raleigh and married the ailing, bedridden Thomas Dixon on March 20, 1939.

It seems doubtful that the long-term relationship between Dixon and Madelyn Donovan was purely platonic. She was certainly never far from Dixon's thoughts, and in June 1935, he had written in his journals, "Madelyn I have a great success waiting for you I want to do it thru you." In her defense, Madelyn never tried to lure Dixon away from his wife. She was "the other woman," who had been part of Dixon's life at least since 1923 if not earlier. She became, as Raymond Rohauer noted, "Dixon's researcher, collaborator, girl Friday and, increasingly through the years, confidante and companion. She became virtually a one-man woman, although the man was not hers to have."[8] She cared for him with deep devotion, and with even greater passion, she defended his memory, ever watchful and paranoid of researchers and would-be biographers and fearful of colleges and universities seeking her husband's papers.

Her husband was neither well nor wealthy. From the Sir Walter Hotel, the couple moved to a small apartment and then a tract home in Raleigh at 1507 Hillsboro Street. There, Thomas Dixon died on April 3, 1946. He was buried the following day at the Sunset Cemetery in Shelby, North Carolina, behind the Episcopal Church of the Redeemer. "Standing there in one spot, you can almost reach out and touch the gravestones of W.J. Cash, Thomas Dixon and my grandmother," notes Charleen Swansea, adding that Cash's final resting place is small and insignificant compared to that of Dixon, "who has a gravestone that looks like the Washington Monument."[9]

Dixon's death was recorded in both *Newsweek* and *Time* (on April 15, 1946). The local newspaper, the *Raleigh News and Observer*, devoted more space to Dixon's passing than it had to the death of President Franklin D. Roosevelt.

Although subject to multiple interpretations, comments by

North Carolina's Governor R. Gregg Cherry cannot be disputed: "North Carolina has lost a distinguished son. Through his long list of popular and worthwhile novels, his activities on the lecture platform and in the pulpit, Thomas Dixon has made a distinctive contribution to North Carolina and to the nation."[10]

Following Dixon's death, his library of books was donated to Gardner-Webb University in Boiling Springs, North Carolina. His widow and the editor of the local newspaper suggested that Dixon be cremated and his ashes kept in the Gardner-Webb library. "That might confer upon us a certain uniqueness, but I confess I'm happier that his final resting place is elsewhere," comments the library's director.[11]

In 1908, Thomas Dixon was described as "the most interesting man the State [of North Carolina] has ever mothered."[12] The same writer also noted, "whoever has heard him speak will never forget the thrill of the man's presence."[13] Almost forty years later, there were few who had such a recollection, whether positive or negative, and almost a century later, there are even fewer familiar with Thomas Dixon's oratory, novels, or motion pictures. In the mid-1930s, Thomas Dixon wrote in his journal, "ask self—if you dropped dead tonight How many people would really miss you, how many lives would really be poorer—because I'd gone." In retrospect, the answer is perhaps very few.

Like Major Daniel Norton in *The Sins of the Father*, Thomas Dixon was caught "in the grip of the sins of centuries" (p. 452)— trapped by the remembrance of the slavery that he abhorred and the price that he believed the United States of America was doomed to pay for that sin. Today, we are no less caught in the grip of the sins of the centuries, but they are of far greater number and offer a far greater threat to our humanity.

13

RAYMOND ROHAUER AND
THE DIXON LEGACY

Had he not been writing or producing films, Thomas Dixon would still have remained in public view, thanks entirely to the continued controversy generated by the many reissues of *The Birth of a Nation*. The first reissue came in 1921 and helped generate additional support for the Ku Klux Klan. When the film played New York in 1922, the *New York Times* (December 6, 1922) reported that Klan members were present, "seen cheering whenever a hooded and gowned figure appeared." In the *New York Daily News* (December 7, 1922), P.W. Gallico wrote, "*The Birth of a Nation* stands up to us not as a relic trotted forth for curiosity's sake but as a powerful motion picture which might have been made only yesterday." Along with Klan approbation, there were massed protests against the film in 1921 in both New York and Detroit. Large numbers of Klansmen attended a February 1924 presentation at the Auditorium Theatre in Chicago, and historian Terry Ramsaye reported, "The patronage of the Ku Klux Klan was credited with giving this run its extraordinary success."[1] Another major reissue in 1926 led *Variety* (January 6, 1926) to comment that the film was "eleven years old next March and still a great picture."

With the coming of sound, *The Birth of a Nation* was recut and reissued as a sound motion picture, with a recorded score based on the original by Joseph Carl Breil and orchestrated by Louis Gottschalk. In the summer of 1930, at the Las Palmas Avenue studios of the Triangle Film Corp. in Hollywood, D.W. Griffith directed a new prologue for the film.[2] The eminent cinematographer Karl Struss, who had photographed Griffith's 1928 production of *The Drums of Love*, was behind the camera, with Bert Sutch credited as assistant director and Edward Seward as head electrician. The five-minute prologue begins as three children, Byron Sage, Betsy Heiler, and Dawn O'Day (who later changed her name to Anne Shirley), spot Griffith and actor Walter Huston (the star of Griffith's *Abraham Lincoln*), dressed in tuxedoes and apparently enjoying an after-dinner smoke. The children creep nearer in order to hear what the two men are saying. Griffith presents Huston with a Civil War sword after first asking him for a nickel or dime in that this is a "sharp" gift. (In order to protect oneself, the recipient of a "sharp" gift such as a sword should always pay for his benefactor's generosity.) Huston asks Griffith if he told his father's story in *The Birth of a Nation*, to which Griffith offers a doubtful No. After quoting Pontius Pilate as to what is the truth, the director then points out—importantly—that the Klan served a purpose then. The film concludes with aerial shots of Atlanta, Forth Worth, Dallas, Houston, New Orleans, and Memphis, with their skyscrapers heralding the rise of the new South; this footage does not survive in extant prints.

The sound reissue was to include at least one talking sequence, written by Walter Huston and Campbell MacCulloch, but that did not materialize, perhaps because of the cost or perhaps because commentators such as Louella Parsons, writing in the *Los Angeles Examiner* (June 15, 1930), asked, "Why not bring it back in its silent version and give those who never saw it a chance to see it? Put in music and sound synchronization, if necessary, but why a talking sequence?" The *New York Times* (December 22, 1930) hailed the film in its sound reissue as "still startling effectively."

Dixon was sent a copy of the cutting continuity for the sound reissue and presumably gave it his approval. Dixon may also have been involved in writing the screenplay for a remake in 1936.[3]

Reviewing the sound reissue, *Variety* (December 24, 1930) wrote, "There's too much epic history involved to ever let the *Nation* die altogether. It's a landmark and certainly the champion reissue film of them all—which it will so remain." In years to come, *The Birth of a Nation* was also to be a reissue nightmare. Because of the age of the film, no effort had been made to obtain a Production Code seal of approval, as was required under the self-regulating and self-censoring efforts of the Hollywood film industry from the 1930s onward. In May 1938, the Royal Film Exchange, Inc., in New York decided to apply for such a seal, and members of the Production Code Administration were forced to sit down and view *The Birth of a Nation*. Staffer Francis Harmon wrote:

> It is my opinion that regardless of any justification which may have existed for those activities of the original Ku Klux Klan, which were without legal sanction, this portrayal creates sympathy for those who take the law into their own hands and approbation for their unlawful acts and tends to inspire in others a desire for imitation. The fact that the victims of the Klan's vengeance are members of another race, accentuates the problem and makes the Code violation more serious.
>
> Another section of the Code states that miscegenation is prohibited and defines this as "sex relationship between the white and black races." While no actual sex relationship of the prohibited kind is shown, the film contains two references to it.

With the passage of time, it would appear that Thomas Dixon's views on miscegenation had become those of a united film industry. Will Hays, president of the Motion Picture Producers and Distributors of America, Inc., spoke with Martin Quigley, publisher of the influential trade paper *Motion Picture Herald* and a leading

197

Catholic responsible for the establishment of the Legion of Decency. Quigley was surprised that there should be anything unsatisfactory with the production. Ultimately, the Production Code Administration decided it might be best to ask the distributor to withdraw his request for a seal, but without putting anything in writing.[4]

Will Hays's successor, Eric Johnson, had a similar problem in 1954 when plans were announced for a remake by a group headed by Ted Thal, president of Thalco and associated with the Owens-Corning Fiberglas Corporation. Thal and his associate Phil L. Ryan claimed to have purchased rights to the film for $750,000 and said the remake would cost $8 million and include a cast of fifteen thousand soldiers. Walter White, executive secretary of the NAACP, wrote Johnson, urging his organization to issue a statement opposing the remake. White stated, "We could conceive of no time when such a picture as *The Birth of a Nation* could do more harm domestically as well as internationally."[5] Happily for all concerned, the remake project fell through, as did plans for a remake in 1960 by King Bros. Productions.

At the time of the planned King Bros. remake, *Variety* (April 13, 1960) estimated that the film had grossed more than $50 million over some forty-five years. While unable to verify the amount, the trade paper pointed out that it made *The Birth of a Nation* the biggest moneymaker of all time, ahead of even *Gone with the Wind*. It was also identified as the most controversial film ever made in the United States, in racial terms matching the notoriety of the Nazi production *Jew Suess*.

The original production continued to be screened and continued to generate controversy. In April 1939, a Denver theatre manager was fined fourteen hundred dollars and sentenced to 120 days in jail for six screenings of *The Birth of a Nation* in violation of a city ordinance prohibiting the showing of motion pictures that were "contrary to good order and morals and the public welfare and which tend to stir up or engender race prejudice, or are calculated to disturb the peace." In a most extraordinary essay by David Platt in the communist *Daily Worker* (February 22, 1940), *The Birth of a Nation* and its maker were accused of setting in motion reactionary forces that led to screen censorship, of being responsible for America's entry into an imperialistic war, and finally, of retarding the real development of motion pictures. In 1946, New York's Museum of Modern Art declined to screen *The Birth of a Nation* as part of its "History of the Motion Picture" cycle, noting, "Fully aware of the greatness of the film and of its artistic and historic importance, we have also had sufficient and repeated evidence of the potency of the anti-Negro bias and believe that exhibiting it at this time of heightened social tensions cannot be justified."

With the production of *Gone with the Wind* in 1939, D.W. Griffith became very concerned that *The Birth of a Nation* might be misplaced in film history. He wrote to Dixon, "You couldn't very well be out of mind what with all the fuss that has been made of *Birth of a Nation* within the past year, with the constant comparisons to *Gone with the Wind*. It seems to the general public, that *Birth of a Nation* is still the yard stick by which all pictures are measured. Little did we what, twenty six years ago, that if we never did another thing, we would still gain quite a slice of immortality. You for the story, and I for the direction." Griffith concluded, "I am thankful indeed that I am in as good health today, as ever in my life, and hope the same is true of you. Hope you have kept your long, lean, aristocratic figure—within reason, and your well remembered oak, or should I say southern walnut, vitality."[6]

Pickets were on hand when the film played at New York's Republic Theatre in October 1947. It was banned by Boston's city censor in April 1952 and by Atlanta's municipal censor in June 1959. In January 1965, the New York state conference of the NAACP announced that it would fight any reissue of *The Birth of a Nation* in that state. Riverside, California, where the film had first been seen, canceled a screening at its municipal museum in March 1978, and in June 1980, vandals attacked the Richelieu Cinema in San Francisco and forced screenings there to end. Like the American South under the Klan, the theatre management admitted that it was "giving in to lawless and mindless assaults."[7]

The Library of Congress became embroiled in the *Birth of a Nation* controversy in 1988, when President Reagan signed what was called the National Film Preservation Act. Despite its title, the act had nothing whatsoever to do with film preservation, but rather established the National Film Registry, to which the Librarian of Congress, in collaboration with an appointed panel, would add twenty-five films a year. This exercise in bureaucratic futility, which cost the taxpayer only a reported quarter million dollars a year and was therefore not worth protesting, required that copyright owners of the registered films could alter them only if they affixed a label to each, advising as to the alteration.

Various self-appointed arbiters of American film art and history were appointed to work with the Librarian of Congress in announcing the first twenty-five films. Despite its obvious and major importance in the development of the art of the motion picture, *The Birth of a Nation* was conspicuously absent from the initial listing. Its inclusion would, of course, have offended African Americans, and the Librarian of Congress and his board were anything if not political. (At one point, a noted feminist on the board refused to consider Alfred Hitchcock's *Psycho* for inclusion because it showed violence against women.) Laughably, although *The Birth of a Nation* was excluded, an obscure 1969 film, *The Learning Tree*, directed by a black American, made the cut. It was not until 1992 that *The Birth of a Nation* was added; "the Library has otherwise treated it as if it were toxic waste," reported the *New York Times*.[8]

A terrified Library of Congress eventually considered the issue of *The Birth of a Nation* on April 25, 1994, when a panel of three "experts" gathered to discuss the film. The "experts" were a white historian of black film history, Thomas Cripps; an obscure and aging black actor, director, and producer named William Greaves; and John Hope Franklin, an African American professor emeritus of history at Duke University. Only Cripps possessed academic qualifications to be described as an expert, and only Cripps adopted a moderate stance, although even William Greaves had to admit that *The Birth of a Nation* is "a hell of a film."

Equally cowardly and indefensible are the actions of the Directors Guild of America, whose life achievement award had long been named in honor of D.W. Griffith. In December 1999, the guild's national board voted unanimously to retire the award, claiming that though its namesake was "a brilliant pioneer director," he had "helped foster intolerable racial stereotypes." The guild membership was not asked for its opinion on the matter, and the guild refused to discuss its decision. At least one organization, the National Society of Film Critics, took issue with the guild, stating, "The recasting of this honor, which had been awarded appropriately in D.W. Griffith's name since 1953, is a depressing example of 'political correctness' as an erasure, and rewriting of American film history, causing a grave disservice to the reputation of a pioneering American filmmaker."

As the Confederate flag ceased to fly over the capital cities of the South, so did elements with American society and the American film industry decide that D.W. Griffith, Thomas Dixon, and *The Birth of a Nation* were to be consigned to the scrap heap of history. Even outside of the United States, *The Birth of a Nation* was at risk. In the United Kingdom, the British Board of Film Classification ruled that the film could only be released on video with a lengthy, six-hundred-word disclaimer describing the production as "inflammatory" and denouncing its maker's "unthinkable racial prejudice" and "distortion of history."

"Certainly this criticism was always there; every time the film was shown, a fresh batch of criticism would appear," said Evelyn Baldwin Griffith, the director's second wife and widow.

It was always there and it did always plague him. I think it's a little ridiculous to put the blame on a man who told the story the way he saw it. The Negro's lot was different in those days. There's no point in getting away from it. I can remember when I was a child. Negroes were not permitted to sit in a theatre; they had to go upstairs. They couldn't sit on a bus; they had to go in the back. They couldn't eat in a restaurant. You know this isn't right, but don't blame the passerby or someone who tells you about it. This is unfair criticism.

I know when we went to Florida, we had a Negro chauffeur, an immaculate and a very nice person. And every time we went in the deep South, we had trouble finding a place for him to stay, a place for him to eat. And one time in a public park, he was mobbed because he wanted to drink from a water fountain. And the people that mobbed him were very dirty, white people who hadn't washed in some time. This upset Mr. Griffith very much indeed. Is this racism? I don't know.[9]

It was claimed that Griffith failed to give Dixon adequate credit or recognition for his contribution to *The Birth of a Nation*, and Harry Aitken's brother, Roy, wrote, "Thomas Dixon smarted under the slight for many years and frequently told Harry and me so."[10] In reality, it was probably Harry Aitken who failed to receive proper credit from Griffith and who was slighted by the lack of publicity in regard to his being the producer of *The Birth of a Nation*. Published reports on the various reissues of the film seldom failed to mention Dixon's involvement.

■ ■ ■ ■ ■

The Thomas Dixon story, particularly as relative to the motion picture, might have ended with his death and the demise of whatever literary status was left him at the end of his life, had it not been for a remarkable, if disreputable, figure named Raymond Rohauer. His presence and his ulterior motives help to update the legend of Thomas Dixon. While perhaps only a footnote to a biography of Thomas Dixon, Raymond Rohauer is prominent in the tale of Dixon as a Southern filmmaker.

Following Dixon's death, his widow, Madelyn, became obsessed with protecting his image, perhaps rightly in view of the extreme prejudice against her husband and his work. She would share information with students and scholars and then almost immediately turn against them. Items were donated to local universities and promptly recalled. When James Zebulon Wright went to see her in connection with his dissertation, she thought he was the young Thomas Dixon. "She was almost insane," recalls Wright. She would insist that he eat something, serve him the same plate of food five times, and then remove it before he could take a bite.[11]

Madelyn Dixon died in a Raleigh, North Carolina, hospital on September 20, 1975, and was buried next to her husband in Shelby, North Carolina. There were no reported survivors, nor money for such survivors to inherit. But there was Raymond Rohauer, and he was not interested in Mrs. Dixon's financial worth but rather in the rights she owned, as Dixon's widow, to the film version of *The Birth of a Nation*.

Born in Buffalo, New York, in 1924, Raymond Rohauer moved to California in 1942 and quickly became an ardent film buff. In 1947, he wrote, produced, directed, and edited a five-reel 16mm experimental psychological drama titled *Whirlpool*. The film failed to serve as a means of entry into the film industry, and instead, Rohauer turned to exhibition, taking over the Coronet Theatre in Los Angeles in 1950 and screening various retrospective series devoted to all aspects of motion picture art and history.[12]

Rohauer did not always bother to clear the rights to the films he screened at the Coronet Theatre, and the more he became involved in acquiring and exhibiting "old" films, the more he realized there was confusion as to their copyright. Under the law as it stood at that time, the original copyright owner was required to renew the copyright twenty-eight years after the initial registration. Failure to do so threw the film into the public domain. Many original registrants had died in the first twenty-eight-year copyright period, and relatives and other heirs were unaware of the need to protect their assets by renewing the copyrights. Raymond Rohauer set out to locate such "heirs" and to acquire the rights from them. He was not always particularly careful as to whether the rights were valid or even if the films were still under copyright.

If a film was out of copyright, Rohauer would quietly reedit it, perhaps add minor additional material, and then copyright it as a new work. If there were no legal successors to the original copyright claimant, Rohauer would track down someone associated with the film in a lesser capacity, perhaps a writer or the long-forgotten star, and obtain from that person a "quit claim." Such "quit claims" did not recognize that the individual concerned had any legitimate claim to the film or right to renew its copyright, but such minor matters of legal nicety did not concern Raymond Rohauer.

Rohauer's first major coup came in 1954 when he began a professional relationship with Buster Keaton. He negotiated control of the rights to Keaton's silent films, and at the same time—and certainly to his credit—he helped revive interest in the comedian's career and enabled him to end his days once again as a celebrity. Among the major names in whose work Rohauer had an interest were Harry Langdon, W.C. Fields, and Charlie Chaplin (through acquisition of the outtakes of the comedian's films that had been abandoned when he was denied reentry to the United States in the early 1950s).

In all, there are 293 entries in the copyright catalog of the Library of Congress in which Rohauer's name appears. On February 22, 1972, he told *Variety* that he had "the rights to about 12,000 films, all American." With his acquisition of these supposed "rights," Raymond Rohauer began harassing those who had innocently been screening early films not for profit but in the public interest. The Film Department of the Museum of Modern Art was a frequent target of his nuisance lawsuits. More and more, individuals and organizations found themselves recipients of threatening letters from Rohauer's army of attorneys. Rohauer had become a monster trying to buy up the golden age of the cinema. As one writer had it, "Rohauer is to the movies what Dr. Jekyll is to medicine."[13]

In 1964, Rohauer contracted with Paul Killiam, a New York classic film distributor, to acquire the theatrical rights to the films of D.W. Griffith, with Killiam retaining television rights. Killiam had acquired the "rights" to the films from the D.W. Griffith estate, but the majority, if not all, of the titles were in the public domain, and the master elements had been deposited and preserved at the Museum of Modern Art (where Griffith had deposited the film elements in 1937). It was obviously not in Rohauer's best interest to control rights to public domain titles, and so it was necessary for him to "revive" the copyrights in at least some of the Griffith features.

"Along about 1964," Rohauer reminisced, "I had reached a point where I felt it would be helpful to clarify the copyright situation of *The Birth*, so that the actual owners could be approached with my plans for future use of the picture."[14] Rohauer discovered that *The Birth of a Nation* had been copyrighted twice. The first copyright was in the name of D.W. Griffith, and the second in the name of Epoch, the corporation created by Harry Aitken to handle distribution of the film. Epoch had renewed its copyright, but Griffith had failed to renew his. The 1930 sound version was not copyrighted until 1972 and 1976, when Rohauer registered it as an unpublished work.

It was generally assumed, since Griffith had failed to renew his copyright, that *The Birth of a Nation* was in the public domain and freely available for exhibition and distribution by any interested party.

Rohauer telephoned Madelyn Dixon in Raleigh, and eventually she agreed to meet him on neutral territory, a hotel lobby. The next day, Rohauer was invited to the Dixon home, where, unlike James Zebulon Wright, he was treated to "a sumptuous meal."[15] Mrs. Dixon agreed that Rohauer might approach Harry Aitken's brother, Roy,[16] on her behalf in an effort to obtain an accounting of revenues from *The Birth of a Nation*, and she assigned to him all of Thomas Dixon's literary rights. "I made it a point to see her several times a year, whether there was business to discuss or not, and in time this became a sort of ritual—especially when she finally accepted the fact that I was not about to betray her confidence."[17]

As "owner" of Dixon's autobiography, Raymond Rohauer permitted a New York University student named Karen Crowe to edit the manuscript as a 1982 dissertation.[18] As such, it is somewhat unsatisfactory in that no footnotes are provided by the editor.

With the ownership of Dixon's share in *The Birth of a Nation*, Rohauer was able to threaten Roy Aitken with legal action over nonpayment of royalties to the Thomas Dixon estate. Basically, Rohauer blackmailed Aitken into selling ownership of Epoch, a corporation whose sole assets would appear to be the screen rights to the novel of *The Clansman* and the expired copyright in *The Birth of a Nation*. To finance the purchase of Epoch, Rohauer brought in Jay Ward Enterprises, best known for its creation of the Rocky and Bullwinkle cartoon series.

Utilizing the Epoch copyright and renewal in *The Birth of a Nation* as legal leverage, Epoch and its agent Raymond Rohauer sued Paul Killiam and the Museum of Modern Art for infringing Epoch's copyright in the film. In the meantime, the American Film Institute had acquired various film elements relating to *The Birth of a Nation*, and these had been deposited at the Library of Congress. In 1972, in a remarkable display of bravura, Epoch filed a copyright infringement suit against the American Film Institute and sent federal marshals with a seizure warrant to the Library of Congress.

The staff of the library's motion picture section was at a loss to know what to do. Since when did federal marshals enter government property and seize government assets? And why had the federal marshals chosen to appear at lunchtime, when senior staff members were conveniently out of the building? Eventually, the library's chief legal counsel was called, and he summoned the library's security guards to eject the federal marshals from the premises. The cans of film were ultimately "seized" and "sealed" but remained physically in the custody of the Library of Congress and stored in its nitrate vaults in Suitland, Maryland. The suit against the American Film Institute was settled in 1974 for the princely sum of $250.

In 1975, Epoch's action against Paul Killiam and the Museum of Modern Art got under way in Room 2704 of the Federal Court House in New York's Foley Square. Lillian Gish was the first witness to be called by the defense, determined to prove that Griffith was the creator of the film and therefore the only one with a legal right to copyright and renew that copyright. Asked her name, she replied, "Lillian Gish," and then proceeded to spell it out, just in case the court stenographer should have any doubt as to her identity. In answer to a question about her profession, she announced, "From the age of five, I have been an actress." When queried whether she was the star of *The Birth of a Nation*, she responded, much to the amusement of the court, "Oh, there were no stars in Mr. Griffith's films."

Miss Gish was followed by Joseph Henabery, who delighted the judge with his confession to having played Abraham Lincoln in *The Birth* and by telling him to keep out of the questioning. Both celebrities, however, carried little weight with the court. The judge dismissed most of their evidence as hearsay, much to the vehement protestations of Miss Gish that she was there and that she should know of what she spoke.

Despite the personalities offered as witnesses by the defendants—Andrew Sarris also appeared to explain the auteur theory to the jury in an attempt to prove that Griffith was the author of *The Birth of a Nation*—the court found largely in favor of the plaintiff. In the verdict handed down on June 27, it was held that Epoch Corporation owned the title to the film, through its copyright and renewal, but the jury agreed that the Museum of Modern Art's license to physical ownership of its materials on *The Birth of a Nation* was in force and that there had been no breach of such license.

The verdict was overturned by the U.S. Circuit Court of Appeals on August 13, 1975, when it ruled that D.W. Griffith was the creator and legal "author" of *The Birth of a Nation*. Epoch Corporation had no right to renew the copyright, and the film was legitimately in the public domain. On March 8, 1976, the U.S. Supreme Court let stand the lower court's dismissal of copyright infringement and refused to review the decision by the U.S. Circuit Court of Appeals. More than a decade after Raymond Rohauer had initiated his various lawsuits and 101 years after the birth of D.W. Griffith, his most famous work, *The Birth of a Nation*, was legally in the public domain.

With the ruling in New York, the case in Washington, D.C., was essentially null and void. There was still arguing between Paul Killiam and Epoch as to ownership of the film elements at the Library of Congress, and eventually in September 1977, the Department of Justice was forced to file suit to determine which party had control of the materials. Following much mediation by American Film Institute archivist Larry Karr, all parties agreed to a secret resolution on November 6, 1979. Thus ended what John Kominski, chief legal counsel for the Library of Congress, had dubbed "The Afterbirth of a Nation."[19]

Raymond Rohauer died of AIDS on November 10, 1987, and left his estate to his partner Kristian Chester. After the latter succumbed to AIDS, the Raymond Rohauer Collection was bequeathed to the couple's two cats. Animal rights activist Thomas Dixon would surely have approved.

FILMOGRAPHY

The Birth of a Nation. Epoch Producing Corp. Director: D.W. Griffith. Screenplay: D.W. Griffith and Frank E. Woods, based on the novel *The Clansman* and the play of the same name by Thomas Dixon. Photography: G.W. Bitzer. With Henry B. Walthall, Miriam Cooper, Mae Marsh, Josephine Crowell, Spottiswoode Aitken, Lillian Gish, Elmer Clifton, and Robert Harron. 12 reels. Premiere screening in Los Angeles on February 8, 1915, and in New York on March 3, 1915.

The Fall of a Nation. National Drama Corp. Director and Screenplay: Thomas Dixon. Photography: William C. Thompson, John W. Boyle, Claude H. "Bud" Wales, and Jack R. Young. With Lorraine Huling, Percy Standing, Arthur Shirley, Flora MacDonald, and Paul Willis. 8 reels. Released on September 18, 1916.

The Foolish Virgin. Clara Kimball Young Film Corp. Director and Screenplay: Albert Capellani, based on the novel by Thomas Dixon. Photography: Jacques Monteran, Hal Young, and George Peters. With Clara Kimball Young, Conway Tearle, Paul Capellani, Catherine Proctor, and Sheridan Tansey. 7 reels. Released on December 18, 1916.

The One Woman. Mastercraft Photo-Play Corp. Director: Reginald Barker. Screenplay: Harry Chandlee and E. Richard Schayer, based on the novel by Thomas Dixon. Photography: Clyde De Vinna. With W. Lawson Butt, Clara Williams, Hershel Mayall, Thurston Hall, Ben Alexander, and Adda Gleason. 6 reels. Released in October 1918.

FILMOGRAPHY

Bolshevism on Trial. Mayflower Photoplay Corp. Director: Harley Knoles. Screenplay: Harry Chandlee, based on the novel *Comrades*, by Thomas Dixon. Photography: Philip Hatkin. With Robert Frazer, Leslie Stowe, Howard Truesdell, Jim Savage, Pinna Nesbit, and Valda Valkyrien. 6 reels. Released on April 19, 1919.

Wing Toy. Fox Film Corp. Director: Howard M. Mitchell. Screenplay: Thomas Dixon, based on the story by Pearl Doles Bell. Photography: Glen MacWilliams. With Shirley Mason, Raymond McKee, Edward McWade, Harry S. Northrup, and Betty Schade. 6 reels. Released on January 30, 1921.

Where Men Are Men. Vitagraph Company of America. Director: William Duncan. Screenplay: Thomas Dixon. Photography: George Robinson. With William Duncan, Edith Johnson, George Stanley, Tom Wilson, Gertrude Wilson, and Harry Lonsdale. 5 reels. Released on September 1, 1921.

Bring Him In. Vitagraph Company of America. Directors: Earle Williams and Robert Ensminger. Screenplay: Thomas Dixon, based on a story by H.H. Van Loan. Photography: Jack MacKenzie. With Earle Williams, Fritzi Ridgeway, Elmer Dewey, Ernest Van Pelt, and Paul Weigel. 5 reels. Released on October 16, 1921.

Thelma. Chester Bennett Productions. Director: Chester Bennett. Screenplay: Thomas Dixon, based on the novel by Marie Corelli. Photography: Jack MacKenzie. With Jane Novak, Barbara Tennant, Gordon Mullen, Bert Sprotte, and Vernon Steele. 6 reels. Released on November 26, 1922.

The Mark of the Beast. Thomas Dixon Productions. Director and Screenplay: Thomas Dixon. Photography: Harry Fischbeck. With Robert Ellis, Madelyn Clare, Warner Richmond, Gustav von Seyffertitz, and Helen Ware. 6 reels. Released on June 24, 1923.

The Foolish Virgin. Columbia Pictures. Director: George W. Hill. Screenplay: Lois Zellner, based on the novel by Thomas Dixon. Photography: Norbert Brodin. With Elaine Hammerstein, Robert Frazer, Gladys Brockwell, Phyllis Haver, Lloyd Whitlock, and Irene Hunt. 6 reels. Released on August 15, 1924.

The Painted Lady. Fox Film Corp. Director: Chester Bennett. Screenplay: Thomas Dixon, based on the *Saturday Evening Post* story by Larry Evans. Photography: Alfred Gosden. With George O'Brien, Dorothy Mackaill, Harry T. Morey, Lucille Hutton, Lucille Ricksen, Margaret McWade, and John Miljan. 7 reels. Released on September 28, 1924.

The Great Diamond Mystery. Fox Film Corp. Director: Denison Clift. Screenplay: Thomas Dixon, based on a story by Shannon Fife. With Shirley Mason, Jackie Saunders, Harry von Meter, John Cossar, Philo McCullough, and William Collier Jr. 5 reels. Released on October 5, 1924.

The Brass Bowl. Fox Film Corp. Director: Jerome Storm. Screenplay: Thomas Dixon, based on the novel by Louis Joseph Vance. With Edmund Lowe, Claire Adams, Jack Duffy, J. Farrell MacDonald, and Leo White. 6 reels. Released on November 16, 1924.

Champion of Lost Causes. Fox Film Corp. Director: Chester Bennett. Screenplay: Thomas Dixon, based on the *Flynn's Magazine* story by Max Brand. Photography: Ernest Palmer. With Edmund Lowe, Barbara Bedford, Walter McGrail, Jack McDonald, and Alec B. Francis. 5 reels. Released on January 22, 1925.

The Trail Rider. Fox Film Corp. Director: William S. Van Dyke. Screenplay: Thomas Dixon, based on the novel by George Washington Ogden. Photography: Reginald Lyons. With Buck Jones, Nancy Deaver, Lucy Fox, Carl Stockdale, and Jack McDonald. 5 reels. Released on February 22, 1925.

The Gentle Cyclone. Fox Film Corp. Director: William S. Van Dyke. Screenplay: Thomas Dixon, based on the *Western Story Magazine* story "Peg Leg and the Kidnapper," by Frank R. Buckley. Photography: Chester Lyons and Reginald Lyons. With Buck Jones, Rose Blossom, Will Walling, Reed Howes, Grant Withers, and Oliver Hardy. 5 reels. Released on January 27, 1926.

Nation Aflame. A Victor and Edward Halperin Production for Treasure Pictures Corp. Director: Victor Hugo Halperin. Original story by Thomas Dixon, in collaboration with Oliver Drake and Rex Hale. Screenplay: Oliver Drake. Additional Dialogue: William Lively. Photography: Arthur Martinelli. With Noel Madison, Norma Trelvar, Lila Lee, Douglas Walton, Harry Holman, and Snub Pollard. 8 reels. Released on October 16, 1937.

NOTES

INTRODUCTION

1. Raymond Allen Cook, "The Literary Principles of Thomas Dixon," *Georgia Review,* p. 97.

2. F. Garvin Davenport Jr., "Thomas Dixon's Mythology of Southern History," p. 350.

3. A statement from 1883 quoted in Paul H. Buck, *The Road to Reunion, 1865–1900,* New York: Vintage Books, 1959, p. 295.

4. *Moving Picture World*, June 3, 1916, p. 1671.

5. When Leni Riefenstahl came to New York in November 1937, she visited a Harlem nightclub and commented on the Negro stage show: "It is breathtaking jungle ability, but no brains and no inspiration. Did a Negro ever make a great invention?" She continued, "The Jews are backing the Negroes politically. Under their influence the Negroes will become communists, and so the Jew and the Negro will bring bolshevism to America." It is a comment with which Dixon would agree in part, but unlike Riefenstahl, he would never denigrate the Jews. See Ernest Jaeger, "How Leni Riefenstahl Became Hitler's Girlfriend," *Hollywood Tribune,* June 2, 1939, p. 11. Riefenstahl's comments echo those of Thomas Dixon in *The Leopard's Spots*: "The African has held one fourth of this globe for 3000 years. He has never taken one step in progress or rescued one jungle from the ape and the adder, except as the slave of a superior race" (p. 441). And also those of Dr. Cameron to Austin Stoneman in *The Clansman*:

> Since the dawn of history the negro has owned the Continent
> of Africa—rich beyond the dream of a poet's fancy, crunching

acres of diamonds beneath his bare black feet. Yet he never picked one up from the dust until a white man showed to him its glittering light. His land swarmed with powerful and docile animals, yet he never dreamed a harness, cart, or sled. A hunter by necessity, he never made an axe, spear or arrow-head worth preserving beyond the moment of its use. He lives as an ox, content to graze for an hour. In a land of stone and timber he never sawed a foot of lumber, carved a block, or built a house save of broken sticks and mud. With league on league of ocean strand and miles of inland seas, for four thousand years he watched their surface ripple upon the wind, heard the thunder of the surf on his beach, the howl of the storm over his head, gazed on the dim blue horizon calling him to worlds that lie beyond, and yet he never dreamed a sail! He lived as his fathers lived—stole his food, worked his wife, sold his children, ate his brother, content to drink, sing, dance, and sport as the ape! (p. 292)

6. Lee B. Weathers, *Thomas Dixon,* p. 1.

7. Thomas Dixon, *Southern Horizons*, p. 312.

8. Irving Harlow Hart, "Best Sellers in Fiction during the First Quarter of the Twentieth Century," *Publishers Weekly*, February 14, 1925, pp. 525–27.

9. *Motion Picture News*, July 7, 1923, p. 46.

10. Quotes from Dixon's entry in Martin Seymour-Smith and Andrew C. Kimmens, *World Authors, 1900–1950*, p. 726.

11. Raymond Allen Cook, *Thomas Dixon*, p. 52.

12. Quotes in *Shelby (N.C.) Cleveland Times*, January 3, 1967, p. 8.

13. May 14, 1924, speech by Dixon to the American Booksellers Association, New York, reported in the *New York Times*, May 15, 1924, p. 21.

14. Brian R. McGee, "Thomas Dixon's *The Clansman*," p. 300.

15. Lynde Denig, "Thomas Dixon Lauds the Cinema," p. 1671.

16. Thomas Dixon, "Booker T. Washington and the Negro," p. 1.

17. Quoted in Raymond Allen Cook, "The Literary Principles of Thomas Dixon," p. 101.

18. Kim Magowan, "Coming between the 'Black Beast' and the White Virgin," p. 18.

1. THE LIFE WORTH LIVING

1. Correctly, the subject of this book is named Thomas Dixon Jr. However, for the purpose of convenience, and because he was generally referred to without it in his lifetime, I am dropping the "Jr." in the text and the notes.

2. Lee B. Weathers, *Thomas Dixon*, p. 5.

3. Thomas Dixon, *Southern Horizons*, p. 1.

4. Ibid, p. 29.

5. Kenneth J. Jackson, *The Ku Klux Klan in the City, 1915–1930*, New York: Oxford University Press, 1967, p. 131.

6. "Klokard Haywood Here to Aid Ku Klux," *New York Times*, February 5, 1923, p. 4. If it was not for the horrific calling of the organization, one might almost laugh at the childish silliness of the Klan's use of words such as Klokard, its constitution being titled a Kloran, and its members holding klonversations.

7. "Dixon Condemns Klan," *New York Times*, August 5, 1924, p. 18.

8. Quoted in Wyn Craig Wade, *The Fiery Cross*, p. 316.

9. Quoted in the *Shelby (N.C.) Cleveland Times*, January 3, 1967. p. 8.

10. James Zebulon Wright, "Thomas Dixon," p. 84.

11. Thomas Dixon, *Southern Horizons*, p. 158.

12. *New York Times*, March 11, 1895, p. 8.

13. Samuel A. Ashe and Stephen B. Weeks, eds., *Biographical History of North Carolina: From Colonial Times to the Present*, Greensboro, N.C.: L. Van Noppen, 1908, vol. 7, p. 92.

14. Raymond Allen Cook, *Fire from the Flint*, p. 103.

2. SOUTHERN HISTORY ON THE PRINTED PAGE

1. W.J. Cash, *The Mind of the South*, pp. 83–84.

2. Mildred Lewis Rutherford, *The South in History and Literature: A Hand-Book of Southern Authors from the Settlement of Jamestown, 1607, to Living Writers*, Atlanta: Franklin-Turner, 1907, p. 607.

3. *New York Times*, December 31, 1894, p. 9. Dixon's views are not shared by modern critics. Rachel Anderson writes in *Twentieth-Century Romance and Historical Writers*, Detroit: St. James Press, 1994, p. 111,

"What is astonishing is that a writer who was so pretentious, so self-important, and whose skill was so inadequate for the task he set himself should ever have been taken seriously in the first place."

4. Thomas Dixon, *Southern Horizons*, p. 263.

5. W.H. Johnson, *Critic*, vol. 45, March 1905, p. 277.

6. Burton J. Hendricks, ed., *The Life and Letters of Walter H. Page*, New York: Doubleday, Page, 1922, pp. 12–13.

7. Raymond Cook claims that Dixon was paid 10 percent for the first 25,000 copies sold, 12.5 percent for the next 25,000 copies sold, 15 percent for the next 25,000, and 20 percent for all copies beyond that. It is not clear whether this applies to the wholesale or retail price. But even at the retail price of $1.50, Dixon's royalties on a million copies at the most would have been $300,000.

8. Joel Williamson, *The Crucible of Race*, p. 165.

9. Ibid, p. 158.

10. James Zebulon Wright, telephone conversation with the author, May 5, 2003. It must be assumed that Dixon's widow chose to destroy these and many other pages of her husband's autobiography that she considered unsuitable for public consumption.

11. Sandra Gunning, *Race, Rape, and Lynching*, p. 37.

12. Philip Dray, *At the Hands of Persons Unknown: The Lynching of Black America*, New York: Modern Library, 2003, p. 82.

13. Contemporary documentation on the Ku Klux Klan indicates that it was involved in sexual assault, sodomy, rape, and sexual humiliation. Because wearing bedsheets and "uniforms" made out of their wives' dresses might make them appear feminine, members of the Spartanburg, South Carolina, Klan padded their crotches "to make them look big—bulging out." See Wyn Craig Wade, *The Fiery Cross*, p. 60.

14. Presumably Dixon never considered the possibility that some "rapes" might have been nothing more than interracial love affairs.

15. *New York Times*, August 9, 1902, p. 538.

16. Sandra Gunning, *Race, Rape, and Lynching*, p. 41.

17. Dixon's library contained three volumes on the Klan, all but one published prior to the appearance of *The Clansman*: Thomas Jefferson Jerome, *Ku Klux Klan No. 40* (1895); John Moffatt Mecklin, *The Ku Klux Klan* (1924); and Charles W. Tyler, *The K.K.K.* (1902). Early volumes on the African American are also present in the library: George Washington Cable, *The Negro Question* (1898); Charles Carroll, *The*

Negro a Beast; or, In the Image of God (1900); David King, *Cotton Is King; or, Slavery in the Light of Political Economy* (1860); Samuel Creed Cross, *The Negro and the Sunny South* (1899); Frederick May Holland, *Frederick Douglass: The Colored Orator* (1891); Thomas Nelson Page, *The Negro: The Southerner's Problem* (1904); Lindley Spring, *The Negro at Home* (1868); William Hannibal Thomas, *The American Negro* (1901); and Booker T. Washington, *Up from Slavery* (1904).

18. *Charlotte Observer*, May 4, 1905, p. 12.

19. Fawn M. Brodie, *Thaddeus Stevens*, p. 371.

20. See Michael Soper, "*The Birth of a Nation*: It's the Most Stupendous Movie of Them All," *Charlotte Observer*, July 14, 1963.

21. Some academics have misread this section of the book, believing that Dr. Cameron does see the image of Gus in the mother's eyes, when Dixon quite obviously writes that it is only in the doctor's imagination. The same academics have also made much of the name Lenoir, meaning the black one.

22. In all certainty, a major exaggeration.

23. Thomas Dixon, *Southern Horizons*, p. 5.

24. Ibid, p. 4.

25. Thomas Dixon, "Booker T. Washington and the Negro," p. 1.

26. Ibid., p. 2.

27. "Thomas Dixon, Novelist, Playwright, Actor, and Host," *New York Dramatic Mirror*, July 12, 1911, p. 5.

28. *New York Times*, June 9, 1903, p. 2.

29. Thomas Dixon to D.W. Griffith, January 4, 1921, in the D.W. Griffith papers at the Museum of Modern Art.

3. SOUTHERN HISTORY ON STAGE

1. Eleven other plays by Bartley Campbell were produced on the New York stage between 1876 and 1905.

2. Copies of the play script are held by the Harvard Theatre Collection, the Library of Congress, and the Museum of Modern Art (as part of the D.W. Griffith papers). An incomplete and substantially variant version, presumed to be an early draft, of act 1 can be found at Duke University.

3. The craze for having live horses on stage originated with Adah Isaacs Menken, who appeared half-nude, tied to a horse galloping across the stage, in *Mazeppa* in the 1860s. While I was in the process of writing

this book, I saw the British National Theatre production of *Jerry Springer—The Opera* in London. The act 1 finale with a stageful of tap-dancing Ku Klux Klansmen against the backdrop of a fiery cross was a truly mind-boggling and also blood-stirring moment in theatrical history.

4. Reported in the *Norfolk Virginian-Pilot*, September 23, 1905.

5. Samuel A. Ashe and Stephen B. Weeks, eds. *Biographical History of North Carolina,* vol. 7, p. 92.

6. This and the quotes in the preceding paragraph of the text are taken from Durant Da Ponte, "The Greatest Play of the South," which is, in turn, based on the scrapbooks of Booker T. Washington at the Library of Congress.

7. Quoted in Thomas Dixon, "Why I Wrote 'The Clansman,'" *Theatre*, January 1906, pp. 20–21.

8. Ibid., pp. 20 and 22.

9. Original copy in author's collection. When I acquired this item through an advertisement on the Internet, the seller advised me that Internet sites such as eBay would no longer permit sales of Klan-related materials such as this.

10. Thomas Dixon, *Southern Horizons*, p. 288.

11. Thomas Dixon, "Booker T. Washington and the Negro," p. 1.

12. *New York Press*, January 29, 1906.

13. Chauncey L. Parsons, "Thomas Dixon," p. 5.

14. Ibid.

15. Quotes are from the *New York Dramatic Mirror*, October 5, 1910, p. 25.

16. Chauncey L. Parsons, "Thomas Dixon," p. 5.

17. Charleen Swansea, telephone conversation with the author, October 30, 2003.

18. Burns Mantle, *The Best Plays of 1919–1920*, New York: Dodd, Mead, 1920, p. 15.

4. SOUTHERN HISTORY ON FILM

1. Mrs. D.W. Griffith, *When the Movies Were Young*, p. 250.

2. William Haddock quoted in Bernard Rosenberg and Harry Silverstein, *The Real Tinsel*, New York: Macmillan, 1970, pp. 324–25.

3. Thomas Dixon, *Southern Horizons*, p. 289.

4. Ibid, p. 295.

NOTES TO PAGES 73–83

5. D.W. Griffith to Thomas Dixon, March 30, 1941, letter in author's collection.

6. James Hart, ed., *The Man Who Invented Hollywood*, p. 89. It is unclear as to Griffith's contribution to his "autobiography."

7. Quoted in Richard Schickel, *D.W. Griffith,* p. 207.

8. There is a puzzling unsigned contract extant in the Thomas Dixon papers at Duke University, whereby the author grants the motion picture rights to the play to the Sterling Camera and Film Company, which may or may not be Harry Aitken's organization. Under the terms of this contract, Dixon is to receive a total of $1,500 in cash along with 25 percent of the net profits. The expenses incurred in the production and exploitation of the film were not to exceed $5,000, and production was to be completed by January 1, 1914. Griffith scholar Arthur Lennig strongly doubts that this contract could have been with Aitken.

9. Roy E. Aitken, as told to Al P. Nelson, *The Birth of a Nation Story*, p. 24.

10. Billy Bitzer to Iris Barry, November 28, 1939, Museum of Modern Art.

11. Frances Oakes, "Whitman and Dixon," p. 334.

12. Thomas Dixon to Joseph Henabery, March 19 [1915], in the Joseph Henabery Collection, Margaret Herrick Library, Academy of Motion Picture Arts and Sciences.

13. Myron Lounsbury, ed., *The Progress and Poetry of the Movies: A Second Book of Film Criticism by Vachel Lindsay*, Lanham, Md.: Scarecrow Press, 1995, p. 259.

14. Vachel Lindsay, *The Art of the Moving Picture*, New York: Macmillan, 1916.

15. Lillian Gish, with Ann Pinchot, *The Movies, Mr. Griffith, and Me*, Englewood Cliffs, N.J.: Prentice-Hall, 1969, p. 132.

16. Scott Simmon, *The Films of D.W. Griffith*, p. 125.

17. Miriam Cooper, interview by the author, October 14, 1973.

18. Madame Sul-te-Wan, interview by Raymond Lee, date unknown. In the interview, the actress claimed to have been under contract to Griffith for seven years and to have been described by him as "the best of the race."

19. Griffith associates Karl Brown and Joseph Henabery both insist that Griffith saw the film in Los Angeles.

20. John Morton Blum, *Woodrow Wilson and the Politics of Morality*, Boston: Little, Brown, 1956, p. 115.

21. Josephus Daniels, *The Life of Woodrow Wilson*, Philadelphia: John C. Winston, 1924, p. 87.

22. August Heckscher, *Woodrow Wilson*, New York: Collier, 1991, p. 293.

23. A copyrighted description of the story at the Library of Congress identifies the film as *The Birth of the Nation*.

24. The clergymen were Rev. Thomas B. Gregory, Universalist; Rev. Charles H. Parkhurst, Presbyterian; and Rev. John Talbot Smith, Roman Catholic. Parkhurst, as a keen campaigner against political corruption and vice, was the most prominent. Gregory was quoted in the *Literary Digest* (March 20, 1915): "I am prepared to say that not one of the more than five thousand pictures that go to make up the wonderful drama is in any essential way an exaggeration. They are one and all faithful to historic fact, so that, looking upon them, you may feel that you are beholding that which actually happened."

25. Francis Hackett, "Brotherly Love," *New Republic*, March 20, 1915, p. 185.

26. The Leo Frank lynching is the subject of two books: Harry Golden, *A Little Girl Is Dead*, Cleveland: World Publishing, 1965; and Leonard Dinnerstein, *The Leo Frank Case*, New York: Columbia University Press, 1968.

27. *Collier's*, July 14, 1928, p. 35.

28. Cedric Robinson, "In the Year 1915," p. 183.

5. *THE FALL OF A NATION*

1. *The Autobiography of Cecil B. DeMille*, ed. Donald Hayne, Englewood Cliffs, N.J.: Prentice-Hall, 1959, p. 125.

2. Ray Stannard Baker, *Woodrow Wilson—Life and Letters*, New York: Doubleday, Doran, 1937, vol. 6, p. 14.

3. Thomas Dixon, *Southern Horizons*, pp. 309–10.

4. Quoted in Roy E. Aitken, as told to Al P. Nelson, *The Birth of a Nation Story*, p. 63.

5. *Moving Picture World*, June 3, 1916, p. 1671.

6. Quoted in Wayne D. Shirley, "A Bugle Call to Arms for National Defense!" p. 37.

7. *Motion Picture News*, May 20, 1916, p. 3056.

8. Thomas Dixon, "Booker T. Washington and the Negro," p. 2.

The somewhat peculiar grammar is as originally published. Nowhere in his writings does Dixon appear to realize that the "Semitic group of the white race" would also include the Arab/Islamic community.

9. "The Negro a Menace Says Thomas Dixon," p. 2.

10. Walter Benn Michaels, *Our America,* p. 10.

11. *Moving Picture World,* June 3, 1916, p. 1671.

12. Quoted in Leif Furhammar and Folke Isaksson, *Politics and Film,* trans. Kersti French, London: Studio Vista, 1971.

6. *THE FOOLISH VIRGIN* AND THE NEW WOMAN

1. *Moving Picture World,* June 3, 1916, p. 1671.

2. F. Garvin Davenport Jr., "Thomas Dixon's Mythology of Southern History," p. 358. Dixon must have been aware of Dorothy Dix's praise of *The Birth of a Nation* in the *New York American* (March 5, 1915): "I never had the slightest conception of what could be done with the moving picture as an art until I saw *The Birth of a Nation.* . . . I had thought that to grip an audience, to melt it to tears with pathos, to thrill it with high heroic sentiment, required the spoken word and the magic of the human voice."

3. Interview with Louella Parsons, *New York Morning Telegraph,* January 12, 1919.

4. James Zebulon Wright, telephone conversation with the author, May 5, 2003.

5. Interview with Louella Parsons, *New York Morning Telegraph,* January 12, 1919.

6. Raymond Allen Cook, *Fire from the Flint,* p. 194. Cook does not indicate the source for this information, but he adds that the sale was for "a large sum" of money. No such contract exists in the Joseph M. Schenck archives.

7. DIXON ON SOCIALISM

1. Raymond Allen Cook identifies the woman as Lilian Lida Bell, whose articles in the *Saturday Evening Post* and *Harper's Bazaar* "seem to express more than academic interest in Dixon the man." See *Thomas Dixon,* pp. 146 and 155.

2. According to *Motion Picture News,* November 16, 1918, p. 2958.

3. Quoted in James Zebulon Wright, *Thomas Dixon*, p. 166.

4. F. Garvin Davenport Jr., "Thomas Dixon's Mythology of Southern History," p. 364.

5. Quoted in Samuel A. Ashe and Stephen B. Weeks, eds., *Biographical History of North Carolina*, vol. 7, p. 91.

6. *Motion Picture News*, February 9, 1918, p. 862.

7. *Motion Picture News*, March 2, 1918, p. 1295.

8. Kevin Brownlow, *Behind the Mask of Innocence*, p. 462. Unfortunately, Brownlow appears too intent on ridiculing the film, referencing Dixon's "politics of the farmyard," to provide an adequate critical discussion.

9. *Motion Picture News*, February 23, 1918, p. 1162.

8. THE RED SCARE

1. Brian R. McGee, "Thomas Dixon's *The Clansman*," p. 304.

2. Robert K. Murray, *Red Scare: A Study of National Hysteria, 1919–1920*, Minneapolis: University of Minnesota Press, 1955, pp. ix, 92. Murray's book remains the only major study of this political phenomenon. Other useful sources are William Preston Jr., *Aliens and Dissenters: Federal Suppression of Radicals, 1903–1933*, Cambridge: Harvard University Press, 1963; and Mari Jo Buhle, Paul Buhle, and Dan Georgakas, eds., *Encyclopedia of the American Left*, New York: Garland, 1990.

3. Reported in *Motion Picture News*, May 10, 1919, p. 3057.

4. The six-page contract survives among Thomas Dixon's papers at Duke University.

5. Kevin Brownlow claims in *Behind the Mask of Innocence* (p. 443) that *Shattered Dreams* was the working title of *Bolshevism on Trial*. This is not correct.

9. MISCEGENATION

1. Emily Wortis Leider, *California's Daughter: Gertrude Atherton and Her Times*, Stanford, Calif.: Stanford University Press, 1991, p. 186. I am grateful to Emily Leider for drawing my attention to Gertrude Atherton's racist attitudes.

2. Thomas Dixon, *Dixon's Sermons*, p. 12.

3. Dixon writes of Captain Shotwell in *Southern Horizons*; he was a

Civil War hero, imprisoned during the Reconstruction period with two Negro felons in an iron cage in the Rutherfordton jail.

4. The white character with whom Norton argues here is perhaps based on Henry Ward Beecher, who preached from his pulpit in Brooklyn, "The Negro is superior to the white race. If the latter do not forget their pride of race and color and amalgamate with the purer, richer blood of the blacks, they will die out." See Thomas Dixon, *Southern Horizons*, p. xxv.

5. Matthew A. Taylor, *Motion Picture News*, February 12, 1921, p. 1387.

6. Robert C. McElravy, *Moving Picture World*, February 12, 1921, p. 817.

10. JOURNEYMAN FILMMAKER

1. The *New York Times* may not have considered Dixon's film career worthy of mention, but according to James Zebulon Wright, the newspaper published more than one hundred articles dealing specifically with Thomas Dixon.

2. Because the film does not survive, it is not clear whether its title is *Mark of the Beast* or *The Mark of the Beast*. All contemporary reviews describe it as *The Mark of the Beast,* and I have followed their example, although I have a strong notion that *Mark of the Beast* is a more compelling title.

3. *New York Times*, June 2, 1923, p. 14.

4. *Motion Picture News*, September 10, 1923, p. 1194.

5. Raymond Cook to the author, October 13, 2002.

6. A copy survives at the Library of Congress.

11. NATION AFLAME

1. Letter headed The Thomas Dixon Corporation, 43 West 37th Street, New York, a copy of which is in the author's collection.

2. *Moving Picture World*, January 22, 1921, p. 425. The footage appeared in *Fox News*, vol. 2, no. 28, and was authorized by the Klan.

3. For more information on the Black Legion, see George Morris, *The Black Legion Rides*, New York: Workers Library Publishers, 1936.

4. It is not part of the Black Legion cycle, but in 1938, Paramount produced *The Texans*, set in Texas immediately after the Civil War, starring Joan Bennett and Randolph Scott and directed by James Hogan, in which the heroine discovers that her fiancé (played by Robert Cummings) is an organizer of the Ku Klux Klan and quickly rejects him.

5. Letter in the files of the Production Code Administration (PCA) at the Margaret Herrick Library of the Academy of Motion Picture Arts and Sciences. Additional information in this chapter is also taken from the PCA file on *Nation Aflame*.

6. I am inclined to believe he is the butler in the governor's mansion.

7. Quoted in Leonard Dinnerstein, *The Leo Frank Case*, New York: Columbia University Press, 1968, p. 149.

8. Kathleen M. Blee, *Women of the Klan: Racism and Gender in the 1920s*, Berkeley: University of California Press, 1991, p. 46.

12. THE FINAL YEARS

1. Thomas Dixon, *Southern Horizons*, p. 315.

2. *Raleigh (N.C.) News and Observer*, May 2, 1937, p. 2.

3. Raymond Allen Cook, *Thomas Dixon*, p. 99.

4. James Zebulon Wright, telephone conversation with the author, May 5, 2003.

5. Reprinted in Richard Howell, ed., *Margaret Mitchell's "Gone with the Wind" Letters, 1936–1949*, New York: Macmillan, 1976, p. 52.

6. Associated Press Biographical Service sketch no. 2952.

7. Bess Ballentine and Nell Joslin Styron, "Tales of the Sir Walter," *The State*, September 1980, p. 16. Those readers who might believe that Dixon's attitude toward the African American was outdated in the author's later years should note that as late as October 1980, the popular North Carolina magazine *The State*, makes reference to a "faithful colored man," whose quoted dialogue is every bit as offensive to a liberal audience as the Negro dialogue found in the pages of Dixon's novels.

8. Thomas Dixon, *Southern Horizons*, p. 336.

9. Charleen Swansea, telephone conversation with the author, October 30, 2003.

10. *Durham (N.C.) Morning Herald*, April 4, 1946.

11. Valerie M. Parry to author, July 23, 1998.

12. "Thomas Dixon, Jr.," in Samuel A. Ashe and Stephen B. Weeks, eds., *Biographical History of North Carolina,* vol. 7, p. 88.

13. Ibid, p. 93.

13. Raymond Rohauer and the Dixon Legacy

1. Terry Ramsaye, *A Million and One Nights,* New York: Simon and Schuster, 1926, p. 642.

2. Information taken from *Exhibitors Herald-World,* July 5, 1930, p. 30.

3. According to Roy E. Aitken, as told to Al P. Nelson, *The Birth of a Nation Story,* p. 36.

4. Information taken from the Production Code Administration files in the Margaret Herrick Library of the Academy of Motion Picture Arts and Sciences.

5. Walter White to Eric Johnson, December 9, 1954, Production Code Administration files.

6. D.W. Griffith to Thomas Dixon, March 30, 1941, letter in author's collection.

7. *Los Angeles Times,* June 13, 1980, p. 17.

8. William Grimes, "Can a Film Be Both Racist and Classic?" p. B1.

9. Evelyn Baldwin Griffith, interview by the author, June 12, 1975.

10. Roy E. Aitken, as told to Al P. Nelson, *The Birth of a Nation Story,* p. 5.

11. James Zebulon Wright, telephone conversation with the author, May 5, 2003.

12. Later, Rohauer would be curator of Huntington Hartford's Gallery of Modern Art in New York, from 1965 to 1967, and again its curator from 1969 to 1970, when the gallery was renamed the New York Cultural Center.

13. John Baxter, "The Silent Empire of Raymond Rohauer," *Sunday Times Magazine* (London), January 19, 1975, p. 32. After Paul Killiam circulated copies of this article in the United States, Raymond Rohauer filed a libel suit against him and the *Sunday Times* for $460 million.

14. Thomas Dixon, postscript to *Southern Horizons,* p. 332.

15. Ibid, p. 333.

16. Harry Aitken had died in 1956; his brother Roy died in 1976.

17. Thomas Dixon, postscript to *Southern Horizons,* p. 335.

18. I have tried without success to contact Karen Crowe and obtain information as to how she and Raymond Rohauer became involved in the autobiography.

19. Much of the information herein is taken from confidential American Film Institute memoranda, dated December 3, 1979, and in the possession of the author. The author must also declare a conflict of interest in the recounting of events in that he was actively involved at the time in researching materials on behalf of Paul Killiam in his long-running feud with Raymond Rohauer.

BIBLIOGRAPHY

Books and articles cited in full in the endnotes are not additionally cited here.

Aitken, Roy E., as told to Al P. Nelson. *The Birth of a Nation Story*. Middleburg, Va.: Denlinger, 1965.

Bell, Lilian Lida. "A Collarless Novelist." *Saturday Evening Post*, May 3, 1903, p. 17. This extremely slight piece is, in fact, unsigned.

———. "Girl in Love." *Harper's Bazaar*, November 1901, pp. 603–8.

———. "The Leopard's Spots." *Saturday Evening Post*, April 12, 1902, p. 15.

Berquist, Goodwin, and James Greenwood. "Protest against Racism: *The Birth of a Nation* in Ohio." *Journal of the University Film Association*, vol. 26, no. 3, 1974, pp. 39–44.

Boeckmann, Cathy. *A Question of Character: Scientific Racism and the Genres of American Fiction, 1892–1912*. Tuscaloosa: University of Alabama Press, 2000.

Brodie, Fawn M. *Thaddeus Stevens: Scourge of the South*. New York: W.W. Norton, 1966.

Brownlow, Kevin. *Behind the Mask of Innocence*. New York: Alfred A. Knopf, 1990.

Bryan, George B. "Edward Sheldon." In *Dictionary of Literary Biography*, ed. Jack MacNicholas, vol. 7, part 2, K–Z, pp. 228–31. Detroit: Gale Research, 1981.

C.M. "After the Play." *New Republic*, August 20, 1919, p. 94.

Campbell, Edward D.C., Jr. *The Celluloid South: Hollywood and the Southern Myth*. Knoxville: University of Tennessee Press, 1981.

Campbell, Russell. "Nihilists and Bolsheviks: Revolutionary Russia in American Silent Film." *Silent Picture*, no. 19, 1974, pp. 4–36.

Cash, W. J. *The Mind of the South*. New York: Alfred A. Knopf, 1941.

"Censorship Means Graft, Says Dixon." *New York Times*, May 15, 1924, p. 21.

Chadwick, Bruce. *The Reel Civil War: Mythmaking in American Film*. New York: Alfred A. Knopf, 2001.

"The Civil War in Film." *Literary Digest*, March 20, 1915, pp. 608–9.

Clements, Kendrick A. *Woodrow Wilson: World Statesman*. Boston: Twayne, 1987.

Cook, Raymond Allen. *Fire from the Flint: The Amazing Careers of Thomas Dixon*. Winston-Salem, N.C.: John F. Blair, 1968.

———. "The Literary Principles of Thomas Dixon." *Georgia Review*, vol. 13, no. 1, spring 1959, pp. 97–102.

———. *Thomas Dixon*. New York: Twayne, 1974.

Cuniberti, John. *The Birth of a Nation: A Formal Shot-by-Shot Analysis together with Microfiche*. Woodbridge, Conn.: Research Publications, 1979.

Da Ponte, Durant. "The Greatest Play of the South." *Tennessee Studies in Literature*, vol. 2, 1957, pp. 15–24.

Davenport, F. Garvin, Jr. "Thomas Dixon's Mythology of Southern History." *Journal of Southern History*, vol. 36, no. 3, August 1970, pp. 350–67.

Dell, Floyd. *Upton Sinclair: A Study in Social Protest*. New York: George H. Doran, 1927.

Denig, Lynde. "Thomas Dixon Lauds the Cinema." *Moving Picture World*, June 3, 1916, p. 1671.

Dixon, Thomas, Jr. "An Author's Answer to His Critics." *New York Times*, August 9, 1902, p. 538.

———. *The Black Hood*. New York: D. Appleton, 1924.

———. "Booker T. Washington and the Negro." *Saturday Evening Post*, August 19, 1905, pp. 1–2.

———. *The Clansman*. New York: Doubleday, Page, 1905.

———. *Companions*. New York: Otis, 1931.

———. *Comrades*. New York: Doubleday, Page, 1909.

———. *Dixon's Sermons: Delivered in the Grand Opera House, New York, 1898–1899*. New York: F.L. Bussey, 1899.

———. *A Dreamer in Portugal: The Story of Bernarr Macfadden's Mission to Continental Europe*. New York: Covici, Friede, 1934.

———. *The Failure of Protestantism in New York and Its Causes*. New York: Victor O.A. Strauss, 1896.

———. *The Fall of a Nation: A Sequel to "The Birth of a Nation."* New York: D. Appleton, 1916.

———. *The Flaming Sword*. Atlanta: Monarch, 1939.

———. *The Foolish Virgin: A Romance of Today.* New York: D. Appleton, 1915.

———. "From the Horrors of City Life." *World's Work*, October 1902, pp. 2603–11.

———. *The Inside Story of the Harding Tragedy*. New York: Churchill Company, 1932.

———. *The Leopard's Spots: A Romance of the White Man's Burden, 1865–1900*. New York: Doubleday, Page, 1902.

———. *The Life Worth Living: A Personal Experience*. New York: Doubleday, Page, 1905.

———. *The Love Complex*. New York: Boni and Liveright, 1925.

———. *The Man in Gray: A Romance of North and South*. New York: D. Appleton, 1921.

———. *A Man of the People: A Drama of Abraham Lincoln*. New York: D. Appleton, 1920.

———. *The One Woman: A Story of Modern Utopia*. New York: Doubleday, Page, 1903.

———. *The Reconstruction Trilogy.* Newport Beach, Calif.: Noontide Press, 1994. Includes *The Leopard's Spots, The Clansman,* and *The Traitor.*

———. Respondent's Brief, Supreme Court of the State of New York, Appellate Division—First Department, New York, Thorne Baker as Trustee in Bankruptcy of National Drama Corporation, Plaintiff-Appellant, against Thomas Dixon, Defendant-Respondent, undated. Thomas Dixon Collection, Duke University.

———. *The Root of Evil*. Garden City, N.Y.: Doubleday, Page, 1911.

———. *The Sins of the Father: A Romance of the South*. New York: D. Appleton, 1912.

———. *The Southerner.* New York: D. Appleton, 1913.

———. *Southern Horizons: The Autobiography of Thomas Dixon*, ed. Karen Crowe. Alexandria, Va.: IWV Publishing, 1984.

———. *The Sun Virgin*. New York: Horace Liveright, 1929.

———. *The Traitor*. New York: Doubleday, Page, 1907.

———. *The Way of a Man: A Story of the New Woman*. New York: D. Appleton, 1919.

———. "Why I Wrote 'The Clansman.'" *Theatre*, January 1906, pp. 20–22.

"Dixon Confers with Mastercraft Heads." *Motion Picture News*, February 9, 1918, p. 862.

"Dixon Denies Race Prejudice." *Moving Picture World*, June 24, 1916, p. 2211.

"Dixon Penniless; $1,250,000 Gone." *New York Times*, April 17, 1934, p. 19.

"Dixon Picture Gives Survey of Human Freedom." *Motion Picture News*, May 20, 1916, p. 3056.

D'Ooge, Craig. "*The Birth of a Nation*: Symposium on Classic Film Discusses Inaccuracies and Virtues." *Library of Congress Information Bulletin*, June 27, 1994, pp. 263–66.

"Dr. Zeb Wright Brilliantly Probes Mind of Cleveland's Thomas Dixon." *Cleveland Times*, January 3, 1967, pp. 1, 8.

Ernst, Robert. *Weakness Is a Crime: The Life of Bernarr Macfadden*. Syracuse, N.Y.: Syracuse University Press, 1991.

"*The Fall of a Nation* Rises to Dramatic Heights." *Motion Picture News*, June 24, 1916, p. 3877.

French, Warren, ed. *The South and Film*. Jackson: University Press of Mississippi, 1981.

Griffith, Mrs. D.W. *When the Movies Were Young*. New York: E.P. Dutton, 1925.

Griggs, Sutton E. *The Hindered Hand; or, The Reign of the Repressionist*. Nashville: Orion, 1905.

Grimes, William. "Can a Film Be Both Racist and Classic?" *New York Times*, April 27, 1994, pp. B1, B4.

Gunning, Sandra. *Race, Rape, and Lynching: The Red Record of American Literature, 1890–1912*. New York: Oxford University Press, 1996.

Hanson, Patricia King, ed. *The American Film Institute Catalog of Motion Pictures Produced in the United States: Feature Films, 1911–1920*. Berkeley: University of California Press, 1988.

Hart, James, ed. *The Man Who Invented Hollywood: The Autobiography of D.W. Griffith*. Louisville, Ky.: Touchstone Publishing, 1972.

Harwell, Richard, ed. *Margaret Mitchell's "Gone with the Wind" Letters, 1936–1949*. New York: Macmillan, 1976.

Huff, Theodore. *A Shot Analysis of D.W. Griffith's The Birth of a Nation*. New York: Museum of Modern Art, 1961.

Johnson, W.H., "The Case of the Negro." *Dial*, May 1, 1903, pp. 299–302.

Kinney, James. *Amalgamation! Race, Sex, and Rhetoric in the Nineteenth-Century American Novel*. Westport, Conn.: Greenwood Press, 1985.

"Klokard Haywood Here to Aid Ku Klux." *New York Times*, February 5, 1923, p. 4.

Lang, Robert, ed. *The Birth of a Nation*. New Brunswick, N.J.: Rutgers University Press, 1994.

Lewis, Warren W. "Why Dixon wrote *One Woman*." *Motion Picture News*, November 16, 1918, p. 2958.

"Little Trips to the Studios." *New York Dramatic Mirror*, November 16, 1918, p. 740.

Magowan, Kim. "Coming between the 'Black Beast' and the White Virgin: The Pressures of Liminality in Thomas Dixon." *Studies in American Fiction*, vol. 27, no. 1, spring 1999, pp. 77–101.

Martin, Jeffrey B. "Film out of Theatre: D.W. Griffith, *Birth of a Nation* and the Melodrama *The Clansman*." *Literature/Film Quarterly*, vol. 18, no. 2, 1990, pp. 87–95.

McGee, Brian R. "Thomas Dixon's *The Clansman*: Radicals, Reactionaries, and the Anticipated Utopia." *Southern Communication Journal*, vol. 65, no. 4, summer 2000, pp. 300–317.

Merritt, Russell. "Dixon, Griffith, and the Southern Legend." *Cinema Journal*, vol. 12, no. 1, fall 1972, pp. 26–45.

Meserve, Walter J., and Mollie Ann Meserve, eds. *Fateful Lightning: America's Civil War Plays*. New York: Feedback TheatreBooks and Prospero Press, 2000.

Michaels, Walter Benn. *Our America: Nativism, Modernism, and Pluralism*. Durham, N.C.: Duke University Press, 1995.

Miller, Kelly. "An Open Letter to Thomas Dixon, Jr." Howard University, Washington, D.C., September 1905.

"The Negro a Menace Says Thomas Dixon." *New York Times*, June 9, 1903, p. 2.

"No Small Features, but Big Operatic Spectacles from Dixon." *Motion Picture News*, June 17, 1916, p. 3758.

Oakes, Frances. "Whitman and Dixon: A Strange Case of Borrowing." *Georgia Review*, vol. 11, no. 3, fall 1957, pp. 333–40.

Parsons, Chauncey L. "Thomas Dixon: Novelist, Playwright, Actor, and Host." *New York Dramatic Mirror*, July 12, 1911, pp. 5, 7.

Parsons, Louella. "Thomas Dixon." *New York Morning Telegraph*, January 12, 1919.

Robinson, Cedric. "In the Year 1915: D.W. Griffith and the Whitening of America." *Social Identities*, vol. 3, no. 2, 1997, pp. 161–92.

Ross, Steven J. *Working-Class Hollywood: Silent Film and the Shaping of Class in America*. Princeton, N.J.: Princeton University Press, 1998.

Schickel, Richard. *D.W. Griffith: An American Life*. New York: Simon and Schuster, 1984.

Seymour-Smith, Martin, and Andrew C. Kimmens. *World Authors, 1900–1950*. New York: H.W. Wilson, 1996.

Shepherd, William G. "How I Put Over the Klan: 'Col.' William Joseph Simmons, Father of the Ku Klux Klan, Tells His Story." *Collier's*, July 14, 1928, pp. 5–7, 32, 34–35.

Shirley, Wayne D. "A Bugle Call to Arms for National Defense! Victor Herbert and His Score for *The Fall of a Nation*." *Quarterly Journal of the Library of Congress*, vol. 40, no. 1, winter 1983, pp. 26–47.

Silva, Fred, ed. *Focus on The Birth of a Nation*. Englewood Cliffs, N.J.: Prentice-Hall, 1971.

Simcovitch, Maxim. "The Impact of Griffith's *Birth of a Nation* on the Modern Ku Klux Klan." *Journal of Popular Film*, vol. 1, no. 1, winter 1972, pp. 45–54.

Simmon, Scott. *The Films of D.W. Griffith*. New York: Cambridge University Press, 1993.

Slide, Anthony. "Dixon, Thomas." In *A Political Companion to American Film*, ed. Gary Crowdus, pp. 115–17. New York: Lakeview Press, 1994.

Stern, Seymour. *The Birth of a Nation*. London: British Film Institute, 1945.

———. "Griffith Not Anti-Negro." *Sight and Sound*, vol. 16, no. 61, spring 1947, pp. 32–35.

"Victor Herbert Writes Opera for Dixon Film." *Motion Picture News*, May 13, 1916, p. 2870.

Wade, Wyn Craig. *The Fiery Cross: The Ku Klux Klan in America*. New York: Simon and Schuster, 1987.

Wagenknecht, Edward, and Anthony Slide. *The Films of D.W. Griffith*. New York: Crown, 1975.

Weathers, Lee B. *Thomas Dixon, Carolina's Most Colorful Character*. Shelby, N.C.: The Author, 1949.

Williamson, Joel. *The Crucible of Race: Black-White Relations in the American South since Emancipation*. New York: Oxford University Press, 1984.

Wright, James Zebulon. "Thomas Dixon: The Mind of a Southern Apologist." Ph.D. diss., George Peabody College for Teachers, 1966.

INDEX

INDEX

238